Buses Restored 2005

Buses Restored 2005

Ian Allan
PUBLISHING

Cover: **The Quantock Heritage fleet contains a number of former Crosville saloons including KA226 (LFM 302), a Weymann-bodied Leyland PS1 seen here in Alton in summer 2004.** *Philip Lamb*

Half title: **Blue Triangle's former London Transport RT 6 RTW75 (KEK 575) is seen at North Weald in 2004.**
Philip Lamb

Title page: **Former Crosville Bristol L5G KG131 (KFM 893) has been restored by Quantock Heritage in dual-purpose livery. It is seen here on a free service at the 2004 Andover Running Day.**
Philip Lamb

First published 2005

ISBN 0 7110 3089 8

All rights reserved. No part of this book may be reproduced or transmitted in any form or by any means, electronic or mechanical, including photocopying, recording or by any information storage and retrieval system, without permission from the Publisher in writing.

© Ian Allan Publishing Ltd 2005

Published by Ian Allan Publishing

an imprint of Ian Allan Publishing Ltd, Hersham,
Surrey KT12 4RG.
Printed in England by Ian Allan Printing Ltd, Hersham,
Surrey KT12 4RG.

Code: 0503/A3

Contents

Introduction 7
What is NARTM? 10
How to Use this Book 12

Part 1
Museums Normally open to the Public
Abbey Pumping Station, Leicester 16
Amberley Museum 17
Aston Manor Road Transport Museum 17
Birmingham & Midland Museum of Transport 19
Black Country Living Museum 21
Bristol Road Transport Collection 22
British Commercial Vehicle Museum, Leyland 23
Castle Point Transport Museum, Canvey Island 24
Cavan & Leitrim Railway, Dromod 25
Cobham Bus Museum 28
Coventry Transport Museum 29
Dover Transport Museum 29
East Anglia Transport Museum, Carlton Colville 30
Grampian Transport Museum, Alford 31
Imperial War Museum, London 32
Ipswich Transport Museum .32
Isle of Wight Bus Museum .33
Keighley Bus Museum 34
Lincolnshire Road Transport Museum 38
London's Transport Museum 39
Manchester Museum of Transport 40
Midland Road Transport Group, Butterley 42
Museum of Transport, Glasgow 43
National Museum of Science and Industry 46
North of England Open Air Museum, Beamish 46
North West Museum of Road Transport 47
Nottingham Transport Heritage Centre 49
Oxford Bus Museum 50
Scottish Vintage Bus Museum, Lathalmond 51
Sheffield Bus Museum 57
Tameside Transport Collection, Mossley 58
Transport Museum Society of Ireland, Howth 59
Trolleybus Museum at Sandtoft 61
Ulster Folk & Transport Museum, Cultra 62
Wirral Transport Museum 63

Note: Please be aware that vehicles on display can vary from time to time as not all museums display their entire 'fleet'. Visitors wishing to see a particular vehicle should make enquiries prior to their visit.

Part 2
Other Collections of Preserved Buses & Coaches

Aldershot & District Bus Interest Group 66
Aycliffe & District Bus Preservation Society 67
Barrow Transport Group 67
Bohemia-Sachsen Transport Heritage Park 67
Bolton Bus Group 68
Bournemouth Heritage Transport Collection 68
Bristol Omnibus Vehicle Collection 69
Bristol Vintage Bus Group 70
British Trolleybus Society 70
Cardiff & South Wales Trolleybus Project 71
Chelveston Preservation Society .71
Cherwell Bus Preservation Group .72
City of Portsmouth Preserved Transport Depot 73
Classic Southdown Omnibuses 76
Devon General Society 76
Dewsbury Bus Museum 77
East Kent Road Car Heritage Trust 78
Eastern Transport Collection Society 78
Friends of King Alfred Buses 79
Glasgow Vintage Vehicle Trust 80
Golcar Transport Collection 81
Halifax Bus Museum 82
Huddersfield & District Transport Museum Society 82
Irish Transport Trust 83
John Shearman Collection 83
Kelvin Amos Collection 86
Lancastrian Transport Trust 86
Legionnaire Group 87
Leicester Corporation Bus Owners Group 87
Medstead Depot Omnibus Group 88
Merseyside Transport Trust 88
Mike Sutcliffe Collection 88
North East Bus Preservation Trust Ltd 89
Peter Stanier Collection 91
Ribble Vehicle Preservation Trust .91
Roger Burdett Collection 92
Rotherham Trolleybus Group 93
RTW Bus Group 95
St Margarets School Transport Society 96
SELNEC Preservation Society 96
Southampton & District Transport Heritage Trust 98
Southdown Historic Vehicle Group 98
Telford Bus Group 99
TH Collection 100
Three Counties Bus and Commercial Vehicle Museum . .100
Wealdstone & District Vintage Vehicle Collection 101
West Country Historic Omnibus & Transport Trust 102
West Midlands Bus Preservation Society 102
West of England Transport Collection 103
Westgate Museum 105
Workington Transport Heritage Trust 105

Part 3
Privately-Owned Vehicles

British Bus Preservation Group 107

Part 4
Heritage Bus Services

Blue Triangle, Rainham 114
Buckland Omnibus Co, Woodbridge 114
Carmel Coaches, Okehampton .114
Cosy Coaches, Killamarsh 115
Cumbria Classic Coaches, Kirkby Stephen 111
Green Bus Service, Great Wyrley 116
MacTours & Majestic Tour, Edinburgh 116
Memory Lane Vintage Omnibus Services, Maidenhead . .117
Quantock Heritage, Wiveliscombe 117
Southcoast Motor Services, Croydon 118

Index of Vehicles by Registration Number 120
Index of Museums and Locations Open to Public . . .127

Useful addresses

NARTM, PO Box 5141, Burton-upon-Trent DE15 OZF.
The Transport Trust, 202 Lambeth Road, London SE1 7JW.
British Bus Preservation Group, 6 Pine Close, Billingshurst RH14 9NL.
The PSV Circle, 26 Ashville Grove, Halifax HX2 OPN.

Introduction

Welcome to the sixth edition of *Buses Restored*. A measure of the book's popularity is that our publishers have decided to significantly increase the amount of colour pictures this year, which is a very welcome improvement. Colour is one of the things that the general public remember most about their local buses and those they rode on when they were children. It is, of course, useful to remember other basic things like the number of the service that will take you home and the fare, but visitors to local museums often say, 'I remember when the buses in x-town were red/green/blue (or whatever colour they were) — they were really good in the old days…' That's a bit unfair on the present bus companies, who often face much more difficult operating conditions than in the past, but that's what nostalgia is all about.

Colour, then! In the middle decades of the 20th century the colour of a town's buses (and trams) really helped to give that town a distinctive look. Yellow buses in Newcastle and Bournemouth, the blues of Walsall or Hull, green in Liverpool and Leeds, and those smart deep maroon and white buses in Edinburgh, which are only now being replaced with a less traditional livery. A yellow bus in Edinburgh or a red one in Hull just wouldn't have looked right. That's part of the fascination for the enthusiasts as well, and they can be quite partisan about the merits of their favourite bus operator — either a local-authority-owned one like Birmingham or Glasgow or one of the well-known bus companies of the past like Midland Red or Alexander. The public also like to see the buses they remember in their local transport museums and you will see from this book that there are museums or collections in most parts of the country today.

This view is something not always appreciated by the professionals in the 'heritage industry', who have been known to look askance at the proliferation of small groups of enthusiasts, each dedicated to preserving its own 'favourite' buses. There are calls for groups to work together, which is a laudable objective, but in practice asking a Lancastrian to work on a bus from Yorkshire would be like asking a Manchester United fan to go and support Leeds United. This is where NARTM, the National Association of Road Transport Museums, comes in — it is a relatively informal network ranging from museums that are open to the public on a regular basis through to smaller groups with perhaps just one or two buses in their care. NARTM provides a forum for an exchange of ideas and information on all subjects, from health and safety policy, through funding and sponsorship, to the best place to buy parts for a prewar Leyland bus.

A few years ago there were calls for a National Bus Museum, along the lines of the splendid National Railway Museum, but, as noted above, buses, much more than trains, are tied to a local area. Given that volunteers run the majority of the projects listed in this book in their own time, not as a full-time occupation, what would be the incentive for those people to travel a considerable distance to a central location? NARTM would rather support the relatively low-cost option of local museums and keep the buses 'in their own environment'. At the same time there are some splendid examples of professionally run transport museums and the London Transport Museum in Covent Garden has perhaps the best interpretative material of the establishments in this book – focusing simply on the public transport of the capital.

This local emphasis keeps the museums and their exhibits close to the public who remember the vehicles and who like to show them to their children and grandchildren. The buses themselves will show local destinations and the unique touches bestowed on them by individualistic general managers over the years. Remembering why we used the buses — to go to school, work, the shops or the cinema — helps to explain to future generations just how much life in Britain has changed over the past century. That is what bus museums should be all about — explaining why the buses were used in each area and just how much a part of everyday life they really were. It is what the heritage professionals call 'interacting with your heritage'. If that experience can sometimes involve taking a ride on an old bus as well, then so much the better.

Historic vehicle rallies and other events where the public can see old buses from the local area give an opportunity to see vehicles that may not be on display in formal museums and a number of the museums listed in *Buses Restored* which cannot be visited instead take their vehicles out to meet the public. This is one area where transport museums have a much easier job than a more static museum or art gallery of engaging with the general public. Several of the museums listed have included details of their events in 2005, others give contact details and many now have websites that are regularly updated. Magazines such as *Buses*,

Bus and Coach Preservation and *Classic Bus* are readily available and give the latest information about where you can see and ride on historic buses.

If you bought last year's *Buses Restored* you may remember that I listed the number of buses that had changed hands since the first edition, and also those that had slipped out of sight. As a result several groups have come forward to let us know that some of these vehicles are safe in their possession. By way of a change I thought I would conclude this Introduction by giving details of some of the buses that have moved from being 'Under Restoration' into the 'Restored' category. Restoration of a bus can be a very protracted business, often depending on the circumstances and other commitments of the vehicle's owners. I should know — we have been working on a Leyland Atlantean bus that had an extended working life of 22 years, followed by five years in storage and then 11 years under restoration (so far, although now it really is quite near to being finished). Why should it take so long? Well, in my case I plead work commitments, living out of the area for some years and, most of all, doing my bit to run the museum where the bus lives.

The first of our restoration cases was funded by the Heritage Lottery Fund, so made much more rapid progress, as described below by Mike Greenwood of the Sheffield Bus Museum Trust.

Sheffield Transport 1954 Leyland PD2/Weymann No 687 (RWB 87)

The year 2004 marked the appearance on the rally scene of restored Sheffield Transport Weymann-bodied Leyland PD2 No 687. Owned by the Sheffield Bus Museum Trust, the bus was the subject of a Lottery-funded restoration that took just three years.

Just before Christmas 2000 the Sheffield Bus Museum heard the good news that its application for a Lottery grant had been successful. A considerable amount of work was required as a number of vital components were missing and, as always seems to be the case with vehicle restoration, unforeseen problems arose at regular intervals! By summer 2002 the mechanical and rewiring work was almost complete and the bodywork was as good as finished, or so the Museum thought! Further unforeseen mechanical woes had to be sorted out,

---

SUNDAY 14TH AUGUST 2005
MIDLANDS BUS & COMMERCIAL SHOW
WALSALL ARBORETUM EXTENSION,
WALSALL, West Midlands
Entries Invited from New and Preserved Buses and Coaches, Miniature Coaches, Commercials, trade and collectors/enthusiasts stalls

Also

SUNDAY 8TH MAY 2005
27th SANDWELL HISTORIC VEHICLE SHOW,
SANDWELL COUNTRY PARK,
WEST BROMWICH, West Midlands

SUNDAY 26TH JUNE 2005
SHEFFIELD FESTIVAL OF TRANSPORT,
GRAVES PARK, SHEFFIELD

Details/Entry Forms:

Transtar Promotions, 9 Newquay Road, Park Hall, Walsall, West Midlands, WS5 3EL
Telephone: 01922 643385
Or visit the website www.transtarpromotions.co.uk

although during this period the lower saloon upholstery was completed and seat frames and seat backs were repaired or made. Due to these inevitable delays the Museum was able to negotiate a final extension of the period of funding and the completion date was put back to the end of December 2003.

The final phase of the project is for the Museum to acquire an Operator's Licence and for No 687 to be upgraded to a Class 6 MOT. Once this is achieved, this 1954 stalwart will be available for private hire, to undertake heritage tours and to assist with educational visits.

Our second case study was a much longer-term job and the bus concerned really 'came back from the dead'. I remember seeing this forlorn-looking London Transport Routemaster at Aston Manor Road Transport Museum in Birmingham many years ago when it looked very sorry for itself.

London Transport 1960 AEC/Park Royal Routemaster RM506 (WLT 506)

Routemaster RM506 finally ended a very long restoration with a successful first-time MOT just in time to get to the RM 50th anniversary celebration event in July 2004. One of the early group of Routemasters to be withdrawn from service, this vehicle was donated to Aston Manor by the West Midlands Probation Service in 1988 and was an early member of the Witton fleet before the Museum opened to the public in 1992. The vehicle was in a heavily vandalised condition, with every piece of glass smashed and most exterior panels having had holes punched in them with a scaffold pole. Work commenced around 1992 and various work parties have been involved in further stripping down of the vehicle, as well as its total refurbishment. Work has included the complete replacement of the interior with parts from other buses (one of the advantages of standardisation and mass-production methods). The exterior has been almost completely repanelled and new glazing has been fitted throughout. Restoration sees it in original condition just as it was delivered in 1960 as a trolleybus replacement bus at Hanwell garage. However, in reality, the true identity is mostly that of RM1818 so there are some body variations that can be spotted!

Our third restoration is of a bus that has been in preservation for even longer than those described above. Bought for preservation in 1981, it changed hands twice before serious restoration began as long ago as 1988.

Rawtenstall Corporation 1950 Leyland Tiger PS2/East Lancs No 55 (MTB 848)

This single-deck bus worked in the Rossendale area of Lancashire for around 20 years before it became the towing bus, based in the Rawtenstall depot. More precisely, it was parked next to a pile of rock salt, which did nothing for the rear chassis, and it had to be extensively plated and welded. The rear part of the floor had to be replaced and the interior was completely refurbished. This work included the fitting of heaters for the first time – they were hardy folk in the Rossendale valley in the 1950s. The bus was completely rewired and one of the last major jobs was to rebuild the radiator. After the usual brake overhaul, oil changes, chassis cleaning and painting, the bus was painted during summer 2004 and is now ready to take its first MOT test for well over 20 years. No 55 can usually be seen at the Museum of Transport in Manchester.

The three very different case studies above represent many thousands of hours of mostly unpaid work, with some excellent end products to show for all that hard labour. When scraping rust off a chassis or cleaning sludge out of the engine sump, often in cold and damp conditions, it can be all too easy to become discouraged and succumb to the temptation to give up and get an easier hobby. However, all the people involved in these projects had the staying power and vision to know that they could finish the huge list of jobs ahead, and now the finished articles show that they were right to carry on. There are many more projects around the country that are nearing completion – some will be seen on the rally fields during 2005 and others will make their debut in 2006. All being well, we will be looking at some of these in the next edition of *Buses Restored*.

In the meantime, read this book, enjoy the pictures and information inside and, most important of all, support as many museums and groups as you can by visiting those projects open to the public and attending the many rallies up and down the country.

Dennis Talbot
Chairman, NARTM

What is NARTM ?

The National Association of Road Transport Museums (NARTM) is an informal organisation of museums and collections. Volunteers operate many of them, although others, such as the Glasgow and London Transport Museums, are managed by full-time staff. This mix of museum types gives the opportunity to share ideas and experiences and the volunteers involved each bring their own professional skills to their projects and best practices can then be shared by all the member collections.

NARTM has been in existence for almost 20 years and now has around 30 member organisations, with more joining each year. The buses and coaches that form part of the NARTM collections are generally regarded as forming the nucleus of the National Collection of Buses and Coaches. However, it must be stressed that many important examples are in private hands outside the scope of NARTM and its members.

What does NARTM do?

Many of the people involved in running transport museums are busy people and have little spare time after making significant contributions to their own projects, such as the Museum in Manchester. This is why NARTM only holds two meetings each year at the various member museums and in recent years we have visited Devon, Lincoln, Glasgow, Oxford and Portsmouth. In between meetings, the quarterly *Bulletin* keeps members in touch with each other and we are often in touch. Indeed, one of the main functions of NARTM is to put people in touch with each other and there are many instances of restoration projects progressing and spare parts being located through NARTM contacts. Discussion topics at recent meetings have included the encouragement and role of Junior members, bus services, grant applications, museum registration, visitor facilities, risk assessment, documentation and links with other bodies.

NARTM's unique service to its members is also as an information exchange about running museums — after all, as so many of our members are volunteers, their skills and experiences are not within the heritage and leisure industry. It is often the case that another project in another area has already been faced with exactly the same issues as we have today, and by sharing ideas and pooling resources, progress can be made more quickly.

Over the years NARTM has also taken a lead role in campaigning on new legislation to lessen its impact on the historic bus preservation movement. Vehicle licensing, driver licensing, tachographs and the retention of original registration numbers have all received our attention, with some success in each case through our work in conjunction with other groups within the movement. NARTM is also a club authorised to endorse applications from historic vehicle owners to retain, or regain, the original registration of their vehicle.

The future

NARTM is currently working closely with the Transport Trust to define the bus preservation sector of the heritage transport industry. It is also addressing the major issues currently facing the movement — storage, documentation, human resources and skills, public access and the future of vehicles in preservation. A database is now maintained which lists all vehicles in NARTM and associated collections and this will eventually form part of a decision-making process to ensure that the most historically important vehicles have a secure long-term future.

For more information about NARTM please contact:
NARTM, PO Box 5141, Burton-upon-Trent, Staffordshire, DE15 0ZF.
Website: www.nartm.org.uk
e-mail: nartm@btinternet.com

Useful addresses

The Transport Trust, 202 Lambeth Road, London SE1 7JW.

British Bus Preservation Group, 18 Greenriggs, Hedley Park, Stopsley, Luton LU2 9TQ.

The PSV Circle, 26 Ashville Grove, Halifax HX2 0PN.

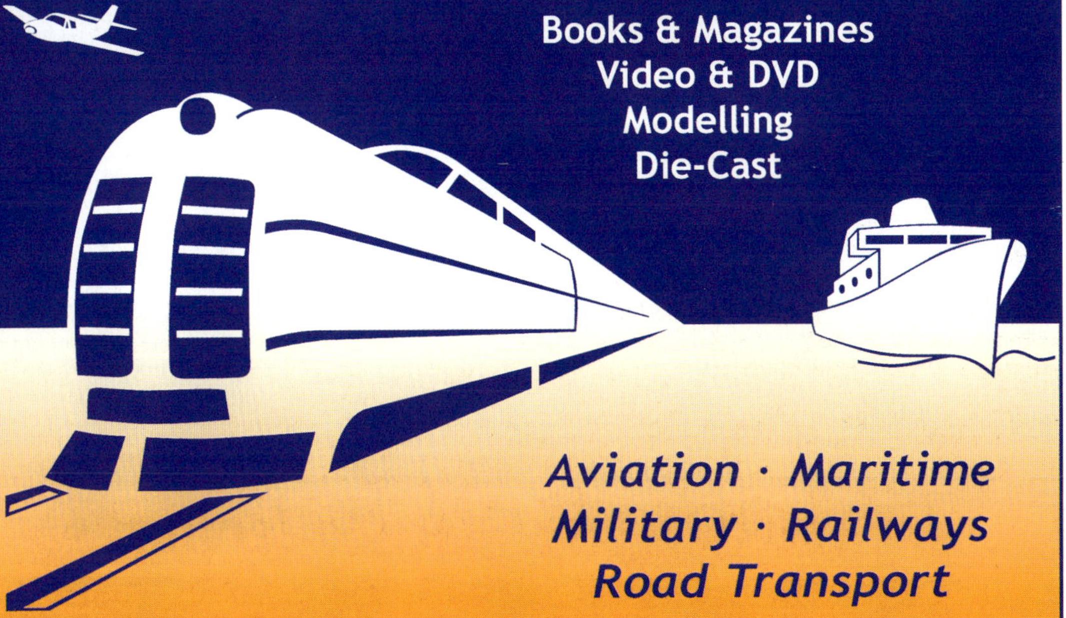

How to Use this Book

This book lists both formal museums and the more informal types of collection, and gives details of opening times, contact addresses and the facilities available, together with a list of the buses, trolleybuses and coaches on display. Many of the sites are open to the public on a regular basis. Admission fees vary and some are even free to visitors, although donations towards the upkeep of the collections are always welcome. Please be aware that the vehicles on display can vary from time to time. Not all museums are able to display their entire 'fleet', and some practise the regular rotation of exhibits for added interest. In addition, some of the vehicles may be in the process of restoration in a workshop off-site, and there is always the possibility that a bus may be on loan to another museum! Visitors wishing to see a particular vehicle should make enquiries prior to the visit.

Some collections are not normally available for public access. However, the owners usually welcome visitors and will arrange for viewing by prior application. In addition, many such groups do have open or public days from time to time. Contact addresses are provided in this book, and those wishing to visit a particular site are asked to contact the address given. Please bear in mind that most are run by volunteers — please enclose a stamped self-addressed envelope when writing and respect the privacy of individuals. This book does not grant or imply any permission whatsoever to enter premises to look at old buses except by the agreement of the group involved. Note that, where buses are licensed for use on public passenger-carrying services, the use of individual vehicles will vary from time to time, as the demands of their preservation dictate.

Whilst some of the restored vehicles detailed here have been 'officially' preserved by their former operators, the majority have been restored and conserved by volunteers, often working in difficult conditions with limited resources of time, money and materials. That there are so many buses and coaches fully restored is a testimony to the

• The NOSTALGIA Collection •

ROAD TRANSPORT HERITAGE

Trams, trolleybuses and motor-buses provide us with the perfect means of travelling down Memory Lane, allowing us to wonder at all the changes in fashions, street scenes, adverts and architecture in these many photographs of the High Streets and suburbs of our towns and cities.

BIRMINGHAM BUSES AT WORK	1 85794 237 X	£15.99
A NOSTALGIC TOUR OF WOLVERHAMPTON BY TRAM, TROLLEYBUS AND BUS		
Part 1 The western routes	1 85794 133 0	£15.99
Part 2 The northern routes	1 85794 192 6	£15.99
Part 3 The eastern routes	1 85794 241 8	£15.99
BIRMINGHAM IN THE AGE OF THE TRAM		
The south-eastern and northern routes	1 85794 181 0	£15.99
LEEDS IN THE AGE OF THE TRAM	1 85794 187 X	£14.99
SHEFFIELD IN THE AGE OF THE TRAM	1 85794 191 8	£15.99

Order by calling or writing to *The NOSTALGIA Collection*
The Trundle, Ringstead Road, Great Addington, Kettering, Northants NN14 4BW

All major credit cards accepted Tel/Fax: 01536 330588 Website: www.nostalgiacollection.com

dedication of bus enthusiasts over the last 40 years or more, and it is intended that the vehicles will have a long and secure future.

The information used in this book is as provided by the organisations listed, for which the authors express their thanks. As far as possible, details are correct to 30 September 1999. Any information on further collections not included in the current edition will be most welcome. If you own vehicles, or are associated wih such an organisation, please contact NARTM at the address given on page 5.

For each vehicle, details given include the present registration number, year first registered, brief chassis and body details (including seating) and original operator. Standard PSV Circle body codes are used, as outlined below.

Body type (before seating capacity)**:**
- A   articulated
- B   single-deck bus
- C   coach (single-deck)
- CH   double-decker coach
- Ch   charabanc
- CO   convertible open-top double-decker
- DP   dual-purpose (eg coach seats in bus shell)
- F   full-front (where not normal for chassis)
- H   Highbridge double-decker
- L   Lowbridge double-decker (ie with sunken side gangway upstairs; all other types — with conventional gangways — are 'H', regardless of overall height)
- O   open-top double-decker
- OB   open-top single-decker
- PO   partially-open-top double decker
- R   single-decker with raised rear saloon (eg over luggage compartment)
- T   Toastrack

Seating capacity:
For double-deckers this is shown with the upper-deck capacity first, eg 43/31

Door position (after seating capacity)**:**
- C   centre entrance/exit
- D   dual doors (usually front entrance and centre exit)
- F   front or forward entrance/exit
- R   open rear platform
- RD   rear entrance/exit with doors
- RO   open rear platform with open staircase
- T   triple doors (eg on articulated vehicles)

Suffix:
- t   fitted with toilet
- l   fitted with wheelchair lift

The restoration state is given in accordance with the following code:
- **R**   restored;
- **RP**   restoration in progress;
- **A**   awaiting restoration.

Note: Please be aware that vehicles on display can vary from time to time as not all museums display their entire 'fleet'. Visitors wishing to see a particular vehicle should make enquiries prior to their visit.

BUS MAGAZINES

from  PUBLISHING

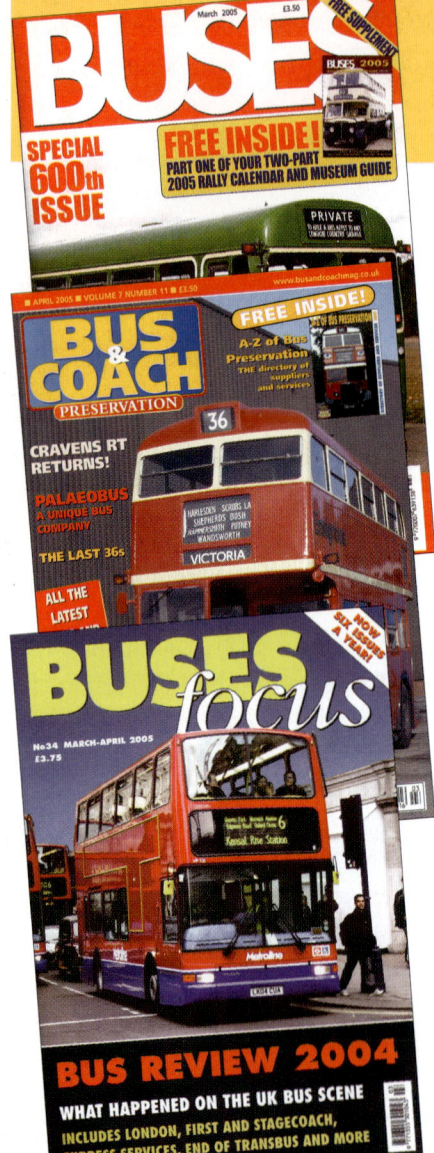

BUSES
Monthly £3.50

Britain's most widely read publication covering the bus and coach industries. *Buses* is written for a readership that appreciates quality editorial and first rate photography. All the latest developments within the UK's bus and coach fleets are covered within the unique 'Fleet News' section of the magazine every month.

BUS & COACH PRESERVATION
Monthly £3.50

The ONLY monthly magazine dedicated to Britain's rich and varied bus preservation movement. Each issue has a wealth of editorial features and news including restoration, events and full colour photography creating an unbeatable read for the enthusiast.

BUSES FOCUS
Bi-monthly £3.75

THE informed voice of the contemporary British Bus scene. Each issue contains authoritative in-depth coverage of key operators and the markets' everchanging requirements.

Available from all leading newsagents, or order direct from:
Subscription Dept, Ian Allan Publishing Ltd, Riverdene Business Park, Molesey Road, Hersham, Surrey KT12 4RG
Tel: 01932 266622 **Fax:** 01932 266633 **e-mail:** subs@ianallanpub.co.uk

Part 1

Museums Normally Open to the Public

Belfast 246 (2206 OI) is currently at the Black Country Museum on loan from the Eat Anglia Transport Museum, The Harkness-bodied Sunbeam F4A was restored there in 2003. *Philip Lamb*

Key to facilities

A	Audio/visual displays	H	Baby-changing facilities
B	Bus rides (regular)	L	Lecture theatre
B(e)	Bus rides (at events)	M	Band stand
C	Children's information pack	P	Car parking
D	Access for disabled	R	Refreshments
E	Picnic facilities	S	Enthusiasts' shop
F	School activity pack	T	Toilets
G	Gift shop		

Note: Please be aware that vehicles on display can vary from time to time as not all museums display their entire 'fleet'. Visitors wishing to see a particular vehicle should make enquiries prior to their visit.

Abbey Pumping Station
Leicester

Contact address: Corporation Road, Leicester LE4 5PX
Phone: 0116 299 5111
Fax: 0116 299 5125
Brief description: The Museum is a Victorian pumping-station dating from 1892 with four beam-engines. The vehicle collection is on view on special open days. On these occasions, one of the beam-engines is steamed.
Events planned: Opening times for special events: Saturdeys 11.00-14.30, Sundays 13.00-17.00
3 April, 7 May, 4 June, 9 July, 6 August, 3 September 2005 — Railway Running Days;
4 June 2005 — Teddy Bears Day
25/26 June 2005 — Urban Rally Weekend
6 August 2005 — Classic Vehicles
11 September 2005 — Steam & Craft Day
1 October 2005 — Smelly Railway Day
30 October 2005 — Halloween and Ghostly Engineers Steam Day
4 December 2005 — Christmas Toys Steam Day
Please see the enthusiast press for further details.
Opening days/times:
Summer opening: From 1 April 2005 Saturday, and Monday to Wednesday 11.00 to 16.30, Sunday 13.00-16.30
Directions by car: A6 (north of Leicester) joins Abbey Lane at Redhill Island. Corporation Road is off Abbey Lane.
Directions by public transport: From City Centre (Charles Street) take bus 54 to top of Corporation Road.
Charges: Free except on special open days.
Facilities: C D E G H P R (on open days) T

Registration	Date	Chassis	Body	New to	Fleet No	Status
CBC 921	1939	AEC Renown O664	Northern Counties H32/32R	Leicester City Transport	329	R
GAY 171	1950	Leyland Tiger PS1/1	Willowbrook DP35F	Allen of Mountsorrel	43	A
MTL 750	1958	Leyland Tiger Cub PSUC1/2	Yeates DP43F	Delaine Coaches of Bourne	47	R
TBC 164	1958	Leyland Titan PD3/1	Willowbrook H41/33R	Leicester City Transport	164	R
JMC 121K	1972	AEC Reliance 6MU4R	Plaxton C34C	Glenton Tours of London	121	R
OUM 727P	1976	Bedford J2SZ10	Caetano C16F	Anderton Tours of Keighley		R
B401 NJF	1984	Ford Transit 190D	Rootes B16F	Midland Fox	M1	R

Notes:
CBC 921 — On view at Snibston Discovery Park
B401 NJF — On view at Snibston Discovery Park

Note: Please be aware that vehicles on display can vary from time to time as not all museums display their entire 'fleet'. Visitors wishing to see a particular vehicle should make enquiries prior to their visit.

Amberley Museum

Contact address: Amberley, Arundel, West Sussex, BN18 9LT
Phone: 01798 831370
Fax: 01798 831831
E-mail: office@amberleymuseum.co.uk
Brief Description: The industrial museum has a wide range of attractions, including rail and bus operations. Some buses in the collection are museum-owned and others are owned by the Southdown Omnibus Trust or are in private hands.
Events planned:
16/17 July 2005 — The *Real* Museum Show (a look behind the scenes of a museum at work);
11 September 2009 — Bus Rally — 90 Years of Southdown.
9 October 2005 — Autumn Vintage Vehicle show
Opening days/times:
March to October: Weds to Sun (also Mon and Tues during school holidays)
Directions by car: Situated close to Amberley railway station on the B2139. Approach from the north and west via the A29 and from the east via the A24 and A283.
Directions by public transport: Hourly rail service calls at Amberley station which is adjacent to the museum.
Charges: Adults £7.50, OAP £6.50.
Facilities: A B B(e) C D E F G H L P R T

Registration	Date	Chassis	Body	New to	Fleet No	Status
IB 552	1914	Tilling Stevens TS3 Petrol Electric	Newman O22/16R	Worthing Motor Services		R
CD 5125	1920	Leyland N	Short O27/24R	Southdown Motor Services	125	R
CD 4867	1923	Tilling Stevens TS3A Petrol Electric	(chassis only)			RP
BP 9822	1924	Shelvoke & Drewery Freighter	Hickman (replica) B18F	Tramocar of Worthing		R
MO 9324	1927	Tilling Stevens B9A	Brush B32R	Thames Valley Traction Co	152	R
UF 1517	1927	Dennis 30cwt	Short B19R	Southdown Motor Services	517	R
BR 7132	1929	Leyland Lion LT1	Leyland B34F	Sunderland Corporation	2	R
UF 4813	1929	Leyland Titan TD1	Brush O27/24R	Southdown Motor Services	813	A
UF 6473	1930	Leyland Titan TD1	Leyland H24/24R	Southdown Motor Services	873	R
UF 6805	1930	Tilling Stevens B10A2	Short B31R	Southdown Motor Services	1205	RP
UF 7428	1931	Leyland Titan TD1	Short H26/24R	Southdown Motor Services	928	R
ECD 524	1937	Leyland Cub KPZ2	Park Royal B20F	Southdown Motor Services	24	A
EUF 184	1938	Leyland Titan TD5	Leyland -	Southdown Motor Services	0184	R

Notes:
IB 552	Petrol-electric Transmission. Body new 1909.	MO 9324	Mechanical Transmission. Restored at Amberley
CD 5125	Restored using a P or Q 5- or 6-ton chassis. Rebodied 1928	BR 7132	Stored off-site
		UF 4813	On loan from Southdown Motor Services Ltd
CD 4867	Petrol-electric. To be restored as Southdown replica charabanc	UF 6805	Mechanical Transmission.
		EUF 184	Converted from bus 184; fitted with breakdown vehicle body ex Leyland TD1 872 (UF 6472)
BP 9822	Solid tyres. Replica body built at Amberley		
UF 1517	All-metal body.		

Aston Manor Road Transport Museum

Contact address: The Old Tram Depot, 208-216 Witton Lane, Aston, Birmingham B6 6QE
Phone: 0121 322 2298
Fax: 0121 308 0544
Web site: www.amrtm.org.uk
Affiliation: NARTM

Brief description: The 19th-century former tram depot houses a selection of buses, coaches, commercial vehicles and tramcar bodies in an authentic setting — the depot still has tram tracks and stone sets in situ. There are also many small exhibits, working model layouts and video presentations.

Events planned:
30 May 2005 — Two Museums Running Day. Bus service linking Aston Manor and Wythall.
10 July 2005 — Open day/vehicle gathering.
10/11 Sept 2005 — Heritage Open Days.
27 Nov 2005 — Collectors' fair with free bus rides.
Please see the enthusiast press for other events.

Opening days/times:
Saturdays, Sundays and Bank Hols 11.00 to 17.00. Other times by arrangement.
Opening times may vary over Christmas/New Year period.

Directions by car: Easy access from M6 junction 6.
Directions by public transport: Rail to Witton Station and a short walk (170yd)
Bus No 7 from Birmingham City Centre or bus No 11, outer circle to Witton Square.

Charges:
Adults £1, Child 50p, Family £2.75.
Admission charges may vary on special event days.

Facilities: A B(e) D H P R S T

Other information: Not all of the vehicles listed are on display at the museum. To view any vehicle not normally accessible, visitors should enquire at the museum as to arrangements for viewing.

Registration	Date	Chassis	Body	New to	Fleet No	Status
note z	1925	AEC S	Buckingham	Birmingham Corporation Tramways	215	A
OP 237	1926	(no chassis)	Short H32/26R	Birmingham Corporation Tramways	208	A
EA 4181	1929	Dennis E	Dixon B32F	West Bromwich Corporation	32	RP
HA 4963	1930	SOS RR	(chassis only)	BMMO ('Midland Red')	963	A
JF 2378	1931	AEC Regal 662	Burlingham C32R	Provincial of Leicester	R1	R
OJ 9347	1933	Morris Commercial Dictator	Metro Cammell B—F	Birmingham Corporation Tramways	47	RP
ANB 851	1934	Crossley Mancunian	Crossley/MCT H28/26R	Manchester Corporation	436	A
AOG 679	1935	Daimler COG5		Birmingham Corporation Tramways	83	A
CDH 501	1935	Dennis Lance	Park Royal H28/24R	Walsall Corporation	110	A
EHA 775	1938	SOS SON	(chassis only)	BMMO ('Midland Red')	2207	A
FON 630	1942	Leyland Titan TD7	(chassis only)	Birmingham City Transport	1330	A
KHA 301	1948	BMMO C1	Duple C30C	BMMO ('Midland Red')	3301	R
KTT 689	1948	Guy Vixen	Wadham FC29F	Court Cars of Tourquay		R
ARC 515+	1949	Sunbeam F4	Brush H30/26R	Derby Corporation	215	A
GUJ 608	1950	Sentinel STC4	Sentinel B40F	Sentinel demonstrator		R
JOJ 222	1950	Leyland Titan PD2/1	Park Royal H29/25R	Birmingham City Transport	2222	RP
JOJ 526	1950	Guy Arab IV	Metro Cammell H30/24R	Birmingham City Transport	2526	A
JOJ 548	1950	Guy Arab IV	Metro Cammell H30/24R	Birmingham City Transport	2548	RP
KEL 131	1950	Leyland Titan PD2/3	Weymann FH33/25D	Bournemouth Corporation	131	RP
KHA 352	1950	BMMO CL2	Plaxton C26C	BMMO ('Midland Red')	3352	RP
SB 8155	1950	Guy Wolf	Ormac B20F	Alexander MacConnacher of Ballachulish		R
JOJ 847	1952	Daimler CVG6	Crossley H30/25RD	Birmingham City Transport	2847	A
LOG 301	1952	Guy Arab IV	Saunders Roe H30/25R	Birmingham City Transport	3001	RP
LJW 336	1953	Guy LUF	Saunders Roe B44F	Guy Demonstrator		R
LOG 302	1954	Daimler CLG5	Metro Cammell H30/25R	Birmingham City Transport	3002	R
MOF 90	1954	Guy Arab IV	Metro Cammell H30/25R	Birmingham City Transport	3090	RP
RRU 903	1955	Leyland Tiger Cub PSUC1/1	Park Royal B40F	Bournemouth Corporation	266	R
773 FHA	1958	BMMO D9	BMMO H40/32RD	BMMO ('Midland Red')	4773	A
1294 RE	1959	Guy Arab LUF	Burlingham C41F	Harper Bros of Heath Hayes	60	R
WLT 506	1960	AEC Routemaster R2RH	Park Royal H36/28R	London Transport	RM 506	R
264 ERY	1963	Leyland Titan PD3A/1	Park Royal O41/33R	Leicester City Transport	264	R
3035 HA	1963	BMMO D9	BMMO O40/32RD	BMMO ('Midland Red')	5035	RP
334 CRW	1963	Daimler CVG6	Metro Cammell H34/29R	Coventry City Transport	334	RP
6370 HA	1964	BMMO D9	BMMO H40/32RD	BMMO ('Midland Red')	5370	R
EHA 415D	1966	BMMO D9	BMMO/Willowbrook H40/32RD	BMMO ('Midland Red')	5415	R
KOX 663F	1967	AEC Swift MP2R	MCW B37D	Birmingham City Transport	3663	RP
LHA 870F	1967	BMMO S21	BMMO DP49F	BMMO ('Midland Red')	5870	R

Registration	Date	Chassis	Body	New to	Fleet No	Status
UHA 969H	1970	BMMO S23	BMMO/Plaxton B51F	BMMO ('Midland Red')	5969	A
XNX 136H	1970	Leyland Leopard PSU3A/4R	Alexander DP49F	Stratford-upon-Avon Blue Motors	36	R
XON 41J	1971	Daimler Fleetline CRG6LX	Park Royal H43/33F	West Midlands PTE	4041	R
GOH 357N	1974	Leyland Leopard PSU3B/2R	Marshall DP49F	Midland Red Omnibus Co	357	R
OFR 989M	1974	AEC Swift 3MP2R	Marshall B47D	Blackpool Corporation	589	RP
PHA 319M	1974	Leyland Leopard PSU3B/2R	Marshall DP49F	Midland Red Omnibus Co	319	RP
JOV 714P	1976	Bristol VRTSL2/6LX	MCW H43/33F	West Midlands PTE	4714	R
OOX 825R	1977	Leyland National 11351A/1R	Leyland National DP45F	West Midlands PTE	6825	RP
BVP 784V	1979	Leyland Leopard PSU3E/4R	Plaxton C53F	Midland Red Omnibus Co	784	A
WDA 700T	1979	Leyland Fleetline FE30AGR	MCW H43/33F	West Midlands PTE	7000	A
F685 YOG	1988	MCW Metrorider MF150/113	MCW B23F	West Midlands PTE	685	A

+ Trolleybus

Notes:
note z	Registration not known	KEL 131	Built with twin staircases and dual doors
HA 4963	Chassis only	LOG 302	Chrome-plated chassis exhibited 1952 Commercial Motor Show
OJ 9347	Renumbered 77 in 1935		
ANB 851	Rebodied 1938	RRU 903	Converted for OMO and rear door removed in 1957
AOG 679	Originally bus 679 with Northern Counties H26/22R body; rebodied 1947 as a van	3035 HA	Originally H40/32RD; converted to open-top by Marshall ('Obsolete Fleet') London (OM6)
EHA 775	Chassis only	264 ERY	Originally H41/33R
KHA 352	Rebodied 1963	OOX 825R	Volvo engine fitted by WM PTE

Birmingham & Midland Museum of Transport
Wythall

Contact address: Chapel Lane, Wythall, Worcestershire, B47 6JX
Phone: 01564 826471
E-mail: enquiries@bammot.org.uk
Web site: www.bammot.org.uk
Affiliations: AIM, NARTM, Transport Trust, MLA West Midlands
Brief description: The collection is based on buses built and/or operated locally, plus others of significant PSV history. In addition, there is a unique collection of battery-operated road vehicles and a miniature passenger-carrying steam railway on site. Museum developed and run by volunteers
Events planned:
Operating days 27/28 March; 1/2, 29 May; 28 August
30 May 2005 — Two Museums Day, half hourly buses to Aston Manor Transport Museum
31 July 2005 — Midland Red in Operation
29 August 2005 — The Big Operating Day
9 October 2005 — Pre-Hibernation Day
Opening days/times: Saturdays, Sundays and Bank Holidays 11.00 to 17.00, Easter Sunday to 9 October.
Directions by car: Wythall is on the main A435 Birmingham-Evesham road. The museum is next to Wythall old church. From M42 use junction 3 and head towards Birmingham.
Directions by public transport: Museum services operate on event days (including ex-Hill St, Birmingham 11.30 on 27/28 March; 1/2, 29 May; 28 August; 9 October.
Bus services serve Wythall from Birmingham and Solihull. Neither operates on Sundays
Wythall rail station is 25min walk from museum.
Charges: £2.00 (£4 on Bank Holiday Mondays, £3 on Sunday operating days). Admission ticket can be upgraded to all-day riding ticket at additional charge of £3 — includes admission to Aston Manor Transport Museum on 30 May
Facilities: B(e) E P S T
Other information: Refreshments available on event days

Note: Please be aware that vehicles on display can vary from time to time as not all museums display their entire 'fleet'. Visitors wishing to see a particular vehicle should make enquiries prior to their visit.

Registration	Date	Chassis	Body	New to	Fleet No	Status
O 9926	1913	Tilling Stevens TTA2	Thomas Tilling O18/16RO	BMMO ('Midland Red')	26	RP
HA 3501	1925	SOS Standard	Ransomes Sims & Jefferies B32F	BMMO ('Midland Red')	501	A
CN 2870	1927	SOS Q	Brush B37F	Northern General Transport Co	321	RP
CC 7745	1928	SOS QL	Brush B37F	Royal Blue of Llandudno		A
OV 4090	1931	Morris Commercial Dictator	Metro Cammell B34F	Birmingham Corporation Tramways	90	A
OV 4486	1931	AEC Regent 661	Metro Cammell H27/21R	Birmingham Corporation Tramways	486	A
OC 527	1933	Morris Commercial Imperial	Metro Cammell H50R	Birmingham Corporation Tramways	527	A
AHA 582	1935	SOS DON	Brush B36F	BMMO ('Midland Red')	1703	A
CVP 207	1937	Daimler COG5	Metro Cammell H30/24R	Birmingham City Transport	1107	R
RC 4615	1937	AEC Regal O662	Willowbrook B34F	Trent Motor Traction Co	714	R
GHA 333	1940	SOS SON	(chassis only)	BMMO ('Midland Red')	2414	RP
GHA 337	1940	SOS SON	Brush B38F	BMMO ('Midland Red')	2418	RP
HHA 637	1946	BMMO S6	Metro Cammell B40F	BMMO ('Midland Red')	3036	A
FFY 402	1947	Leyland Titan PD2/3	Leyland O30/26R	Southport Corporation	85	RP
GUE 247	1948	Leyland Tiger PS1	Northern Coachbuilders B34F	Stratford-upon-Avon Blue Motors	41	A
HOV 685	1948	Leyland Titan PD2/1	Brush H30/24R	Birmingham City Transport	1685	R
JRR 404	1948	Leyland Titan PD1	Duple L29/26F	Barton Transport of Chilwell	473	RP
JXC 432	1948	AEC Regent III O961 RT	Weymann H30/26R	London Transport	RT 624	A
KAL 579	1948	Daimler CVD6	Massey H33/28RD	W Gash & Sons of Newark	DD2	R
FDM 724	1949	Foden PVD6	Massey H30/26R	E H Phillips Motor Services of Holywell		A
FJW 616+	1949	Sunbeam F4	Park Royal H28/26R	Wolverhampton Corporation	616	A
HDG 448	1949	Albion Venturer CX19	Metro Cammell H30/26R	Cheltenham District Traction Co	72	R
HWO 334	1949	Guy Arab III	Duple L27/26R	Red & White Services	34	R
JOJ 245	1950	Leyland Tiger PS2/1	Weymann B34F	Birmingham City Transport	2245	R
JOJ 533	1950	Guy Arab IV	Metro Cammell H30/24R	Birmingham City Transport	2533	R
JUE 349	1950	Leyland Tiger PS2/3	Northern Counties H35/28F	Stratford-upon-Avon Blue Motors	33	RP
KFM 775	1950	Bristol L5G	ECW B35R	Crosville Motor Services	KG126	R
NHA 744	1950	BMMO S12	Brush B44F	BMMO ('Midland Red')	3744	RP
NHA 795	1950	BMMO D5B	Brush H30/26RD	BMMO ('Midland Red')	3795	A
ORB 277	1950	Daimler CVD6	Duple C35F	Tailby & George ('Blue Bus Services') Willington		R
MXX 23	1952	AEC Regal IV 9821LT RF	Metro Cammell B41F	London Transport	RF 381	R
JOJ 976	1953	Guy Arab IV	Metro Cammell H30/25R	Birmingham City Transport	2976	R
PDH 808	1953	Leyland Royal Tiger PSU1	Park Royal DP40F	Walsall Corporation	808	R
RDH 505	1953	Leyland Titan PD2/12	Roe FH33/23RD	Walsall Corporation	815	A
SHA 431	1953	Leyland Titan PD2/12	Leyland H30/26RD	BMMO ('Midland Red')	4031	RP
FRC 956	1954	Leyland Titan PD2/12	Leyland H32/26RD	Trent Motor Traction Co	1256	R
UHA 255	1955	BMMO S14	BMMO B44F	BMMO ('Midland Red')	4255	R
XHA 482	1956	BMMO D7	Metro Cammell H37/26RD	BMMO ('Midland Red')	4482	R
XHA 496	1956	BMMO D7	Metro Cammell	BMMO ('Midland Red')	4496	A
SUK 3	1957	Guy Arab IV	Metro Cammell H33/27R	Wolverhampton Corporation	3	RP
UTU 596J	1957	Guy Otter NLLODP	Mulliner B26F	Douglas Corporation	9	A
VVP 911	1958	Bedford SB3	Duple C41F	Sandwell Motor Co of Birmingham		R
WDF 569	1959	Leyland Tiger Cub PSUC1	Willowbrook DP41F	Soudley Valley Coaches of Cinderford		R
871 KHA	1960	BMMO D9	BMMO H40/32RD	BMMO ('Midland Red')	4871	RP
943 KHA	1960	BMMO D10	BMMO H43/35F	BMMO ('Midland Red')	4943	R
802 MHW	1961	Bristol Lodekka FSF6G	ECW H34/26F	Cheltenham District Traction Co	6037	R
3016 HA	1962	BMMO D9	BMMO/LPC O40/32RD	BMMO ('Midland Red')	5016	R
5073 HA	1962	BMMO S15	BMMO B40F	BMMO ('Midland Red')	5073	R
5212 HA	1962	Leyland Leopard PSU3/4R	Willowbrook B53F	BMMO ('Midland Red')	5212	A
SBF 233	1962	Leyland Titan PD2/28	Northern Counties -	Harper Bros of Heath Hayes	25	R
248 NEA	1963	Daimler CVG6-30	Metro Cammell H41/33R	West Bromwich Corporation	248	R
6545 HA	1964	BMMO S16	BMMO B52F	BMMO ('Midland Red')	5545	R
BHA 399C	1965	BMMO D9	BMMO H40/32RD	BMMO ('Midland Red')	5399	R
BHA 656C	1965	BMMO CM6T	BMMO C44Ft	BMMO ('Midland Red')	5656	R
BON 474C	1965	Daimler Fleetline CRG6LX	Marshall B37F	Birmingham City Transport	3474	R
CUV 219C	1965	AEC Routemaster R2RH/1	Park Royal CH36/29RD	London Transport	RCL 2219	R
EHA 767D	1966	BMMO S17	BMMO/Plaxton B52F	BMMO ('Midland Red')	5767	R
GHA 415D	1966	Daimler Fleetline CRG6LX	Alexander H44/33F	BMMO ('Midland Red')	6015	RP
GRY 60D	1966	Leyland Titan PD3A/1	Park Royal H41/33R	Leicester City Transport	60	R

Registration	Date	Chassis	Body	New to	Fleet No	Status
HBF 679D	1966	Leyland Titan PD2A/27	Metro Cammell H36/28RD	Harper Bros of Heath Hayes	27	R
Q124 VOE	1966	Leyland Leopard PSU4/4R	Plaxton -	Midland Red Omnibus Co	5826	A
JHA 868E	1967	BMMO S21	BMMO DP49F	BMMO ('Midland Red')	5868	R
KHW 306E	1967	Bristol RELL6L	ECW B53F	Cheltenham District Traction Co	1000	R
NJW 719E	1967	Daimler Roadliner SRC6	Strachan B54D	Wolverhampton Corporation	719	R
KOX 780F	1968	Daimler Fleetline CRG6LX	Park Royal H43/33F	Birmingham City Transport	3780	R
NEA 101F	1968	Daimler Fleetline CRG6LX	Metro Cammell H42/31F	West Bromwich Corporation	101	RP
XDH 56G	1968	Daimler CRC6-36	Northern Counties H51/34D	Walsall Corporation	56	RP
OTA 632G	1969	Bristol RELH6G	ECW C45F	Southern National Omnibus Co (Royal Blue)	1460	R
SHA 645G	1969	Leyland Leopard PSU4A/4R	Plaxton C36F	BMMO ('Midland Red')	6145	R
SOE 913H	1969	Daimler Fleetline CRG6LX-33	Park Royal H47/33D	West Midlands PTE	3913	RP
UHA 956H	1969	BMMO S23	BMMO/Plaxton B51F	BMMO ('Midland Red')	5956	R
XDH 516G	1969	Daimler Fleetline CRG6LX	Northern Counties H41/27D	Walsall Corporation	116	R
FRB 211H	1970	Bristol VRTSL2/6LX	ECW H39/31F	Midland General Omnibus Co	322	R
UHA 941H	1970	BMMO S23	BMMO B51F	BMMO ('Midland Red')	5941	A
UHA 981H	1970	BMMO S23	BMMO/Plaxton B51F	BMMO ('Midland Red')	5981	R
WNG 864H	1970	Bristol RELL6G	ECW DP50F	Eastern Counties Omnibus Co	RLE 864	R
AHA 451J	1971	Leyland Leopard PSU4B/4R	Plaxton C36F	BMMO ('Midland Red')	6451	R
OWE 271K	1972	Bristol VRTSL2/6LX	East Lancs H43/30F	Sheffield Transport	271	RP
PDU 135M	1973	Daimler Fleetline CRG6LX	East Lancs H44/30F	Coventry City Transport	135	RP
TCH 274L	1973	Bristol RELH6G	ECW DP49F	Midland General Omnibus Co	274	R
PHA 370M	1974	Ford R1014	Plaxton/Midland Red DP23F	Midland Red Omnibus Co	370	R
JOV 613P	1975	Daimler Fleetline CRG6LX	Park Royal H43/33F	West Midlands PTE	4613	R
99-64-HB	1976	Den Oudsten LOK	Den Ousden B35D	VAD of Ermele (Netherlands)	5656	A
KON 311P	1976	Leyland Fleetline FE30 ALR	Metro Cammell H43/33F	West Midlands PTE	6311	R
NOE 544R	1976	Leyland National 11351A/1R	Leyland National B49F	Midland Red Omnibus Co	544	R
BOK 1V	1979	MCW Metrobus DR102/12	MCW H43/30F	West Midlands PTE	2001	A

+ Trolleybus

Notes:

RC 4615	Rebodied 1950	3016 HA	Originally H40/32RD; converted to open-top by Marshall ('Obsolete Fleet') London (OM5)
GHA 333	Converted to works tug with AEC engine by Midland Red c. 1960.	5073 HA	Reseated from DP40F in 1969
FFY 402	Originally H30/26R	SBF 233	Rebuilt as towing tender 1981
KAL 579	Rebodied 1958	Q124 VOE	Rebuilt as towing tender 1977
JUE 349	Rebodied 1963	PHA 370M	Shortened to B27F by Midland Red in 1979. Reseated to DP23F in 1983.
PDH 808	Originally B42F		
XHA 496	Converted to Breakdown Vehicle 1972	99-64-HB	Netherlands registration
UTU 596J	Originally registered WMN 485	KON 311P	Gardner engine fitted in 1981
943 KHA	Entered service 1961		

Black Country Living Museum Transport Group
Dudley

Contact address: Tipton Road, Dudley, West Midlands DY1 4SQ
Phone: 0121 557 9643
Web site: www.bclm.co.uk
Brief description: Tramway operation daily. Trolleybus operation on Sundays and Bank Holidays.
Opening days/times: Summer: daily 10.00-17.00. Winter: Wednesdays to Sundays 10.00-16.00. Some evening openings
Events planned: Please contact for details

Note: Please be aware that vehicles on display can vary from time to time as not all museums display their entire 'fleet'. Visitors wishing to see a particular vehicle should make enquiries prior to their visit.

Directions by car: M5 (jct 2) signposted on Motorway. follow signs on A4123 to 'Black Country Living Museum'.
Directions by public transport: Central Trains to Tipton station. Travel West Midlands 224, 263, 270, 311-313 to Museum.
Facilities: A, B, B(e)C, D, E, F, G, H, L, P, R, T
Contact (Transport Group): Black Country Museum Transport Group, 28 Farm Close, Etchinghill, Rugeley, Staffs WS15 2XT.

Registration	Date	Chassis	Body	New to	Fleet No	Status
UK 9978+	1931	Guy BTX	Guy H26/24R	Wolverhampton Corporation	78	A
HA 8047	1933	SOS REDD	Metro Cammell H26/26R	BMMO ('Midland Red')	1047	RP
DKY 735+	1946	Karrier W	East Lancs H37/29F	Bradford Corporation	735	RP
DUK 833+	1946	Sunbeam W	Roe H32/28R	Wolverhampton Corporation	433	R
FEA156	1949	Daimler CVG5	Metro Cammell B38R	West Bromwich Corporation	156	RP
GEA 174	1952	Daimler CVG6	Weymann H30/26R	West Bromwich Corporation	174	RP
TDH 912+	1955	Sunbeam F4A	Willowbrook H36/34RD	Walsall Corporation	862	R
SCH 237+	1960	Sunbeam F4A	Roe H37/28R	Derby Corporation	237	R
UCX 275	1961	Guy Wulfrunian	Roe H43/32F	County Motors of Lepton	99	R
6342 HA	1963	BMMO D9	BMMO H40/32RD	BMMO ('Midland Red')	5342	RP
GHA 327D	1965	Leyland Leopard PSU4/4R	Plaxton -	Midland Red Omnibus Co	5827	R
XDH 519G	1969	Daimler Fleetline CRG6LX	Northern Counties H41/27D	Walsall Corporation	119	RP

+ Trolleybus

Notes:
HA 8047	Sole surviving SOS double decker	UCX 275	On loan from Dewsbury Bus Museum
DKY 735	Rebodied 1959.	GHA 327D	Converted to breakdown vehicle in 1979.
DUK 833	Rebodied in 1959		

Bristol Road Transport Collection

Contact address: William Staniforth, 37 Corbett Road, Birmingham B47 5LP (SAE please)
E-mail: william.staniforth@virgin.net
Brief Description: A display of Bristol buses housed at Bristol Aero Collection. Only certain vehicles are on show and visitors wishing to see specific vehicles should enquire first.
Opening days/times: Sunday/Monday and Good Friday, Easter to end October, 10.00-16.00
Directions by car: Hangar A1, Kemble Airfield, Nr Cirencester, Glous GL7 6BA

Registration	Date	Chassis	Body	New to	Fleet No	Status
FAE 60	1938	Bristol L5G	-	Bristol Omnibus Co	W75	RP
AJA 118	1938	Bristol L5G	Burlingham B35R	North Western	364	R
KHU 28	1948	Bedford OB	Duple C29F	Wessex Coaches		A
KHW 630	1948	Leyland Titan PD1	ECW H30/26R	Bristol Tramways	C4019	A
JEL 257	1949	Bristol K5G	ECW L27/28R	Hants & Dorset Motor Services	1238	A
LHW 918	1949	Bristol L5G	ECW B35R	Bristol Tramways	2410	A
MHU 49	1949	Bedford OB	Duple B30F	Bristol Tramways	207	RP
GAM 216	1950	Bristol L6B	Portsmouth Aviation C32R	Wilts & Dorset Motor Services	297	A
LFM 753	1950	Bristol L6B	ECW DP31R	Crosville Motor Services	KW172	R
CNH 699	1952	Bristol KSW6B	ECW L27/28R	United Counties Omnibus Co	860	A
UHY 359	1955	Bristol KSW6B	ECW H32/28R	Bristol Tramways	C8319	A
YHT 958	1958	Bristol Lodekka LD6B	ECW O33/25RD	Bristol Omnibus Co	L8462	R
904 OFM	1960	Bristol SC4LK	ECW C33F	Crosville Motor Services	CSG655	R
57 GUO	1961	Bristol MW6G	ECW C39F	Western National Omnibus Co (Royal Blue)	2268	A
Q507 OHR	1961	Bristol MW6G	ECW	Bristol Omnibus Co	W151	RP
507 OHU	1962	Bristol Lodekka FLF6G	ECW H38/32F	Bristol Omnibus Co	7062	RP
862 RAE	1962	Bristol SUS4A	ECW B30F	Bristol Omnibus Co	301	RP
RDB 872	1964	Dennis Loline III	Alexander H39/32F	North Western Road Car Co	872	RP
DFE 963D	1966	Bristol Lodekka FS5G	ECW H33/27RD	Lincolnshire Road Car Co	2537	R
OHU 770F	1968	Bristol RELL6L	ECW B53F	Bristol Omnibus Co	1071	R

Registration	Date	Chassis	Body	New to	Fleet No	Status
LRN 60J	1970	Bristol VRL/LH/6L	ECW CH42/18Ct	W C Standerwick	60	R
GYC 160K	1971	Bristol LH6L	ECW B45F	Hutchings & Cornelius Services of South Petherton		RP
PUO 331M	1974	Bristol LH6L	Plaxton C41F	Western National Omnibus Co (Royal Blue)	1331	RP
HAX 399N	1975	Bristol LHS6L	Duple C35F	R I Davies & Son of Tredegar		RP
KHU 326P	1976	Bristol LH6L	ECW B43F	Bristol Omnibus Co	376	RP
KOU 791P	1976	Bristol VRTSL3/6LXB	ECW H39/31F	Bristol Omnibus Co	5505	RP
TWS 910T	1979	Bristol VRTSL3/6LXB	ECW H43/27D	Bristol Omnibus Co	5129	R
VAE 499T	1979	Leyland National 10351L/1R	Leyland B44F	Bristol Omnibus Co	700	R
C416 AHT	1986	Ford Transit	Carlyle B16F	Bristol	7416	A

Notes:
FAE 60   Originally bus 2086, converted to tower wagon in 1956.
YHT 958   Originally H33/25RD
Q507 OHR Originally coach 2111 registered 404 LHT; converted to breakdown vehicle in 1974
507 OHU   On display at Aston Manor Road Transport Museum

British Commercial Vehicle Museum
Leyland

Contact address: King Street, Leyland, Lancashire, PR25 2LE
Phone: 01772 451011
Fax: 01772 451015
Brief description: A unique line-up of historic commercial vehicles and buses spans a century of truck and bus building. More than 50 exhibits are on display in this national collection.
Events planned: Please see the enthusiast press for details.
Opening days/times:
April to end of September: Sundays, Tuesdays, Wednesdays, Thursdays and Bank Holidays, 10.00 to 17.00
October: Sundays only, 10.00 to 17.00
Directions by car: Close to the M6 Junction 28.
Directions by public transport:
By train to Leyland station (on West Coast main line).
Buses from Preston and Chorley bus stations.
Charges: Adult £4, Child/OAP £2, Family £10.
Facilities: A B(e) D F G L P R S T

Registration	Date	Chassis	Body	New to	Fleet No	Status
note t	1896	Horse bus	O14/12R	Edinburgh & District Tramways		R
XW 9892	1925	Tilling Stevens TS7	Tilling B30R	Thomas Tilling	0172	R
YT 3738	1927	Leyland Lioness PLC1	Thurgood C22F	King George V		R
KGU 284	1949	Leyland Titan 7RT	Park Royal H30/26R	London Transport	RTL 325	R
JRN 29	1956	Leyland Tiger Cub PSUC1/2	Burlingham C41F	Ribble Motor Services	963	R
OED 217	1956	Foden PVD6	East Lancs H30/28R	Warrington Corporation	112	R
301 LJ+	1962	Sunbeam MF2B	Weymann H37/28D	Bournemouth Corporation	301	R

+ Trolleybus

Notes:
note t   Unregistered
301 LJ   On loan from Bourne

Note: Please be aware that vehicles on display can vary from time to time as not all museums display their entire 'fleet'. Visitors wishing to see a particular vehicle should make enquiries prior to their visit.

Castle Point Transport Museum
Canvey Island

Contact address: 105 Point Road, Canvey Island, Essex SS8 7TP
Phone: 01268 684272
Affiliation: NARTM
Brief description: This historic former Canvey & District bus depot, built in 1935, houses approximately 35 commercial vehicles spanning the years 1944 to 1988. Exhibits include buses, coaches, lorries, fire engines and military vehicles. They can be seen in varying stages from the totally restored to those in need of complete restoration. Completely run by volunteers, membership of the society is available at £10 per annum.
Events planned: Please see enthusiast press for details
Opening days/times: Open on 1st/3rd Sundays, April to mid October.
Directions by car: A130 to Canvey Island; follow brown tourism signs on reaching the island.
Directions by public transport: By rail to South Benfleet, then by bus to Leigh Beck, Canvey Island.
Charges: Free admission. Donations welcome. A charge is made on the Transport Show day in October.
Facilities: B(e) P T
Other information: Hot drinks available.

Registration	Date	Chassis	Body	New to	Fleet No	Status
BTW 488	1935	Dennis Lancet I	(chassis only)	Eastern National Omnibus Co	3549	A
FOP 429	1944	Daimler CWA6	Duple O33/26R	Birmingham Corporation Tramways	1429	R
JVW 430	1944	Bristol K5G	ECW L27/28R	Eastern National Omnibus Co	3885	R
MPU 52	1947	Leyland Titan PD1A	ECW L27/26R	Eastern National Omnibus Co	3991	RP
CFV 851	1948	Bedford OB	Duple C29F	Seagull Coaches of Blackpool		R
LHY 937	1949	Bristol K6B	ECW H31/28R	Bristol Tramways	3774	RP
LYR 997	1949	AEC Regent III O961 RT	Weymann H30/26R	London Transport	RT 2827	RP
NEH 453	1949	Leyland Titan OPD2/1	Northern Counties L27/26RD	Potteries Motor Traction Co	L453	R
ONO 49	1950	Bristol L5G	ECW B35R	Eastern National Omnibus Co	4029	R
PTW 110	1950	Bristol L6B	ECW FC31F	Eastern National Omnibus Co	4107	RP
WNO 478	1953	Bristol KSW5G	ECW O33/28R	Westcliff-on-Sea Motor Services		R
XVX 19	1954	Bristol Lodekka LD5G	ECW H33/25R	Eastern National Omnibus Co	4208	R
381 BKM	1957	AEC Reliance MU3RV	Harrington C41F	Maidstone & District Motor Services	C381	RP
PHJ 954	1958	Leyland Titan PD3/6	Massey L35/32R	Southend Corporation	315	RP
217 MHK	1959	Bristol MW6G	ECW DP41F	Eastern National Omnibus Co	480	R
236 LNO	1959	Bristol Lodekka LDL6LX	ECW H37/33R	Eastern National Omnibus Co	1541	RP
VLT 44	1959	AEC Routemaster	Park Royal H36/28R	London Transport	RM 44	RP
SGD 407	1960	Leyland Titan PD3/2	Alexander H41/31F	Glasgow Corporation	L405	RP
373 WPU	1961	Guy Arab IV	Massey L34/33R	Moore Bros of Kelvedon		R
138 CLT	1962	AEC Routemaster R2RH	Park Royal H36/28R	London Transport	RM 1138	R
28 TKR	1962	AEC Reliance 2MU3RV	Harrington C29F	Maidstone & District Motor Services	C28	R
918 NRT	1963	AEC Regent V MD3RV	Massey H33/28R	Lowestoft Corporation	8	RP
SDX 57	1963	AEC Regent V 2D2RA	East Lancs Neepsend H37/28R	Ipswich Corporation	57	RP
CUV 233C	1965	AEC Routemaster R2RH/1	Park Royal H36/29RD	London Transport	RCL 2233	R
NTW 942C	1965	Bristol Lodekka FLF6G	ECW H38/32F	Eastern National Omnibus Co	2849	R
AVX 975G	1968	Bristol Lodekka FLF6LX	ECW H38/32F	Eastern National Omnibus Co	2614	RP
CPU 979G	1968	Bristol VRTSL6LX	ECW H39/31F	Eastern National Omnibus Co	3000	R
GNM 232N	1975	Bristol LHS6L	Plaxton C33F	Epsom Coaches		RP

Notes:
JVW 430 Renumbered 1274 in 1954
FOP 429 Originally H33/26R; later operated by Eastern National Omnibus Co and Southend Corporation (244)
MPU 52 Renumbered 1121 in 1954
LYR 997 In Osbornes of Tollesbury livery
LHY 937 Renumbered 1541 in 1964
ONO 49 Renumbered 309 in 1954 and 1107 in 1964
PTW 110 Renumbered 328 in 1954
WNO 478 Built as H33/28R; numbered 1423 in 1954; passed to Eastern National Omnibus Co in 1955; renumbered 2380 in 1964 and converted to open-top in 1965/6
XVX 19 Renumbered 1431 in 1954 and 2400 in 1964
VLT 44 In Southend Transport livery
236 LNO Renumbered 2510 in 1964
217 MHK Renumbered 1402 in 1964
AVX 975G Delivered as CH37/18F; fitted with bus seats and renumbered 2946 in 1969

Cavan & Leitrim Railway
Dromod

Contact address: Cavan & Leitrim Railway, Narrow Gauge Station, Station Road, Dromod, Co Leitrim, Eire
Phone/fax: 00353 71 9638599
Brief description: Half mile 3ft gauge steam railway with a collection of railway vehicles (steam, diesel, carriages, wagons and railcars) together with a selection of vintage road vehicles, military equipment and vintage aircraft.
Opening days/times:
Daily April-September. Rest of year by request
Directions by car: to Dromod on N4 from Dublin. R202 from Dromod, 500yds.
Directions by public transport: Train to Dromod Irish Rail station from Dublin Connolly (Dublin-Sligo line). Narrow gauge station next to main line
Charges: Adult 6 Euro, Child 4 Euro, Family 14 Euro
Facilities: B(e) C D E G R (on request) S T

Registration	Date	Chassis	Body	New to	Fleet No	Status
KID 154	1947	Leyland Tiger PS1	Northern Ireland Road Transport Board B34R	Northern Ireland Road Transport Board	A8520	A
FCI 323	1950	Bristol LL5G	ECW B39R	Crosville Motor Services	KG156	RP
ZJ 5904	1950	Leyland Tiger OPS3/1	CIE	CIE	P164	R
IY 7383	1951	GNR Gardner	Park Royal/GNR B33R	Great Northern Railway (Ireland)	G389	R
IY 8044	1952	GNR Gardner	Park Royal/GNR B33R	Great Northern Railway (Ireland)	G396	A
ZO 6960	1953	Leyland Titan OPD2/1	CIE H37/31R	CIE	R541	RP
ZU 5000	1953	Leyland Royal Tiger PSU1/9	Saunders Roe B44C	Irish Army		RP
ZY 1715	1955	AEC Regal IV	Park Royal/GNR B40F	Great Northern Railway (Ireland)	345	R
ILI 98	1958	Bristol SC4LK	ECW B35F	Eastern National Omnibus Co	455	RP
OST 502	1959	AEC Reliance 2MU3RV	Alexander B41F	Highland Omnibuses	B24	RP
3945 UE	1960	Leyland Tiger Cub PSUC1	Park Royal B45F	Stratford-upon-Avon Blue Motors	45	A
71 AHI	1960	Leyland Tiger Cub PSUC1/2	Metro Cammell B41F	Western Welsh Omnibus Co	1274	A
AZD 203	1964	Leyland Leopard L2	CIE B45F	CIE	E140	R
BLH 123B	1964	Bedford VAS2	Duple (Midland) B—F	London County Council		RP
EZH 155	1965	Leyland Leopard PSU3/4R	CIE B—F	CIE	C155	A
EZH 170	1966	Leyland Leopard PSU3/4R	CIE B45F	CIE	C170	R
UZH 258	1966	Leyland Leopard PSU3/4R	CIE B55F	CIE	C258	R
ZS 8621	1971	Daimler Fleetline CRG6LX	Park Royal H—/—F	West Midlands PTE	4130	A
177 IK	1972	Leyland Leopard PSU5/4R	CIE B48F	CIE	M177	A
78 D 140	1978	Bedford SB5	Marshall B40F	Royal Navy		R
78 D 824	1978	Bristol RELL6G	Alexander (Belfast) B52F	Ulsterbus	2193	R
85 D 2412	1978	Bedford SB5	Marshall B40F	Royal Air Force		A
643 MIP	1980	Volvo B58	Duple C—F	North West Coachlines		A

Notes:

KID 154	Originally registered GZ7588	AZD 203	Worked on hire to County Donegal Railways
FCI 323	Original Registration LFM737	EZH 155	Converted to mobile workshop
ZJ 5904	Converted to recovery vehicle by CIE in 1971	ZS 8621	Converted to Playbus. Originally registered YOX 130K.
ZU 5000	Spent 28 years as garden shed	177 IK	Daf engine fitted early 1980s.
ZO 6960	Sole survivor of a batch of 6 Airport buses	78 D 140	Originally registered 42 RN 98
ZY 1715	Converted to 3ft gauge railway carriage 1971	85 D 2412	Originally registered 48 AC 14
ILI 98	Original registration 9579 F	78 D 824	Originally registered POI 2193
71 AHI	Originally registered UKG 274	643 MIP	Original registration GRN 896W

Note: Please be aware that vehicles on display can vary from time to time as not all museums display their entire 'fleet'. Visitors wishing to see a particular vehicle should make enquiries prior to their visit.

27
KINGS HEATH & WEST HEATH
VIA NORTHFIELD
JOJ 245

BUS STOP
MR 3879

Above left: **Weymann-bodied Leyland PS1 2245 (JOJ 245) is resident at the Birmingham and Midland Museum of Transport at Wythall, where its restoration was completed in 2004. It is seen here though on a visit to the Black Country Museum.**
Philip Lamb

Left: **Visitors to the Black Country Museum are sometimes treated to a sighting of resident MR 3879, a 14-seat Reo Speedwagon dating from 1925.**
Philip Lamb

Above: **Part of the large collection of buses and Coaches which go to make up Aston Manor Road Transport Museum's collection is Leyland Leopard /Alexander DP49F Stratford Blue 36 (XNX 136H).**
Philip Lamb

Right: **Dudley's Black Country Museum is home to a number of working trolley-buses including Willowbrook-bodied Sunbeam F4A Walsall 862 (TDH 912).**
Philip Lamb

Cobham Bus Museum

Contact address: Redhill Road, Cobham, Surrey, KT11 1EF
Phone/Fax: 01932 868665
Web site: www.lbpt.org.uk
E-mail: cobhambusmuseum@aol.com
Affiliation: AIM, NARTM
Brief description: This well-established museum is home to the London Bus Preservation Trust. It was formed by a small group of enthusiasts in 1966. The collection has steadily grown over the years and now over 30 preserved buses, coaches and service vehicles are located at Cobham.
Events planned: Please see the enthusiast press for details.
Opening days/times: Open days as advertised.
Viewing possible at weekends 11.00 to 17.00 but please telephone in advance to confirm.
Directions by car: From M25 junction 10 take A3 north and turn left on to A245. Museum is 1 mile on left.
Directions by public transport: Museum bus service from Weybridge station on main events. Network of special services on annual open day. Infrequent bus service at other times to Brooklands Road/Byfleet.
Charges: £4 but higher charges on open days.
Facilities: B B(e) G P R(limited) S T

Registration	Date	Chassis	Body	New to	Fleet No	Status
XX 9591	1925	Dennis 4-ton	Dodson O24/24RO	Dominion Omnibus Co		R
UU 6646	1929	AEC Regal 662	LGOC B30R	London General Omnibus Co	T 31	R
GJ 2098	1930	AEC Regent 661	Thomas Tilling H27/25RO	Thomas Tilling	ST 922	RP
GN 8242	1931	AEC Regal 662	Weymann B30F	Queen Line Coaches of London	T357	A
GO 5170	1931	AEC Renown 664	LGOC B35F	London General Omnibus Co	LT 1059	A
AXM 693	1934	AEC Regent 661	LPTB H30/26R	London Transport	STL 441	RP
CGJ 188	1935	AEC Q O762	Birmingham R C & W B35C	LPTB	Q 83	R
CXX 171	1936	AEC Regal O662	Weymann C30F	LPTB	T 448	RP
DLU 92	1937	AEC Regent O661	LPTB H30/26R	LPTB	STL 2093	A
EGO 426	1937	AEC Regent O661	LPTB H30/26R	LPTB	STL 2377	R
ELP 228	1938	AEC Regal)662	LPTB C30F	LPTB	T 504	R
HGC 130	1945	Guy Arab II	Park Royal UH30/26R	LPTB	G 351	RP
HLX 410	1948	AEC Regent III O961 RT	Weymann H30/26R	London Transport	RT 593	R
JXC 288	1949	Leyland Tiger PS1	Mann Egerton B30F	London Transport	TD 95	R
KGK 803	1949	Leyland Titan 7RT	Park Royal H30/26R	London Transport	RTL 139	R
MYA 590	1949	Leyland Comet CPO1	Harrington C29F	Scarlet Pimpernel of Minehead		R
LUC 210	1951	AEC Regal IV 9821LT RF	Metro Cammell DP35F	London Transport	RF 10	RP
LYR 826	1952	AEC Regent III O961 RT	Park Royal H30/26R	London Transport	RT 2775	RP
LYR 910	1952	AEC Regent III O961 RT	Park Royal H30/26R	London Transport	RT 3491	R
MLL 740	1953	AEC Regal IV 9822E	Park Royal RC37C	British European Airways		R
MXX 334	1953	Guy Special NLLVP	ECW B26F	London Transport	GS 34	R
NLE 672	1953	AEC Regal IV 9821LT RF	Metro Cammell B41F	London Transport	RF 672	R
CDX 516	1954	AEC Regent III 9613E	Park Royal H30/26R	Ipswich Corporation	16	R
SLT 58	1958	Leyland Routemaster R2RH	Weymann H34/30R	London Transport	RML 3	R
461 CLT	1962	AEC Routemaster	Park Royal H32/25RD	London Transport	RMC 1461	R
EGN 369J	1971	AEC Swift 4MP2R	Park Royal B33D	London Transport	SMS 369	R
JPA 190K	1972	AEC Reliance 6U2R	Park Royal DP45F	London Country Bus Services	RP 90	R
WYW 6T	1979	MCW Metrobus DR101/8	MCW H43/28D	London Transport	M 6	R

Notes:

XX 9591	Restored as London General Omnibus Co D142	MYA 590	Converted from petrol to diesel in 1966
GJ 2098	On loan to BMMO during World War 2	JXC 288	Toured Europe and USSR 1963-1967
CXX 171	Used as an ambulance during World War 2	LYR 826	Toured USA and Canada when new
DLU 92	Original metal-framed Park Royal body replaced in 1949	LYR 910	Fitted with AEC 11.3 litre engine in 1998
ELP 228	Used as an ambulance during World War 2	SLT 58	Prototype Leyland Routemaster; renumbered RM3 in 1961
HGC 130	Only remaining example of a London utility bus		

Coventry Transport Museum

Contact address: Coventry Transport Museum, Millenium Place, Hales Street, Coventry CV1 1PN
Phone: 024 7683 2425
Fax: 024 7683, 2465
E-mail: enquiries@transport-museum.com
Brief Description: The museum has over 230 cars and commercial vehicles, over 90 motorcycles and around 240 bicycles. Various tableaux chart the development of the motor vehicle from the early years and Coventry's contribution to this can be seen in the many marques on display. Other exhibits include the Thrust 2 and Thrust SSC land speed record car, several thousand die-cast models and a walk through audio visual display of the Coventry Blitz experience.
Opening days/times:
Open all year, 10.00-17.00 (last admission 016.30) except 24/25/26 December.
Directions by car: Coventry ring road circles the city centre and is encountered whichever direction you come from. Once on it follow the brown 'Motor Museum' signs and turn off at junction 1. Nearest car park (pay & display) is signposted and is in Tower Street at the back of the Museum.
Directions by public transport: The Museum is opposite Pool Meadow bus/coach station. Use Travel West Midlands bus 17 or 27 from Coventry railway station to Broadgate (5min walk downhill to Museum from Broadgate).
Facilities: R, T, L, D, S, G, F, Be, H
Note: The vehicles are frequently stored off site while new developments are built. Please phone to check which vehicles are on display

Registration	Date	Chassis	Body	New to	Fleet No	Status
SR 1266	1916	Maudslay Subsidy A	(chassis only)			A
EKV 966	1944	Daimler CWA6	Roe H31/25R	Coventry Corporation	366	R
JNB 416	1948	Maudslay Marathon II	Trans-United C33F	Hackett's of Manchester		R
KOM 150	1950	Daimler CVD6	Wilsdon -	Birmingham Post & Mail		R
SRB 424	1953	Daimler CD650	Willowbrook L27/28RD	Tailby & George ('Blue Bus Services') Willington		R
PBC 734	1954	Karrier Bantam Q25	Reading C14F	Mablethorpe Homes of Leicester		R
333 CRW	1963	Daimler CVG6	Metro Cammell H34/29R	Coventry Corporation	333	R
PDU 125M	1973	Daimler Fleetline CRG6LX	East Lancs O44/30F	Coventry Corporation	125	R
K232 DAC	1993	Peugeot J5	C11F	Peugeot UK		A

Notes:

SR 1266	To be restored as replica of 1921 Hickman bodied bus for Coventry Corporation		Mail and currently used as museum promotional vehicle
EKV 966	Rebodied 1951; converted to mobile repair workshop (O2) in 1960	PBC 734	Welfare bus
		PDU 125M	Originally H44/30F; converted to open top in 1986
KOM 150	Built as mobile print shop for the Birmingham Post and	K232 DAC	Prototype electric minibus

Dover Transport Museum
Whitfield

Contact address: Willingdon Road, Port Zone White Cliffs Business Park, Whitfield, Dover, CT16 2HJ
Phone: 01304 822409
Affiliation: NARTM, Transport Trust, AIM, ASTRO
Brief description: The museum displays local transport and social history. Road vehicles of all types. A maritime room, railway room, bygone shops and a garage. Hundreds of transport models including a working model tramway.
Events planned: Please see the enthusiast press for details.

Note: Please be aware that vehicles on display can vary from time to time as not all museums display their entire 'fleet'. Visitors wishing to see a particular vehicle should make enquiries prior to their visit.

Opening days/times: Easter to end September — Sundays and Bank Holidays 10.00 to 17.00; Wednesday, Thursdays and Fridays 14.00 to 17.00. Last entry 45 minutes before closing
Open at other times for pre-arranged groups.
Directions by car: Approximately one mile from the A2 Whitfield roundabout on the Dover bypass.
Directions by public transport: Dover Priory station then bus to Old Park, Whitfield.
Charges: Adult £2, Senior Citizen £1.50, Child £1, Family £5.
Facilities: B(e) D E G P R T

Registration	Date	Chassis	Body	New to	Fleet No	Status
CC 9305	1929	Dennis G	Roberts T19	Llandudno UDC	4	R
CJG 959	1947	Leyland Titan PD1A	Leyland L27/26R	East Kent Road Car Co		A
569 KKK	1960	AEC Reliance 2MU3RA	Duple C41C	Ayers Coaches of Dover		R
WFN 513	1961	AEC Reliance 2MU3RV	Park Royal DP41F	East Kent Road Car Co		R
WFN 912	1961	Ford 570E	Duple C41F	Seath Coaches		A
GJG 751D	1966	AEC Regent V 2D3RA	Park Royal O40/32F	East Kent Road Car Co		R

Notes:
GJG 751D   Originally H40/32F; used as promotional vehicle

East Anglia Transport Museum
Carlton Colville

Contact address: Chapel Road, Carlton Colville, Lowestoft, Suffolk, NR33 8BL
Phone: 01502 518459
Affiliation: NARTM, London Trolleybus Preservation Society, Transport Trust.
Brief description: A working transport museum on a four-acre site, first opened in 1972 and run entirely by volunteers. Tram and trolleybus services operate regularly within a developing street scene and the tramway has a woodland section. There is also a narrow-gauge railway. A wide variety of other vehicles on display and sometimes operated includes buses, lorries, steam rollers, battery-electrics, tower wagons and a London taxi. The museum is a registered charity.
Events planned:
27 March 2005 — Launch of Blackpool Vambac tram.
11/12 June 2005 — Steam & Vintage Weekend.
10 July 2005 — Bus Event with free bus service to Lowestoft and Beccles.
10/11 September 2005 — Trolleybus Weekend with a London theme. Free bus service to Lowestoft and Beccles.
Opening days/times: At Easter to end of September:
Sundays and Bank Holidays — 11.00 to 17.00;
Wednesdays and Saturdays (June to Sept) — 14.00 to 17.00;
Daily, except Mondays (late July and Aug) — 14.00 to 17.00.
Last entry 1 hour before closing.
Directions by car: Situated just off the A1384. Follow the brown signs from the A12, A146 and A1117. Free car parking.
Directions by public transport:
Monday to Saturday: Eastern Counties bus 111 or 112 from Lowestoft bus station to Carlton Colville Church.
Every day X2 Lowestoft to Norwich, to Carlton Crown PH then 5min walk.
By train to Oulton Broad South then 35min walk or bus 607.
Bus service 607 links Oulton Broad North and Oulton Broad South railway stations with the museum (Chapel Road bus stop), also gives a direct link to Great Yarmouth (Mondays to Saturdays only). For more details of this or other public transport information please ring the travel line on 08459 583358.
Charges: £5.00 adults, £3.50 children/OAPs. Admission includes free rides within the museum.
Facilities: B(e) D E F G H P R S T
Other information: Regular tram, train and trolleybus rides

Registration	Date	Chassis	Body	New to	Fleet No	Status
AH 79505+	1926	Garrett O type	Strachan & Brown B26D	NESA Copenhagen	5	RP
KW 1961	1927	Leyland Lion PLSC3	Leyland B35F	Blythe & Berwick of Bradford		A
ALJ 986+	1935	Sunbeam MS2	Park Royal O40/29R	Bournemouth Corporation	202	R
CUL 260+	1936	AEC 664T	Metro Cammell H40/30R	London Transport	260	R

Registration	Date	Chassis	Body	New to	Fleet No	Status
EXV 201+	1938	Leyland LPTB70	Leyland H40/30R	London Transport	1201	R
FXH 521+	1940	Metro Cammell	Metro Cammell H40/30R	London Transport	1521	R
GBJ 192	1947	AEC Regent II O661	ECW H30/26R	Lowestoft Corporation	21	R
BDY 809+	1948	Sunbeam W	Weymann H30/26R	Hastings Tramways Co	34	RP
KAH 408	1948	Bristol L4G	ECW B35R	Eastern Counties Omnibus Co	LL 108	A
note d+	1948	Berna	Hess B37D	Biel (Switzerland)	39	R
LLU 829	1950	Leyland Titan 7RT	Park Royal H30/26R	London Transport	RTL 1050	R
NBB 628+	1950	BUT 9641T	Metro Cammell H40/30R	Newcastle Corporation	628	A
ERV 938+	1951	BUT 9611T	Burlingham H28/26R	Portsmouth Corporation	313	RP
SG 2030+	1952	Henschel ÅHIII/s	Uerdingen B32T	Solingen (Germany)	1	R
DRC 224+	1953	Sunbeam F4	Willowbrook H32/28R	Derby Corporation	224	R
LCD 52+	1953	BUT 9611T	Weymann H30/26R	Brighton Corporation	52	R
YTE 826+	1956	BUT 9612T	Bond H32/28R	Ashton-under-Lyne Corporation	87	A
2206 OI+	1958	Sunbeam F4A	Harkness H36/32R	Belfast Corporation	246	R
YLJ 286+	1959	Sunbeam MF2B	Weymann H35/28D	Bournemouth Corporation	286	R
557 BNG	1962	Bristol Lodekka FL6G	ECW H37/33RD	Eastern Counties Omnibus Co	LFL 57	R
AEX 85B	1964	AEC Reliance 2MU3RA	Pennine B39F	Great Yarmouth Corporation	85	RP
YRT 898H	1969	AEC Swift 2MP2R	ECW B45D	Lowestoft Corporation	4	R
OCK 985K	1972	Bristol VRTSL2/6LX	ECW H39/31F	Ribble Motor Services	1985	R
D103 DAJ	1986	Mercedes 608D	Reeve Burgess B20F	Hartlepool Transport	13	R

+ Trolleybus

Notes:
AH 79505	Danish registration	OCK 985K	Acquired by Eastern Counties Omnibus Co (VR385) in 1985
ALJ 986	Converted to open top 1958		
note d	Swiss Trolleybus; unregistered	D103 DAJ	Restored in Lincolnshire Road Car (Roadrunner) livery
SG 2030	German registration		
LCD 52	Built 1950. First used 1953; Preserved in colours of subsequent operator Maidstone Corporation		

Grampian Transport Museum
Alford

Contact address: Alford, Aberdeenshire AB33 8AE
Phone: 01975 562292
Fax: 01975 562180
E-mail: info@g-t-m.freeserve.co.uk
Web site: www.gtm.org.uk
Brief description: Dramatic displays, working exhibits and video presentations trace the history of travel and transport.
Opening days/times: April to October inclusive, 10.00 to 17.00.
Directions by car: On A944 west from Aberdeen (27 miles).
Directions by public transport: Stagecoach bus services from Aberdeen.
Charges: £4.80 Adults, £4.20 Senior Citizens, £2.30 Children, £12.Family.
Facilities: A B(e) C D E FG H L M P R S T

Registration	Date	Chassis	Body	New to	Fleet No	Status
SP 5139	1922	Ford Model T	B6	Lochgelly Post Office		R
JFM 238D	1966	Bristol Lodekka FS6G	ECW H33/27RD	Crosville Motor Services	DFG238	R
NRG 154M	1974	Leyland Atlantean AN68/1R	Alexander H45/29D	Grampian Regional Transport	154	R

Notes:
SP 5139	Post Bus. On loan from Drambuie Liqueur Co Ltd.
JFM 238D	Last rear entrance Bristol ever built
NRG 154M	Used as a video theatre

Note: Please be aware that vehicles on display can vary from time to time as not all museums display their entire 'fleet'. Visitors wishing to see a particular vehicle should make enquiries prior to their visit.

Imperial War Museum
London

Contact address: Lambeth Road, London SE1 6HZ
Phone:
020 7416 5320
0891 600140 (Recorded information)
E-mail: website: www.iwm.org.uk
Brief description: Revel in the history of the nation, through the world wars and much more besides. Regular exhibitions and displays of considerable educational value. The one bus in the collection fills a significant gap in transport history and is on display in museum atrium.
Opening days/times: Daily 10.00 to 18.00 (closed 24, 25 and 26 December)
Directions by car: South of Waterloo Station, close to the Elephant & Castle. Parking difficult but Coach Park at Vauxhall Bridge and disabled parking by prior arrangement only — phone 020 7416 5397.
Directions by public transport:
Underground to Lambeth North, Waterloo or Elephant & Castle.
Rail to Waterloo.
Bus routes 1, 3, 12, 53, 59, 68, 148, 155, 159, 168, 171, 172, 176, 188, 344, 453, 468 and C10 with 45, 63, 100 nearby.
Charges: Free entry to main displays.
Facilities: A C D G H R T

Registration	Date	Chassis	Body	New to	Fleet No	Status
LN 4743	1911	LGOC B	LGOC O18/16RO	London General Omnibus Co	B 43	R

Notes:
LN 4743   Named 'Ole Bill' after wartime cartoon character

Ipswich Transport Museum

Contact address: Old Trolleybus Depot, Cobham Road, Ipswich IP3 9JD
Phone: 01473 715666
E-mail: www.ipswichtransportmuseum.co.uk.html
Affiliation: NARTM, ASTRO, SEMS, AFSM
Brief description: The collection includes most forms of road transport from the last 200 years, including bicycles, horse-drawn vehicles, trucks and service vehicles. There are displays of vehicles and other products of Ipswich engineering companies including six mobile cranes.
Events planned: Please see enthusiast press for details
Opening days/times: March to November: Sundays and Bank Holidays 11.00 to 16.00. School holidays, Monday to Friday 13.00 to 16.00
Directions by car: From A12/A14 junction with A1189 (Nacton and Ipswich East) head towards Ipswich on Nacton Road. Turn right into Lindburgh Road. Museum is on left in Cobham Road.
Directions by public transport: By train to Ipswich. Take any bus to Tower Ramparts bus station. Then IB route 6
Then take bus 2 to Cobham Road (Mon-Fri) or bus 75/76/77 (Suns) to Felixstowe Road railway bridge.
Charges: Adult £3.00, Child £2.00, Concessions £2, Family £8.50. Special event rates may apply
Facilities: A B(e) D G P R T, picnic area

Registration	Date	Chassis	Body	New to	Fleet No	Status
DX 3988+	1923	Railless	Short B30D	Ipswich Corporation	2	R
DX 5610+	1926	Ransomes Sims & Jefferies D	Ransomes Sims & Jefferies B31D	Ipswich Corporation	9	A
DX 5629+	1926	Garrett O type	Strachan & Brown B31D	Ipswich Corporation	26	A
DX 6591	1927	Tilling Stevens B9B	Eastern Counties B36R	Eastern Counties Road Car Co	78	A
VF 2788	1928	ADC 425A	Eastern Counties B36R	United Automobile Services	J379	A
DX 7812	1929	Tilling Stevens B10A2	(chassis only)	Eastern Counties Road Car Co	116	R
VF 8157	1930	Chevrolet LQ	Bush & Twiddy C14D	Final of Hockwold		RP
WV 1209	1932	Bedford WLB	Waveney B20F	Alexander of Devizes		A

Registration	Date	Chassis	Body	New to	Fleet No	Status
PV 817+	1933	Ransomes Sims & Jefferies	Ransomes Sims & Jefferies H24/24R	Ipswich Corporation	46	A
CVF 874	1939	Bristol L5G	ECW B35R	Eastern Counties Omnibus Co	LL 574	A
CAH 923	1940	Dennis Ace	ECW B20F	Eastern Counties Omnibus Co	D 23	A
PV 8270+	1948	Karrier W	Park Royal H30/26R	Ipswich Corporation	105	RP
KAH 407	1949	Bristol L4G	ECW B35R	Eastern Counties Omnibus Co	LL 407	R
KNG 374	1949	Bristol K6B	ECW L27/28R	Eastern Counties Omnibus Co	LK 374	RP
PV 9371	1949	Bedford OB	Duple C27F	Mulleys Motorways		R
ADX 1	1950	AEC Regent III 9612E	Park Royal H30/26R	Ipswich Corporation	1	R
ADX 196+	1950	Sunbeam F4	Park Royal H30/26R	Ipswich Corporation	126	R
MAH 744	1951	Bristol LSX4G	ECW B42F	Eastern Counties Omnibus Co	LL 744	R
BPV 9	1953	AEC Regal IV 9822E	Park Royal B42D	Ipswich Corporation	9	A
ADX 63B	1964	AEC Regent V 2D2RA	Massey H37/28R	Ipswich Corporation	63	R
APW 829B	1964	Bristol MW6G	ECW C39F	Eastern Counties Omnibus Co	LS 829	R
GNG 125C	1965	Bristol Lodekka FS5G	ECW H33/27RD	Eastern Counties Omnibus Co	LFS 125	RP
DPV 68D	1966	AEC Regent V 2D2RA	East Lancs Neepsend H37/28R	Ipswich Corporation	68	A
JRT 82K	1971	AEC Swift 2MP2R	Willowbrook B40D	Ipswich Corporation	82	R
MRT 6P	1976	Leyland Atlantean AN68/1R	Roe H43/29D	Ipswich Corporation	6	R
XNG 770S	1978	Leyland National 11351/1R	Leyland National B53F	Eastern Counties Omnibus Co	LN 770	A

+ Trolleybus

Notes:
DX 3988	Believed the oldest trolleybus on display in the world	PV 817	First Ipswich double decker
DX 5610	Changed from solid to pneumatic tyres in 1930	CVF 874	Originally numbered LL74
DX 6591	New with charabanc body; rebuilt in 1934	CAH 923	Originally fitted with Gardner 4LK engine
VF 2788	Original United body replaced in 1934	PV 8270	Originally fitted with wooden seats
DX 7812	Rebodied twice while with Eastern Counties	KNG 374	Engine changed Gardner 5LW by Eastern Counties OC
VF 8157	Body swapped with VF9126; acquired by Mulleys Motorways of Ixworth in 1940	ADX 1	Ipswich Corporation's first motor bus
		MAH 744	Bristol LS prototype

Isle of Wight Bus Museum
Newport (IoW)

Contact address: Seaclose Quay, Newport, Isle of Wight, PO30 2EF
Phone: 01983 533352
Affiliation: NARTM
Brief description: The collection ranges from a 1927 Daimler CK to a 1979 Ford R-series. Many of the vehicles are of Southern Vectis origin.
Events planned: Running day in October, please contact for details.
Opening days/times: 13-27 April: daily 10.00-16.00;
29 May-September: Tuesdays, Wednesdays, Thursdays and Sundays 10.00-16.00
27 July-31 August: daily 10.30 to 16.00
5-8 October: Sundays and Tuesdays 10.00-16.00
Directions by car: Access off Medina Way relief road and Sea Street. Left on to Quay. Bus museum is adjacent to Boat Museum (both sign-posted).
Directions by public transport: Bus to Newport bus station. Walk 12min to north of town.
Charges: £3 Adult, £2.50 Senior Citizen, £1.50 child.
Facilities: B(e) D G S
Other information: Car parking nearby. Refreshments and toilets at adjacent Boat Museum.

Registration	Date	Chassis	Body	New to	Fleet No	Status
DL 5084	1927	Daimler CK	Dodson B26R	Dodson Bros ('Vectis')	11	A
NG 1109	1931	Reo Pullman	Taylor Ch26D	Reynolds of Overstrand		

Note: Please be aware that vehicles on display can vary from time to time as not all museums display their entire 'fleet'. Visitors wishing to see a particular vehicle should make enquiries prior to their visit.

Registration	Date	Chassis	Body	New to	Fleet No	Status
JT 8077	1937	Bedford WTB	Duple C25F	South Dorset Coaches		R
CAP 234	1940	Bristol K5G	ECW O30/26R	Brighton Hove & District	6350	RP
FDL 676	1949	Bedford OB	Duple C29F	Southern Vectis Omnibus Co	216	
GDL 764	1950	Leyland Titan PD2/1A	Leyland L27/26R	Seaview Services		R
ODL 400	1957	Bedford SBG	Duple C41F	Moss Motor Tours of Sandown		RP
PDL 519	1958	Bristol Lodekka LD6G	ECW CO33/27R	Southern Vectis Omnibus Co	559	A
SDL 268	1959	Bristol Lodekka LD6G	ECW H33/27R	Southern Vectis Omnibus Co	563	R
ADL 459B	1964	Bedford SB3	Duple C41F	Pauls Tours of Ryde	9	RP
CDL 479C	1965	Bristol Lodekka FLF6G	ECW H38/32F	Southern Vectis Omnibus Co	611	R
FDL 927D	1966	Bristol MW6G	ECW B43F	Southern Vectis Omnibus Co	806	R
KDL 885F	1968	Bristol RESH6G	Duple C45F	Southern Vectis Omnibus Co	301	R
SDL 638J	1971	Bristol VRT/SL6G	ECW H39/31F	Southern Vectis Omnibus Co	628	
TDL 564K	1971	Bristol RELL6G	ECW OB50F	Southern Vectis Omnibus Co	864	R
VDL 264K	1972	Bedford YRQ	Plaxton B47F	Seaview Services		A
MDL 880R	1976	Leyland National 11351A/1R	Leyland National B52F	Southern Vectis Omnibus Co	880	A
YDL 135T	1979	Ford R1014	Duple B47F	Isle of Wight County Council	5809	A

Notes:

CAP 234	Originally H30/26R Converted to open top 1952. To Southern Vectis in 1960.	FDL 927D	Owned by Southern Vectis and loaned to museum
		KDL 885F	Owned by Southern Vectis and loaned to museum
PDL 519	Originally H33/27R		
CDL 479C	Owned by Southern Vectis and loaned to museum		

Keighley Bus Museum
Keighley & Denholme

Contact address: 47 Brantfell Drive, Burnley, Lancs BB12 8AW
Phone: 01282 413179
Web site: www.kbmt.org.uk
Affiliation: FBHVC, NARTM, Y&HMC
Brief description: A collection of 60 buses, coaches and ancillary vehicles. Some 50% are owned by the Trust and others by private individuals. The Trust aims to establish a permanent home for the collection in central Keighley.
Events planned:
19 June 2005 — Keighley Historic Vehicle Rally
Opening days/times: Old Dalton Lane Tuesdays and Thursdays evenings 19.00-22.00, and most Sundays (please check in advance). The site was due to be vacated during December 2004, please contact for details of alternative location
Denholme is normally open only on open days and by prior arrangement.
The Museum is located on two sites: Old Dalton Lane (Keighley) adjacent to railway station and at Denholme behind the Parish Church.
Directions by car: Between Keighley and Halifax, at Denholme on A629.
Directions by public transport: Keighley (adjacent to main line station) and 5min walk from bus station. Frequent buses from Keighley and Bradford to Denholme.
Charges: Special events: £2 Adult, £1 concession. Otherwise free but donations welcome.
Facilities: B(e) P T

Registration	Date	Chassis	Body	New to	Fleet No	Status
WT 7101+	1924	Straker Clough	Brush H50R	Keighley Corporation Tramways	5	R
KW 2260	1927	Leyland Lion PLSC3	Leyland B35R	Bradford Corporation	325	A
KY 9106	1931	AEC Regent I	MCW	Bradford Corporation	046	A
TF 6860	1931	Leyland Lion LT3	Leyland B36R	Rawtenstall Corporation	61	RP
ANW 682	1934	AEC Regent 661	Roe H30/26R	Leeds City Transport	139	R
DKT 11	1937	Leyland Tiger TS7	Harrington C32R	Maidstone & District Motor Services	CO553	A
CFM 354	1938	Leyland Titan TD5	ECW L26/26R	Crosville Motor Services	M52	RP
CWX 671	1938	Bristol K5G	Roe L27/28R	Keighley-West Yorkshire Services	KDG 26	R
EUF 198	1938	Leyland Titan TD5	Short -	Southdown Motor Services	0198	R
RN 8622	1939	Leyland Titan TD5	Alexander L27/26R	Ribble Motor Services	2057	R

Registration	Date	Chassis	Body	New to	Fleet No	Status
FWX 914+	1948	Sunbeam F4	East Lancs H37/29F	Mexborough & Swinton Traction Co		R
MNW 86	1948	Leyland Tiger PS1	Roe B36R	Leeds City Transport	28	R
LFM 767	1950	Bristol LL6B	ECW B39R	Crosville Motor Services	SLB186	RP
JWU 886	1951	Bristol LL5G	ECW B39R	West Yorkshire Road Car Co	SGL16	R
LYR 533	1951	AEC Regent III O961 RT	Park Royal H30/26R	London Transport	RT 3314	R
HKW 82	1952	AEC Regent III 9613E	East Lancs H31/28R	Bradford Corporation	82	R
SVS 904	1954	Bristol LS6G	ECW C35F	Southern National Omnibus Co	1381	R
UUA 214	1955	Leyland Titan PD2/11	Roe H33/25R	Leeds City Transport	214	RP
GJX 331	1956	Daimler CVG6	Roe H37/26R	Halifax Corporation	119	R
VTU 76	1956	Daimler CVG6	Northern Counties H35/23C	SHMD Board	76	R
XLG 477	1956	Atkinson Alpha PL745H	Northern Counties B34C	SHMD Board	77	A
7514 UA	1959	Daimler CVG6-30	Roe H38/32R	Leeds City Transport	514	A
PJX 232	1962	Leyland Leopard L1	Weymann B44F	Halifax Joint Omnibus Committee	232	R
WJY 758	1962	Leyland Atlantean	MCW	Plymouth Corporation	158	R
WBR 246	1963	Atkinson Alpha PM746HL	Marshall B45D	Sunderland Corporation	46	RP
6203 KW	1964	AEC Regent V 2D3RA	Metro Cammell H40/30F	Bradford Corporation	203	A
6204 KW	1964	AEC Regent V 2D3RA	Metro Cammell H40/30F	Bradford Corporation	204	A
6220 KW	1964	AEC Regent V 2D3RA	MCW H40/30F	Bradford Corporation	220	R
TRN 731	1964	Leyland Leopard PSU3/3R	Plaxton C49F	Ribble Motor Services	7315	R
ENW 980D	1966	AEC Regent V 2D2RA	Roe H39/31R	Leeds City Transport	980	RP
HNW 131D	1966	Daimler Fleetline CRG6LX	Roe H45/33F	Leeds City Transport	131	R
KVH 473E	1966	Daimler Fleetline CRG6LX	Roe H44/31F	Huddersfield Corporation	473	R
KWT 642D	1966	Bristol Lodekka FS6B	ECW H33/27RD	West Yorkshire Road Car Co	DX210	R
NWU 265D	1966	Bristol Lodekka FS6B	ECW H33/27RD	York - West Yorkshire	YDX221	R
TWW 766F	1967	Bristol RELH6G	ECW C47F	West Yorkshire Road Car Co	CRG6	R
YLG 717F	1967	Bristol RESL6G	Northern Counties B43F	SHMD Board	117	A
LAK 309G	1969	Leyland Titan PD3A/12	Alexander H41/29F	Bradford Corporation	309	R
LAK 313G	1969	Leyland Titan PD3A/12	Alexander H41/29F	Bradford Corporation	313	RP
TKU 467K	1971	Leyland Atlantean PDR2/1	Alexander H47/29D	Bradford Corporation	467	RP
WFM 801K	1972	Leyland National 1151/2R/0403	Leyland National B44D	Crosville Motor Services	SNL801	R
XAK 355L	1972	Daimler Fleetline CRL6	Alexander H43/31F	Bradford Corporation	355	RP
GWY 690N	1975	Leyland Leopard PSU4B/4R	Plaxton C45F	West Yorkshire PTE	64	A
CWU 136T	1978	Daimler Fleetline FE30AGR	Roe H43/33F	West Yorkshire PTE	7136	A
JUM 505V	1980	MCW Metrobus DR101/7	MCW H43/30F	West Yorkshire PTE	7505	A
KWY 228V	1980	Leyland Atlantean AN68A/1R	Roe H43/32F	West Yorkshire PTE	6228	RP
PUA 294W	1980	Leyland Atlantean AN68C/1R	Roe H43/33F	West Yorkshire PTE	7294	A
PUM 149W	1980	Bristol VRTSL3/6LXB	ECW H43/31F	West Yorkshire Road Car Co	1746	A
NKU 245X	1981	Leyland National 2 NL116AL11/1R	Leyland National B52F	Yorkshire Traction	245	A
D275 OOJ	1987	Freight Rover Sherpa	Carlyle B20F	Carlyle Works Demonstrator		RP

+ Trolleybus

Notes:

WT 7101	Solid tyres
KY 9106	Former double decker converted to gritter. On loan from Bradford Museums Service
TF 6860	Used as a tow bus and snow plough 1950-1963
CWX 671	Rebodied 1950
EUF 198	Converted to a towing vehicle from bus 198 in 1957
RN 8622	Chassis refurbished and rebodied in 1949
FWX 914	Originally single deck. Rebodied as d/deck Bradford Corporation 1963
JWU 886	Single block experimental Gardner engine
SVS 904	Originally registered OTT 90
UUA 214	Leeds City Transport driver trainer 1972 to 1978
WJY 758	Converted to open top in 1975. Restored as Keighley Corporation Tramways 59
NWU 265D	Renumbered 3821 in 1971
KWT 642D	Renumbered 1810 in 1971
TWW 766F	Renumbered 1019 in 1971; restored in later guise as 2508
WFM 801K	Second production Leyland National; operated single door with Greater Manchester Buses (South)

Note: Please be aware that vehicles on display can vary from time to time as not all museums display their entire 'fleet'. Visitors wishing to see a particular vehicle should make enquiries prior to their visit.

Above: **Birmingham pre-selector Guy Arab IV/Metro Cammell no2976 (JOJ 976) is seen at Birmingham and Midland Museum of Transport's base at Wythall on the South-west outskirts of Birmingham.** *Philip Lamb*

Above right: **One of the highlights of 2004 was the return of Cobham Bus Museum's RML3 (SLT 58) to original front-end configuration. The bus is seen here soon after the work was completed in July 2004.** *Philip Lamb*

Right: **Derby 224 (DRC 224) is a 1953 Sunbeam F4 with Willowbrook body. It is seen here on the turning circle of the combined tram and trolleybus terminus at the East Anglia Transport Museum, at Carlton Colville near Lowestoft.** *Philip Lamb*

37

Lincolnshire Road Transport Museum
North Hykeham

Contact address: Whisby Road, North Hykeham, Lincoln LN6 3QT
Phone: 01522 689497
Web site: www.lvvs.org.uk
Affiliation: NARTM
Brief description: An impressive collection of over 50 vehicles including classic cars, commercials, buses and motor cycles, mostly with Lincolnshire connections. Sixty years of road transport history is represented in the museum hall, which was built in 1993. An extension to the hall is planned.
Events planned: Please see enthusiast press and web site.
27 March 2005 — Easter Sunday open day
6 November 2005 — Autumn open day
Opening days/times:
May to October: Monday to Friday 12.00 to 16.00; Sunday 10.00 to 16.00;
November to April: Sunday 13.00 to 16.00. Other times by appointment.
Directions by car: Just off A46 Lincoln by-pass on Whisby Road, which links A46 to B1190.
Directions by public transport:
1 mile from North Hykeham railway station.
Whisby Road is just off Doddington Road, served by several bus routes from city centre.
Charges: £2 adult. Accompanied children free. Other charges may apply at special events — please see web site.
Facilities: A B(e) D P T
Other information: Refreshments available on open days.

Registration	Date	Chassis	Body	New to	Fleet No	Status
KW 474	1927	Leyland Lion PLSC1	Leyland B31F	Blythe & Berwick of Bradford		R
TE 8318	1929	Chevrolet LQ	Spicer C14D	Jardine of Morcambe		R
VL 1263	1929	Leyland Lion LT1	Applewhite B32R	Lincoln Corporation	5	R
WH 1553	1929	Leyland Titan TD1	Leyland L27/24RO	Bolton Corporation	54	R
KW 7604	1930	Leyland Badger TA4	Plaxton B20F	Bradford Education Committee	023	R
TF 818	1930	Leyland Lion LT1	Roe B30F	Lancashire United Transport	202	R
FW 5698	1935	Leyland Tiger TS7	Burlingham B35F	Lincolnshire Road Car Co	1411	R
RC 2721	1935	SOS DON	Brush B—F	Trent Motor Traction Co	321	R
FHN 833	1940	Bristol L5G	ECW B35F	United Automobile Services	BG 147	RP
BFE 419	1941	Leyland Titan TD7	Roe H30/26R	Lincoln Corporation	64	R
AHE 163	1946	Leyland Titan PD1	Roe H31/25R	Yorkshire Traction	726	RP
DBE 187	1946	Bristol K6A	ECW H30/26R	Lincolnshire Road Car Co	2115	R
DFE 383	1948	Guy Arab III	Guy H30/26R	Lincoln Corporation	23	R
HPW 133	1949	Bristol K5G	ECW H30/26R	Eastern Counties Omnibus Co	LKH 133	R
OHK 432	1949	Daimler CVD6	Roberts H30/26R	Colchester Corporation	4	R
ONO 59	1949	Bristol K5G	ECW L-/-R	Eastern National Omnibus Co	4038	R
FFU 860	1950	AEC Regal III 9621E	Willowbrook DP35F	Enterprise of Scunthorpe	60	R
FDO 573	1953	AEC Regent III 9613E	Willowbrook H32/28RD	J W Camplin & Sons ('Holme Delight') of Donington		RP
OLD 714	1954	AEC Regent III O961 RT	Weymann H30/26R	London Transport	RT 4494	R
LFW 326	1955	Bristol Lodekka LD6B	ECW H33/25RD	Lincolnshire Road Car Co	2318	R
RFE 416	1961	Leyland Titan PD2/41	Roe H33/28R	Lincoln Corporation	89	R
952 JUB	1964	AEC Regent V 2D2RA	Roe H39/31R	Leeds City Transport	952	RP
CVL 850D	1966	Bristol RELH6G	ECW C47F	Lincolnshire Road Car Co	1431	RP
EVL 549E	1967	Leyland Panther PSUR1/1R	Roe DP45F	Lincoln Corporation	41	RP
UVL 873M	1973	Bristol RELL6L	Alexander B48F	Lincoln Corporation	73	RP
PFE 542V	1980	Bristol VRTSL3/6LXB	ECW H43/31F	Lincolnshire Road Car Co	1958	R

Notes:

KW 474	Restored as Lincoln Corporation No 1	ONO 59	Renumbered 1427 in 1954 and 2255 in 1964; subsequently converted to caravan
FW 5698	Originally fleet No 368. Rebodied in 1949		
FHN 833	Originally fleet No BLO 133.	FFU 860	Passed to Lincolnshire Road Car Co (860) in 1950
DBE 187	Originally fleet No 661. Rebuilt by ECW in mid 1950s.	CVL 850D	Later renumbered 2231
DFE 383	Ruston Hornsby air cooled engine		

London's Transport Museum
Covent Garden

Contact address: 39 Wellington Street, London WC2E 7BB.
Phone: 020 7379 6344; recorded information 020 7565 7299
E-mail: resources@ltmuseum.co.uk
Web site: www.ltmuseum.co.uk
Affiliation: NARTM
Brief description: Visit London's Transport Museum and see how public transport has transformed the capital and lives of Londoners since the early 1800s. It's trams, trains, buses and much more. A truly memorable hands-on experience.
Opening days/times: Please telephone in advance for details of opening times.
Directions by car: Limited parking at parking meters in Covent Garden, Holborn/Kingsway area. Congestion charge payable.
Directions by public transport:
Buses to Strand or Aldwych: 1, 4, 6, 9, 11, 13, 15, 23, 26, 59, 68, 76, 77A, 91, 139, 168, 171, 172, 176, 188, 243, 341, 521 and RV1
Underground to Covent Garden, Leicester Square or Holborn.
Charges: Adult £5.95, Concession £4.50, Accompanied children under 16s free, other prices available — contact the Museum for details. For school rates please telephone Resource Centre.
Facilities: A C D F G H L R S T

Registration	Date	Chassis	Body	New to	Fleet No	Status
note m	1829	Horse bus	LGOC	George Shillibeer		R
note n	1875	Horse bus	Thomas Tilling -24-	Thomas Tilling		R
note p	1888	Horse bus	LGOC -26-	London General Omnibus Co		R
LC 3701	1906	De Dion	(chassis only)	London General Omnibus Co	L 7	R
LA 9928	1911	LGOC B	LGOC O18/16RO	London General Omnibus Co	B 340	R
XC 8059	1921	AEC K	LGOC O24/22RO	London General Omnibus Co	K 424	R
MN 2615	1923	Tilling Stevens TS3A Petrol Electric	(chassis only)	Douglas Corporation	10	R
XM 7399	1923	AEC S	LGOC O28/26RO	London General Omnibus Co	S 742	R
YR 3844	1926	AEC NS	LGOC H28/24RO	London General Omnibus Co	NS 1995	R
GK 3192	1931	AEC Regent 661	LGOC H28/20R	London General Omnibus Co	ST 821	R
GK 5323	1931	AEC Renown 663	LGOC H33/23R	London General Omnibus Co	LT 165	R
GK 5486	1931	AEC Regal 662	Duple C30F	London General Omnibus Co	T 219	R
GO 5198	1931	AEC Renown 664	LGOC B–F	London General Omnibus Co	LT 1076	RP
HX 2756+	1931	AEC 663T	UCC H32/24R	London United Tramways	1	R
AXM 649	1934	AEC Regent 661	Chalmers -	London Transport	STL 390	R
AYV 651	1934	AEC Regent 661	LPTB H30/26R	London Transport	STL 469	R
BXD 576	1935	AEC Q 0762	Birmingham R C & W B35C	London Transport	Q 55	R
CLE 122	1936	Leyland Cub KP03	Weymann B20F	London Transport	C 94	R
EXV 253+	1939	Leyland LPTB70	Leyland H40/30R	London Transport	1253	R
FJJ 774	1939	Leyland FEC	LPTB B34F	London Transport	TF 77	R
HYM 768+	1948	BUT 9641T	Metro Cammell H40/30R	London Transport	1768	R
MXX 364	1953	Guy Special NLLVP	ECW B26F	London Transport	GS 64	R
NLE 537	1953	AEC Regal IV 9821LT RF	Metro Cammell B39F	London Transport	RF 537	R
NXP 997	1954	AEC Regent III O961 RT	Park Royal H30/26R	London Transport	RT 4712	R
OLD 589	1954	AEC Regent III O961 RT	Park Royal H30/26R	London Transport	RT 4825	R
SLT 56	1956	AEC Routemaster	Park Royal/LTE H36/28R	London Transport	RM 1	R
SLT 57	1957	AEC Routemaster	Park Royal/LTE H36/28R	London Transport	RM 2	R
737 DYE	1963	AEC Routemaster 2R2RH	Park Royal H36/28R	London Transport	RM 1737	R
CUV 229C	1965	AEC Routemaster R2RH/1	Park Royal H36/29RD	London Transport	RCL 2229	R
KGY 4D	1966	AEC Routemaster FR2R	Park Royal H41/31F	London Transport	FRM 1	R
AML 582H	1969	AEC Merlin 4P2R	MCW B25D	London Transport	MBA 582	R
EGP 1J	1970	Daimler Fleetline CRG6LXB	Park Royal H44/24D	London Transport	DMS 1	R
KJD 401P	1976	Bristol LH6L	ECW B39F	London Transport	BL 1	A
TPJ 61S	1977	Bristol LHS6L	ECW B35F	London Country Bus Services	BN 61	R

Note: Please be aware that vehicles on display can vary from time to time as not all museums display their entire 'fleet'. Visitors wishing to see a particular vehicle should make enquiries prior to their visit.

Registration	Date	Chassis	Body	New to	Fleet No	Status
NUW 567Y	1982	Leyland Titan TNLXB/2RR	Leyland H44/24D	London Transport	T 567	R
C526 DYT	1986	Volkswagen LT55	Optare B25F	London Transport	OV 2	R
F115 PHM	1988	Volvo B10M-50	Alexander H46/29D	Grey Green	VA115	R
note r	1993	Optare Metrorider	Optare B26F	London Transport	MRL 242	R
+ Trolleybus						

Notes:

note m	Unregistered reconstruction		SLT 57	Prototype new 1955. First Registered 5/1957.
note n	Unregistered; Knifeboard type		TPJ 61S	Support collection vehicle
note p	Unregistered; Garden Seat type		F115 PHM	On loan from Arriva London
AXM 649	Rebuilt with Breakdown Vehicle body in 1950		note r	Unregistered sectioned exhibit built especially for LT Museum
NXP 997	Currently in gold livery			
SLT 56	Prototype new 9/1954. First Registered 1/1956.			

Manchester Museum of Transport
Cheetham

Contact address: Boyle Street, Cheetham, Manchester M8 8UW
Phone/Fax: 0161 205 2122
E-mail: busmuseum@btconnect.com
Web site: www.gmts.co.uk or www.manchester.bus.museum
Affiliation: NARTM
Brief description:
The museum houses over 70 buses and coaches from the Greater Manchester area, from an 1876 horse bus to a 1990 Metrolink tram. Travel back to a time of twopenny singles and coach trips to Blackpool. Extensive displays of photos, uniforms and models complement the vehicles, and visitors may enter many of the vehicles and view the museum's workshop.
Events planned:
19/20 March 2005 — Spring Transport Festival
7/8 May 2005 — Rear Engined Buses Event
18/19 June 2005 — Accessible Transport Weekend
4 September 2005 — Trans-Lancs Rally
9 October 2005 — Rover Car Club Event
3/4 December 2005 — Christmas Cracker Collectors Fair
Opening days/times: Wednesdays, Saturdays, Sundays & Bank Holidays: 10.00-17.00 March to October, 10.00 to 16.00 November-February inclusive (please phone for Christmas/New Year opening)
Directions by car:
From M62/M60 junction 18, follow 'Castlefields' signs to Cheetham Hill; from City, follow A665 (Cheetham Hill Road) — Museum signposted.
Directions by public transport:
Bus 135 or 59 to Queen's Road; Metrolink tram to Woodlands Road (10min walk)
Charges: £3.00 adult, £1.75 concession, £9 family. Season tickets available. School parties free
Facilities: B(e) C D F G H P R S T
Other information: Archives available for study by arrangement.

Registration	Date	Chassis	Body	New to	Fleet No	Status
note b	1876	Horse bus	Manchester Carriage Co O18/14RO	Manchester Carriage Co	2	R
DB 5070	1925	Tilling Stevens TS6 Petrol Electric	Brush O54RO	North Western Road Car Co	170	R
CK 3825	1927	Leyland Lion PLSC1	Leyland B31F	Ribble Motor Services	295	R
VM 4439	1928	Leyland Tiger TS1	Metro Cammell/Crossley B—R	Manchester Corporation	138	A
VY 957	1929	Leyland Lion PLSC1	Ribble B32R	York Corporation	2	R
VR 5742	1930	Leyland Tiger TS2	Manchester Corporation Car Works B30R	Manchester Corporation	28	R
AXJ 857	1934	Leyland Titan TD3	(chassis only)	Manchester Corporation	526	R

Registration	Date	Chassis	Body	New to	Fleet No	Status
JA 7585	1935	Leyland Tiger TS7	English Electric B35C	Stockport Corporation	185	A
RN 7824	1936	Leyland Cheetah LZ2	Brush C31F	Ribble Motor Services	1568	RP
EFJ 92	1938	Bedford WTB	Heaver C25F	Taylor of Exeter		RP
AJA 152	1939	Bristol K5G	Willowbrook L27/26R	North Western Road Car Co	432	R
BBA 560	1939	AEC Regent O661	Park Royal H26/22R	Salford Corporation	235	R
JP 4712	1940	Leyland Titan TD7	Leyland L24/24R	Wigan Corporation	70	RP
BJA 425	1946	Bristol L5G	Willowbrook B38R	North Western Road Car Co	270	R
HTB 656	1946	Leyland Tiger PS1	Roe B35R	Ramsbottom U D C	17	R
HTF 586	1947	Bedford OB	Scottish Motor Traction C29F	Warburton Bros of Bury		R
CDB 224	1948	Leyland Titan PD2/1	Leyland L27/26R	North Western Road Car Co	224	R
CWH 717	1948	Leyland Titan PD2/4	Leyland	Bolton Corporation	367	R
JND 791	1948	Crossley DD42/8S	Crossley H32/26R	Manchester Corporation	2150	R
JNA 467	1949	Leyland Titan PD1/3	Metro Cammell H32/26R	Manchester Corporation	3166	RP
LMA 284	1949	Foden PVSC6	Lawton C35F	Coppenhall of Comberbach		R
BEN 177	1950	AEC Regent III 9613A	Weymann H30/26R	Bury Corporation	177	R
CWG 206	1950	Leyland Tiger PS1	Alexander C35F	W Alexander & Sons	PA164	R
LTC 774+	1950	Crossley Empire TDD42/2	Crossley H30/26R	Ashton-under-Lyne Corporation	80	RP
MTB 848	1950	Leyland Tiger PS2/1	East Lancs B35R	Rawtenstall Corporation	55	R
EDB 549	1951	Leyland Titan PD2/1	Leyland O30/20R	Stockport Corporation	295	R
EDB 562	1951	Leyland Titan PD2/1	Leyland H30/26R	Stockport Corporation	308	A
EDB 575	1951	Crossley DD42/7	Crossley H30/26R	Stockport Corporation	321	R
JND 646	1951	Leyland Titan PD2/3	Metro Cammell H32/26R	Manchester Corporation	3245	R
JVU 755+	1951	Crossley Dominion TDD64/1	Crossley H36/30R	Manchester Corporation	1250	R
NNB 125	1953	Leyland Royal Tiger PSU1/13	Northern Counties B41C	Manchester Corporation	25	R
UTC 672	1954	AEC Regent III 9613S	East Lancs L27/28RD	Bamber Bridge Motor Services	4	R
UMA 370	1955	Atkinson PD746	Northern Counties H35/24C	SHMD Board	70	R
JBN 153	1956	Leyland Titan PD2/13	Metro Cammell H34/28R	Bolton Corporation	77	R
NDK 980	1956	AEC Regent V D2RA6G	Weymann H33/28R	Rochdale Corporation	280	R
PND 460	1956	Leyland Titan PD2/12	Metro Cammell H36/28R	Manchester Corporation	3460	R
DJP 754	1957	Leyland Titan PD2/30	Northern Counties H33/28R	Wigan Corporation	115	R
NBU 494	1957	Leyland Titan PD2/20	Roe H31/29R	Oldham Corporation	394	R
116 JTD	1958	Guy Arab IV	Northern Counties H41/32R	Lancashire United Transport	21	R
122 JTD	1958	Guy Arab IV	Northern Counties H41/32R	Lancashire United Transport	27	R
TNA 496	1958	Leyland Titan PD2/40	Burlingham H37/28R	Manchester Corporation	3496	R
TNA 520	1958	Leyland Titan PD2/34	Burlingham H37/28R	Manchester Corporation	3520	R
UNB 629	1960	Leyland Atlantean PDR1/1	Metro Cammell H43/33F	Manchester Corporation	3629	R
YDK 590	1960	AEC Reliance 2MU3RA	Harrington C37F	Yelloway Motor Services of Rochdale		R
HEK 705	1961	Leyland Titan PD3A/2	Massey H41/29F	Wigan Corporation	57	A
TRJ 112	1962	Daimler CVG6	Metro Cammell H37/28R	Salford City Transport	112	R
414 CLT	1963	AEC Routemaster 2R2RH	Park Royal H36/28R	London Transport	RM 1414	R
4632 VM	1963	Daimler CVG6K	Metro Cammell H37/28R	Manchester Corporation	4632	R
REN 116	1963	Leyland Atlantean PDR1/1	Metro Cammell H41/33F	Bury Corporation	116	A
8860 VR	1964	AEC Regent V 2D3RA	East Lancs Neepsend H41/32R	A Mayne & Son of Manchester		R
BND 874C	1965	Leyland Panther Cub	Park Royal B43D	Manchester Corporation	74	R
DBA 214C	1965	Leyland Atlantean PDR1/1	Metro Cammell H43/33F	Salford City Transport	214	R
DDB 174C	1965	Daimler Fleetline CRG6LX	Alexander H44/31F	North Western Road Car Co	174	R
PTC 114C	1965	AEC Renown 3B3RA	East Lancs H41/31F	Leigh Corporation	15	R
PTE 944C	1965	Leyland Titan PD2/37	Roe H37/28F	Ashton-under-Lyne Corporation	44	R
FRJ 254D	1966	Leyland Titan PD2/40	Metro Cammell H36/28F	Salford City Transport	254	R
JRJ 281E	1967	Leyland Titan PD2/40	Metro Cammell H36/28F	Salford City Transport	281	R
HVM 901F	1968	Leyland Atlantean PDR1/1	Park Royal H45/28D	Manchester City Transport	1001	R
KDB 408F	1968	Leyland Leopard PSU4/1R	East Lancs B43D	Stockport Corporation	408	RP
KJA 871F	1968	Leyland Titan PD3/14	East Lancs H38/32R	Stockport Corporation	71	R
MJA 891G	1969	Leyland Titan PD3/14	East Lancs H38/32R	Stockport Corporation	91	R
MJA 897G	1969	Leyland Titan PD3/14	East Lancs O38/32F	Stockport Corporation	97	R

Note: Please be aware that vehicles on display can vary from time to time as not all museums display their entire 'fleet'. Visitors wishing to see a particular vehicle should make enquiries prior to their visit.

Registration	Date	Chassis	Body	New to	Fleet No	Status
TTD 386H	1969	Leyland Titan PD3/14	East Lancs H41/32F	Ramsbottom U D C	11	R
TXJ 507K	1972	Leyland National 1151/2R/0202	Leyland National B46D	SELNEC PTE	EX30	R
VNB 101L	1972	Leyland Atlantean AN68/1R	Park Royal H43/32F	SELNEC PTE	7001	R
XVU 352M	1974	Seddon Pennine IV-236	Pennine B19F	Greater Manchester PTE	1722	R
GNC 276N	1975	Seddon Lucas	Pennine B19F	Greater Manchester PTE	EX62	R
HVU 244N	1975	AEC Reliance 6U3ZR	Plaxton C49F	Yelloway Motor Services of Rochdale		R
XBU 17S	1978	Leyland Fleetline FE30AGR	Northern Counties H43/32F	Greater Manchester PTE	8017	A
ORJ 83W	1981	MCW Metrobus DR102/21	MCW H43/30F	Greater Manchester PTE	5083	A
A706 LNC	1984	Leyland Atlantean AN68D/1R	Northern Counties H43/32F	Greater Manchester PTE	8706	A
C208 FVU	1986	MCW Metrobus DR153/8	Northern Counties CH43/29F	Greater Manchester PTE	5208	RP
D63 NOF	1986	Freight Rover 400 Special	Carlyle B18F	Manchester Minibuses (Bee Line Buzz Co.)		A
D676 NNE	1987	MCW Metrorider MF151/3	MCW B23F	Greater Manchester Buses	1676	R
M939 XKA	1994	Mercedes Benz 609D	Mercedes - Devon Conversion	Greater Manchester Accessible Transport Ltd		R

+ Trolleybus

Notes:

note b	Largest surviving horse bus.	122 JTD	Gardner 6LX from new.
DB 5070	Petrol Electric transmission	TNA 520	Fully auto transmission when new and converted to semi-auto in 1963
CK 3825	Body rebuilt 1981		
VM 4439	Body new 1935	414 CLT	Loaned to Manchester Corporation when new in Feb 1963
VY 957	Body rebuilt 1983; restored to Ribble livery		
VR 5742	Rebodied 1937	HVM 901F	First 'Mancunian' double-decker
BBA 560	Training bus with dual controls 1948-70. Renumbered 98 in 1950.	KJA 871F	Restored as GMPTE 5871
		MJA 891G	Last open-rear-platform double-decker delivered to a British operator
AJA 152	Rebodied 1951		
BJA 425	Originally numbered 125; rebodied 1958 with 1952 body	TTD 386H	Last half-cab double-decker delivered to a British operator
CWH 717	Originally H30/26R; converted to tower wagon 1963.	MJA 897G	Originally H38/32F; converted to open-top in 1982
LMA 284	Body new 1954	VNB 101L	First SELNEC Standard double-decker
EDB 562	Used as training bus 1968-1978	TXJ 507K	First production Leyland National
EDB 549	Originally H30/26R. Converted to open top in 1968.	GNC 276N	Battery-powered
UMA 370	Only Atkinson double-decker bodied. Originally H35/25C.	M939 XKA	Wheelchair lift at rear

Midland Road Transport Group — Butterley

Contact address: 21 Ash Grove, Mastin Moor, Chesterfield S43 3AW
Phone: Midland Road Transport Group — 01246 473619
Midland Railway 01773 747674, Visitor Information Line (01773) 570140.
Brief Description: A large purpose-built museum building housing a collection of buses, lorries and fork lift trucks fully or partially restored. Situated at the Swanwick Junction site of the Midland Railway Centre. All vehicles are all privately-owned by individual preservaionists who co-operated together to provide finances to build the museum which was completed in 2004
Events planned:
10 July 2005 — 2nd Annual Road Transport Rally (date to be confirmed)
Opening days/times:
See Railways Restored for details
Directions by car: To Swanwick Junction.
From the north, M1 Jcn 28, follow A38 southbound to B600, turn left to Somercotes, right on to B6016 through Riddings. Follow signs to Codnor/Heanor and turn right onto Coach Road at the bottom of descent from Riddings. Half mile along this narrow lane, take right fork after speed bumps.
From the south, M1 Jcn 26, follow A610 northbound to Codnor, turn right and right again onto B6016 Alfreton/Somercotes. Travel along for three

miles and turn left onto Coach Road at bottom of hill after wooded areas on B6016.
Directions by public transport: Trent Barton service H1 from Derby, Heanor or Alfreton. Half mile walk from end of Coach Road, ask for Riddings Dale
Charges: X
Facilities: R, S, T

Registration	Date	Chassis	Body	New to	Fleet No	Status
ESV 811	1947	AEC Regal III	Weymann B30D	Carris of Lisbon	141	R
HVO 937	1947	AEC Regent II	Weymann H30/26R	Mansfield District	126	R
KRR 255	1949	AEC Regal III	Weymann B35F	Mansfield District	9	R
NRA 78F	1968	Bedford TK	Reeves Burgess	Derbyshire County Council		RP
PNU 114K	1971	Leyland Atlantean PDR1A/1	Northern Counties H44/28D	Chesterfield Corporation	114	RP
RCH 629L	1972	Bristol VRT/SL6G	ECW H43/34F	Trent Motor Traction Co	629	R
NNU 123M	1973	Daimler Fleetline CRL6-30	Roe H42/29D	Chesterfield Corporation	123	R
NNU 124M	1973	Daimler Fleetline CRL6-30	Roe H42/29D	Chesterfield Corporation	124	R
SHN 80L	1973	Bristol RELH6G	ECW DP49F	United Automobile Services	6080	R
UOA 322L	1973	Leyland National 1151/1R/0401	Leyland National B52F	Eastern National Omnibus Co	1702	RP
LRA 801P	1975	Bristol VRT/SL3/501	ECW H43/34F	Midland General Omnibus Co	801	RP

Notes:
ESV 811 Original Portugese registration II-14-49
NRA 78F Library Bus
LRA 801P Original Leyland 501 engine replaced by Gardner unit 1980

Museum of Transport
Glasgow

Contact address: Kelvin Hall, 1 Bunhouse Road, Glasgow G3 8DP
Phone: 0141 287 2720 (school bookings on 0141 565 4112/3)
Fax: 0141 287 2692
Affiliation: NARTM
Brief description: The museum displays many items of transport history dating from the 1870s.
Opening days/times: Monday to Thursday and Saturday, 10.00 to 17.00; Friday and Sunday 11.00 to 17.00 (closed 25/26 December and 1/2 January)
Directions by car: From M8 junctions 17 or 19
Directions by public transport: Bus from City Centre (Dumbarton Road) to Kelvin Hall; Underground to Kelvin Hall; nearest main-line railway station is Partick.
Charges: Free admission
Facilities: D F G H R T
Other information: Guided tours and exhibitions also held.

Registration	Date	Chassis	Body	New to	Fleet No	Status
EGA 79	1949	Albion Venturer CX 37S	Croft H30/26R	Glasgow Corporation	B92	R
FYS 988+	1958	BUT RETB1	Burlingham B50F	Glasgow Corporation	TBS13	R
FYS 998	1958	Leyland Atlantean PDR1/1	Alexander H44/34F	Glasgow Corporation	LA1	R

+ Trolleybus

Notes:
FYS 988 Exhibited at the 1958 Commercial Motor Show

Note: Please be aware that vehicles on display can vary from time to time as not all museums display their entire 'fleet'. Visitors wishing to see a particular vehicle should make enquiries prior to their visit.

X50
SERVICE X50
KGY 4D

9 2X
MANCHESTER
CORPORATION
2150
JND 791

Above left: **London's Transport Museum's collection includes unique Routemaster FRM1, the front-entrance, rear-engined prototype of which no production examples were built. FRM1 is seen here at Finsbury Park in 2004 on the occasion of an event marking the 50th anniversary of the introduction into service of the very first Routemaster, RM1.** *Philip Lamb*

Left: **The Manchester Museum of Transport has a fine collection of local buses including Manchester 1948 all-Crossley no2150 (JND 791), seen here outside the museum's Cheetham Hill premises.** *Philip Lamb*

Above: **Few utility buses remain; generally accepted to be the best surviving example in original condition is Swindon 51 (DHR 192), a Weymann-bodied Guy Arab II. Presently the Guy is part of the Science Museum collection to be found at Wroughton Airfield, located just outside its home town.** *Philip Lamb*

National Museum of Science and Industry
Wroughton

Contact address: Exhibition Road, London SW7 2DD
Phone: 0207 942 4105 or 01793 814466
E-mail: s.evans@nmsi.ac.uk
Brief description: The bus collection is located at Wroughton airfield (hangar 4), near Swindon, Wiltshire.
Events planned: Open days are held and details of these may be found in the enthusiast press.
Opening days/times: Open only on Transport Festival and Open Days.
Directions by car: On A4361 approx 4 miles south of Swindon.
Directions by public transport: Publicised for Open Days
Charges: Published for each event.

Registration	Date	Chassis	Body	New to	Fleet No	Status
LMJ 653G	1913	Fiat 52B		(operator unknown) Yugoslavia		RP
JCP 60F	1928	Leyland Lion PLSC1	Leyland B31F	Jersey Railways & Tramways		A
DR 4902	1929	Leyland Titan TD1	Leyland L51RO	National Omnibus & Transport Co	2849	A
DX 8871+	1930	Ransomes Sims & Jefferies D	Ransomes Sims & Jefferies B31D	Ipswich Corporation	44	A
GW 713	1931	Gilford 1680T	Weymann C30D	Valiant of Ealing		A
VO 6806	1931	AEC Regal 662	Cravens B32F	Red Bus of Mansfield		A
JN 5783	1935	AEC Q 762	(chassis only) -	Westcliff-on-Sea Motor Services		A
CPM 61+	1939	AEC 661T	Weymann H28/26R	Brighton Hove & District	6340	A
FR 1347	1940	Saurer CRD		GFM (Switzerland)	52	A
DHR 192	1943	Guy Arab II	Weymann UH30/26R	Swindon Corporation	51	A
KPT 909	1949	Leyland Titan PD2/1	Leyland L27/26R	Weardale Motor Services of Frosterley		R
LTA 772	1951	Bristol LWL5G	ECW B32R	Western National Omnibus Co	1613	A
HET 513	1953	Crossley DD42/7	Crossley H30/26R	Rotherham Corporation	213	A
NLP 645	1953	AEC Regal IV 9822E	Park Royal RDP37C	British European Airways	1035	A
OTT 55	1953	Bristol LS5G	ECW B41F	Southern National Omnibus Co	1701	A
OLJ 291	1954	Bedford CAV	Bedford B12	Non-psv use		A
VLT 140	1960	AEC Routemaster R2RH	Park Royal H36/28R	London Transport	RM 140	R
504 EBL	1963	Bedford VAL14	Duple C52F	Reliance Motor Services of Newbury	87	A
note u	1970	Moulton MD	Moulton C23F	Moulton Development vehicle		A
BCD 820L	1973	Leyland National 1151/1R/0102	Leyland National B49F	Southdown Motor Services	20	A
+ Trolleybus						

Notes:
LMJ 653G Yugoslavia
JCP 60F Originally registered J 4601
FR 1347 Displays original Swiss registration FR1347
note u Eight wheeled integral development vehicle (unregistered)

North of England Open Air Museum
Beamish

Contact address: Beamish, Co Durham, DH9 0RG
Phone: 0191 370 4000
Fax: 0191 370 4001
E-mail: museum@beamish.org.uk
Web site: www.beamishmuseum.co.uk

Brief description: Beamish is an open-air museum which vividly recreates life in the North of England in the early 1800s and early 1900s Buildings from throughout the region have been brought to Beamish, rebuilt and furnished as they once were. Costumed staff welcome visitors and demonstrate the past way of life in The Town, Colliery Village, Home Farm, Railway Station, Pockerley Manor and 1825 Railway. A one-mile circular period tramway carries visitors around the Museum and a replica 1913 Daimler bus operates between The Town and Colliery Village.
Events planned: (transport related, please contact for non-related events) please contact to confirm actual dates
1 May 2005 — Power from the Past
15 May 2005 — Morgan Car Meeting
4 Sept 2005 — Triumph Stag car day
25 Sept 2005 — Classic car day
Opening days/times: 2005
Summer: 19 March to 30 October: (open every day)
Winter 31 October to 31 March 2006: 10.00 to 16.00 (closed Mondays and Fridays); also closed 12 December to 2 January 2006 (inclusive).
Reduced operations in winter.
Last admission always 15.00.
Directions by car: Follow A1(M) to junction 63 (Chester-le-Street exit). Take A693 towards Stanley and follow Beamish Museum signs.
Directions by public transport: Buses 709 from Newcastle, 720 from Durham and 775/778 from Sunderland all serve Beamish.
Charges: — 2005 rates, under 5s free
Summer: Adult £14, Child £9, Over 60s £12.
Winter: £6 per person.
Group rates available in summer for parties of 20 or more.
Facilities: B E F G H M P R T
Other information: Beamish is not ideal for wheelchair users. Free leaflet available in advance for visitors with disabilities and mobility limitations.
Some vehicles not on display. Please telephone for information

Registration	Date	Chassis	Body	New to	Fleet No	Status
WT 7108+	1924	Straker Clough T29	Brush B32F	Keighley Corporation Tramways	12	A
UP 551	1928	BMMO SOS QL	Brush Replica B37F	Northern General Transport Co	338	RP
VK 5401	1931	Dodge UF30A	Robson of Consett B14F	Baty of Rookhope		A
LTN 501+	1948	Sunbeam S7	Northern Coachbuilders H39/31R	Newcastle Corporation	501	R
J 2503	1988	Renault	Osborne O18/14RO	Beamish of the North of England Open Air Museum		R

+ Trolleybus

Notes:
UP 551   Replica body in the course of construction
J 2503   Replica of 1913 Daimler.

North West Museum of Road Transport

Contact address: The Old Bus Depot, 51 Hall Street, St Helens, WA10 1DU
Phone: 01744 451681
E-mail: email@sthelenstransportmuseum.co.uk
website: www.sthtm.freeserve.co.uk
Affiliation: NARTM
Brief description: A collection of over 100 historic vehicles representing the transport heritage of the northwest of England. There is also a small exhibits section containing ticket machines, uniforms, signs and other transport-related items.
Events planned: Please see the enthusiast press for details
Opening days/times: Museum building currently under restoration. Expected to be open to the public during 2005.
Facilities: A B(e) D G T

Note: Please be aware that vehicles on display can vary from time to time as not all museums display their entire 'fleet'. Visitors wishing to see a particular vehicle should make enquiries prior to their visit.

Registration	Date	Chassis	Body	New to	Fleet No	Status
ED 6141	1930	Leyland Titan TD1	Massey H28/26R	Warrington Corporation	22	A
KR 1728	1930	Leyland Titan TD1	Short H48R	Maidstone & District Motor Services	321	A
KJ 2578	1931	Leyland Titan TD1	Weymann	Redcar Motor Services of Tunbridge Wells		A
AFY 971	1934	Leyland Titan TD3	English Electric O26/25R	Southport Corporation	43	A
ATD 683	1935	Leyland Lion LT7	Massey B30R	Widnes Corporation	39	A
RV 6360	1935	Leyland Titan TD4	English Electric O26/24R	Portsmouth Corporation	117	R
FTB 11	1942	Leyland Titan TD7	Northern Coachbuilders UL27/26R	Leigh Corporation	84	A
DKY 713+	1945	Karrier W	East Lancs H37/29F	Bradford Corporation	713	A
EWM 358	1945	Daimler CWA6	Duple UH30/26R	Southport Corporation	62	A
ANQ 778	1946	AEC Regent III	Commonwealth Engineering	Dept of Road Transport & Tramways of Sydney	1984	A
DED 797	1946	Leyland Titan PD1	Alexander H30/26R	Warrington Corporation	16	RP
HLW 159	1947	AEC Regent III O961 RT	Park Royal H30/26R	London Transport	RT 172	R
FFY 401	1947	Leyland Titan PD2/3	Leyland O30/26R	Southport Corporation	84	A
FFY 403	1947	Leyland Titan PD2/3	Leyland O30/26R	Southport Corporation	86	A
FFY 404	1947	Leyland Titan PD2/3	Leyland O30/26R	Southport Corporation	87	R
BCB 341	1948	Leyland Tiger PS1	Crossley B32F	Blackburn Corporation	8	A
KTD 768	1948	Leyland Titan PD2/1	Lydney L27/26R	Leigh Corporation	16	R
ACB 902	1949	Guy Arab II	Northern Coachbuilders H30/26R	Blackburn Corporation	74	A
ACC 88	1949	Bedford OB	Duple C29F	Deiniolen Motors		A
FBU 827	1949	Crossley DD42/8	Crossley H30/26R	Oldham Corporation	368	A
KTC 615	1949	Guy Arab III	Guy B33R	Accrington Corporation	10	A
GFY 406	1950	Leyland Titan PD2/3	Leyland H30/26R	Southport Corporation	106	A
BDJ 808	1952	AEC Regent III O961 RT	Park Royal	St Helens Corporation	D8	A
NTF 466	1952	Daimler CVG5	Northern Counties B32F	Lancaster City Transport	466	R
CDJ 878	1954	Leyland Titan PD2/9	Davies H30/26R	St Helens Corporation	E78	A
RFM 644	1954	Guy Arab IV	Guy/Park Royal H30/26R	Chester Corporation	4	R
434 BTE	1957	Crossley Regent V D3RV	East Lancs H31/28RD	Darwen Corporation	17	R
GDJ 435	1957	AEC Regent V MD3RV	Weymann H33/26R	St Helens Corporation	H135	A
KRN 422	1957	Leyland Titan PD2/10	Crossley H33/29R	Preston Corporation	31	R
FHF 456	1959	Leyland Atlantean PDR1/1	Metro Cammell H44/33F	Wallasey Corporation	6	A
KDJ 999	1959	AEC Regent V 2D3RA	East Lancs H41/32F	St Helens Corporation	K199	A
MSD 407	1959	Leyland Titan PD3/6	Alexander L35/32RD	Western SMT Co	AD1543	A
PFR 346	1959	Leyland Titan PD2/27	Metro Cammell FH35/28RD	Blackpool Corporation	346	A
LDJ 985	1960	Leyland Titan PD2A/27	Weymann H30/25RD	St Helens Corporation	K175	A
562 RTF	1961	Leyland Titan PD2/40	East Lancs H37/28R	Widnes Corporation	31	R
574 TD	1962	Guy Arab IV	Northern Counties H41/32R	Lancashire United Transport	110	R
PSJ 480	1962	Leyland Titan PD2A/27	Massey H37/27F	Wigan Corporation	35	RP
TRJ 109	1962	AEC Reliance 2MU3RV	Weymann B45F	Salford City Transport	109	RP
201 YTE	1963	Leyland Titan PD2/37	East Lancs O37/28F	Lancaster City Transport	201	R
6219 TF	1963	Guy Arab IV	Northern Counties H41/32R	Lancashire United Transport	135	R
TDJ 612	1963	AEC Reliance 2MU3RA	Marshall B45F	St Helens Corporation	212	R
4227 FM	1964	Bristol Lodekka FS6G	ECW H33/27RD	Crosville Motor Services	DFG157	R
AJA 139B	1964	Bedford VAL 14	Strachan B52F	North Western Road Car Co	139	RP
HTF 644B	1964	Leyland Titan PD2/40	East Lancs H37/28R	Widnes Corporation	38	R
JTD 300B	1964	Guy Arab V	Northern Counties H41/32R	Lancashire United Transport	166	A
BCK 367C	1965	Leyland Titan PD3/6	Leyland/Preston Corporation H38/32F	Preston Corporation	61	A
BED 731C	1965	Leyland Titan PD2/40 Special	East Lancs H34/30F	Warrington Corporation	50	R
FFM 135C	1965	Guy Arab V	Massey H41/32F	Chester Corporation	35	RP
MDJ 555E	1967	Leyland Titan PD2A/27	East Lancs H37/28R	St Helens Corporation	55	A
HCK 204G	1968	Leyland Panther PSUR1A/1R	MCW B47D	Preston Corporation	204	RP
KJA 299G	1968	Bristol RESL6G	Marshall B43F	North Western Road Car Co	299	R
AFM 103G	1969	Bristol RELH6G	ECW C47F	Crosville Motor Services	CRG103	RP
DFM 347H	1969	Guy Arab V	Northern Counties H41/32R	Chester Corporation	47	R
JFM 650J	1970	Daimler Fleetline CRG6LX	Northern Counties H43/29F	Chester Corporation	50	RP
SRJ 328H	1970	Leyland Atlantean PDR2/1	MCW H47/31D	SELNEC PTE	1205	RP

Registration	Date	Chassis	Body	New to	Fleet No	Status
JDJ 260K	1972	AEC Swift 3MP2R	Marshall B44D	St Helens Corporation	260	R
PDJ 269L	1972	AEC Swift 3MP2R	Marshall B42D	St Helens Corporation	269	RP
RTC 645L	1972	Leyland National 1151/1R/0101	Leyland National B52F	Widnes Corporation	1	R
LED 71P	1976	Bristol RESL6G	East Lancs B41D	Warrington Corporation	71	R
CFM 86S	1978	Leyland Fleetline FE30AGR	Northern Counties	Chester City Transport	86	A
VBA 151S	1978	Leyland Atlantean AN68A/1R	Northern Counties H43/32F	Greater Manchester PTE	8151	A
CWG 696V	1979	Leyland Atlantean AN68A/1R	Alexander	South Yorkshire PTE	1696	R
XLV 140W	1980	Leyland National 2 NL116AL11/1R	Leyland National B49F	Merseyside PTE	6140	R
YMA 99W	1981	Dennis Dominator DD121B	Northern Counties H43/29F	Chester City Transport	99	RP
LFR 866X	1981	Leyland National 2 NL106AL11/1R	Leyland National B44F	Ribble Motor Services	866	A

+ Trolleybus

Notes:

KJ 2578	Originally H24/24R; converted to canteen by Liverpool Corporation (CL4)	PSJ 480	Originally registered JJP 502
		201 YTE	Originally H37/28F
AFY 971	Originally H26/25R	BCK 367C	Rebuilt from Leyland PD2 by Preston Corporation
RV 6360	Originally H26/24R; renumbered 6 following open-top conversion	HCK 204G	Relocated away from museum during refurbishing works
DKY 713	Rebodied 1960	AFM 103G	Relocated away from museum during refurbishing works
HLW 159	Acquired by Bradford City Transport (410) in 1958		
FFY 404	Originally H30/26R	DFM 347H	Last Guy Arab delivered to a British operator
FFY 403	Originally H30/26R	LED 71P	Relocated away from museum during refurbishing works
FFY 401	Originally H30/26R		
BDJ 808	Converted to breakdown vehicle by Harper Bros of Heath Hayes		

Nottingham Transport Heritage Centre
Ruddington

Contact address: Mere Way, Ruddington, Nottingham NG11 6NX
Phone: 0115 940 5705
E-mail: aecley@aol.com
Web site: http://www.nthc.co.uk
Affiliation: NARTM
Brief description: The centre offers exhibits covering road and rail transport, and provides the opportunity to experience travel of a bygone age.
Events planned: Please see enthusiast press for details.
Opening days/times: Easter to mid-October: Sundays and Bank Holiday Mondays (10.45-17.00).
Directions by car: 3 miles south of Nottingham just off A52 ring-road and main A60 road via small roundabout at Ruddington.
Directions by public transport: Buses from Nottingham pass near museum
Charges: Not finalised at time of publication, all rides inclusive of steam train rides.
Facilities: B B(e) D E G H P R S T

Registration	Date	Chassis	Body	New to	Fleet No	Status
VO 8846	1932	Leyland Lion LT5	Willowbrook DP32F	South Notts Bus Co of Gotham	17	A
DJF 349	1947	Leyland Titan PD1	Leyland H30/26R	Leicester City Transport	248	RP
JVO 230	1948	Leyland Titan PD1A	Duple L29/26F	Barton Transport of Chilwell	507	R
MAL 310	1951	Leyland Royal Tiger PSU1/11	Duple DP45F	South Notts Bus Co of Gotham	42	A
APR 167A	1953	Leyland Titan PD2/12	Leyland H30/26RD	Barton Transport of Chilwell	732	A
OTV 161	1953	AEC Regent III 9613E	Park Royal H30/26R	Nottingham City Transport	161	R
PFN 865	1959	AEC Regent V 2LD3RA		East Kent Road Car Co		R

Note: Please be aware that vehicles on display can vary from time to time as not all museums display their entire 'fleet'. Visitors wishing to see a particular vehicle should make enquiries prior to their visit.

Registration	Date	Chassis	Body	New to	Fleet No	Status
866 HAL	1960	AEC Reliance 2MU3RV	Plaxton C41F	Barton Transport of Chilwell	866	RP
80 NVO	1962	Leyland Titan PD3/4	Northern Counties L33/32F	South Notts Bus Co of Gotham	80	RP
YRC 194	1962	Leyland Tiger Cub PSUC1/1	Alexander DP41F	Trent Motor Traction Co	194	R
APA 46B	1964	AEC Reliance 4MU3RA	Willowbrook B—F	Safeguard of Guildford		RP
DAU 370C	1965	AEC Renown 3B3RA	Weymann H40/30F	Nottingham City Transport	370	R
ETO 452C	1965	Leyland Atlantean PDR1/1	Metro Cammell	Nottingham City Transport	452	RP
EOD 524D	1966	AEC Regent V 2D3RA	MCW H34/25F	Devon General	524	R
FEL 751D	1966	Bristol MW6G	ECW C39F	Hants & Dorset Motor Services	904	R
LNN 89E	1967	Albion Lowlander LR3	Northern Counties H41/30F	South Notts Bus Co of Gotham	89	RP
RCH 518F	1968	Daimler Fleetline CRG6LX	Alexander H44/33F	Trent Motor Traction Co	518	A
STO 523H	1970	Leyland Atlantean PDR1A/1	Northern Counties H47/30D	Nottingham City Transport	523	R
KVO 429P	1975	Leyland National 11351/2R	Leyland National B50F	Trent Motor Traction Co	429	A
ORC 545P	1976	Leyland Atlantean AN68/1R	ECW	Northern General Transport Co	3299	R
GTX 761W	1980	Bristol LHS6L	ECW DP27F	National Welsh Omnibus Services	MD8026	R
LVR 508W	1981	Bedford YRT	Plaxton C53F			RP
SCH 117X	1981	Leyland Fleetline FE30ALR	ECW H44/31F	South Notts Bus Co of Gotham	117	R
VRC 612Y	1982	Leyland Leopard PSU3G/4R	Plaxton C53F	Barton Transport of Chilwell	612	RP

Notes:
APR 167A	Originally registered RAL334	KVO 429P	Originally B44D
PFN 865	Recovery vehicle	ORC 545P	Originally H45/27D and registered MPT299P; used as promotional vehicle
LNN 89E	Last Albion Lowlander delivered Badged Leyland		

Oxford Bus Museum
Long Hanborough

Contact address: Station Yard, Long Hanborough, Witney, Oxfordshire, OX29 8LA
Phone: 01993 883617 (Answerphone) or 01993 881662
Affiliation: NARTM
Brief description: Over 30 buses dating from 1915 to 1994, mainly from City of Oxford Motor Services and other local companies. The collection includes many vehicles of AEC manufacture plus cars, fire engines and support vehicles.
Events planned: Please see enthusiast press for details.
Opening days/times: Sundays and Bank Holiday Mondays, 10.30 to 16.30. Saturdays open from Easter until the last Saturday in October, 10.30-16.30. Bus rides at 15.00 on the first Sunday of each month from the first Sunday in April to the first Sunday in October inclusive.
Directions by car: The entrance is on the south side of the A4095 (Witney-Bicester), between the villages of Bladon and Long Hanborough.
Directions by public transport: Museum is adjacent to Hanborough railway station on the Oxford-Worcester line, Sunday train services (journey time Oxford 10mins, London Paddington 70mins). Stagecoach bus service from George Street Oxford, weekdays, hourly to Long Hanborough village centre (1 mile)
Charges: Adults £2.50, Children £1.50, OAP £2.00, Family (2+2) £6.
Facilities: B(e) D P R S T
Other information: School parties welcome by arrangement — please telephone for booking.

Registration	Date	Chassis	Body	New to	Fleet No	Status
DU 4838	1915	Daimler Y	City of Oxford Electric Tramways B32R	City of Oxford Electric Tramways	39	A
note e	1916	Daimler Y	(chassis only)			A
note f	1916	Daimler Y	(chassis only)			A
note ao	1917	Daimler Y	O18/16RO	City of Oxford Electric Tramways		RP
YL 740	1925	Morris Commercial 1 ton	Ch14			R
JO 5032	1932	AEC Regal 642	(chassis only)	City of Oxford Motor Services	GC41	R
JO 5403	1932	AEC Regent 661	Brush O28/24R	City of Oxford Motor Services	GA16	R
DBW 613	1948	Bedford OB	Duple C29F	Oliver of Long Handborough		A
JVF 528	1949	Bedford OB	Duple C29F	Bensley of Martham		R
NJO 703	1949	AEC Regal III 9621A	Willowbrook DP32F	City of Oxford Motor Services	703	R
OFC 393	1949	AEC Regent III 9612A	Weymann H30/26R	City of Oxford Motor Services	H892	A

Registration	Date	Chassis	Body	New to	Fleet No	Status
OFC 205	1950	AEC Regal III 6821A	Duple C32F	South Midland Motor Services	66	A
PWL 413	1950	AEC Regent III 9613A	Weymann L27/26R	City of Oxford Motor Services	L166	RP
GJB 254	1952	Bristol LWL6B	ECW B39R	Thames Valley Traction Co	616	R
SFC 610	1952	AEC Regal IV 9821S	Willowbrook C37C	City of Oxford Motor Services	610	R
TWL 928	1953	AEC Regent III 9613S	Park Royal H30/26R	City of Oxford Motor Services	H928	RP
956 AJO	1957	AEC Regent V MD3RV	Park Royal H33/28R	City of Oxford Motor Services	H956	R
YNX 478	1958	AEC Reliance MU3RA	Duple Midland B44F	Chiltern Queens of Woodcote		RP
756 KFC	1960	AEC Reliance 2MU3RV	Park Royal B44F	City of Oxford Motor Services	756	R
14 LFC	1961	Morris FF	Wadham C27F	Morris Motors		A
304 KFC	1961	Dennis Loline II	East Lancs H35/28F	City of Oxford Motor Services	304	R
305 KFC	1961	Dennis Loline II	East Lancs H35/28F	City of Oxford Motor Services	305	R
850 ABK	1962	AEC Reliance 2MU3RA	Duple C43F	Don Motor Coach Co of Southsea		RP
YWB 494M	1964	International Harvester 1853FC	Superior of Ohio B44F	United States Air Force		RP
FWL 371E	1967	AEC Renown 3B3RA	Northern Counties H38/27F	City of Oxford Motor Services	371	RP
NAC 416F	1967	Leyland Atlantean PDR1A/1	Northern Counties H44/31F	Stratford-upon-Avon Blue Motors	10	A
UFC 430K	1971	Daimler Fleetline CRL6	Northern Counties H43/27D	City of Oxford Motor Services	430	A
EUD 256K	1972	AEC Reliance 6MU4R	Plaxton B47F	Chiltern Queens of Woodcote		R
VER 262L	1972	AEC Reliance 6U3ZR	Alexander C53F	Premier Travel of Cambridge	262	RP
HUD 476S	1977	Bristol VRTSL3/6LXB	ECW H43/27D	City of Oxford Motor Services	476	R
BBW 21V	1980	Leyland Leopard PSU3	Duple C49F	City of Oxford Motor Services	21	R
JUD 597W	1980	Ford R1014	Plaxton C45F	House of Watlington		R
A869 SUL	1983	Leyland Titan TNLXB/2RRSP	Leyland H44/26D	London Transport	T869	R
B106 XJO	1985	Ford Transit 160D	Carlyle B16F	South Midland of Witney	SM6	RP
C724 JJO	1986	Ford Transit	Carlyle DP20F	City of Oxford Motor Services	724	R
D122 PTT	1987	Ford Transit 190D	Mellor B16F	Thames Transit	122	R
L247 FDV	1994	Fiat 49-10	Mellor B13D	Bay Line of Exeter		A

Notes:

DU 4838	Body new 1920
note e	Chassis only
note f	Chassis only
note ao	Body ex-London built 1906
JO 5032	Passed to Mascot Motors in Jersey and subsequently converted to lorry. Body removed. To be exhibited as chassis.
JO 5403	Originally H28/24R
JVF 528	Restored in Mulleys livery.
OFC 205	Displayed as an unrestored vehicle
YNX 478	Carries 1956 body transferred from Dennis Pelican chassis
305 KFC	Sectioned museum display showing body construction method
14 LFC	Originally used for Morris Motors band
850 ABK	Acquired by Chiltern Queens of Woodcote in 1964
YWB 494M	Original USAF Identity 64 B 2428
NAC 416F	Acquired by City of Oxford Motor Services (905) in 1970
A869 SUL	Acquired by City of Oxford Motor Services (975) in 1993
L247 FDV	Bi-mode Minibus

Scottish Vintage Bus Museum
Lathalmond

Contact address: M90 Commerce Park, Lathalmond, Fife, KY12 OSJ
Phone: 01383 623380
E-mail: website: www.busweb.co.uk/svbm
Affiliation: NARTM
Brief description: The collection of over 160 buses was, in the main, operated or manufactured in Scotland, from the late 1920s to the early 1980s. Vehicles are generally owned by private individuals or groups. A fully-equipped workshop enables comprehensive restoration to be undertaken. The 42-acre site is a former Royal Navy depot.

Note: Please be aware that vehicles on display can vary from time to time as not all museums display their entire 'fleet'. Visitors wishing to see a particular vehicle should make enquiries prior to their visit.

Events planned: Open weekend — please see enthusiast press for details.
Opening days/times: Easter to end of September, Sundays 13.00 to 17.00
Directions by car: Use M90 junction 4. Take B914 Dollar road. Left B915 Dunfermline (2 miles). 2 miles to M90 Commerce Park on right.
Directions by public transport: Nearest bus/train Dunfermline. No public transport to site.
Charges: Sunday opening £3. Other charges apply at special events.
Facilities: B B(e) D E P R S T

Registration	Date	Chassis	Body	New to	Fleet No	Status
CD 7045	1922	Leyland G7	Short O27/24R	Southdown Motor Services	135	R
GE 2446	1928	Leyland Titan TD1	Leyland L27/24RO	Glasgow Corporation	111	R
RU 8678	1929	Leyland Lion PLSC3	Leyland B35F	Hants & Dorset Motor Services	268	RP
SO 3740	1929	Leyland Tiger TS2	Alexander B32F	Scottish General (Northern) Omnibus Co	P63	R
VD 3433	1934	Leyland Lion LT5A	Alexander B36F	Central SMT Co		R
AAA 756	1935	Albion Victor PK114	Abbott C20C	King Alfred Motor Services		R
WG 3260	1935	Leyland Lion LT5A	Alexander B35F	W Alexander & Sons	P705	A
WS 4522	1935	Leyland Tiger TS7	Cowieson B—R	Scottish Motor Traction Co		RP
ATF 477	1937	Leyland Tiger TS7T	Fowler B39F	Singleton of Leyland		A
AUX 296	1939	Sentinel-HSG	Cowieson B32R	Sentinel of Shrewsbury (demonstrator)		RP
WG 8107	1939	Leyland Tiger TS8	Alexander -	W Alexander & Sons	P528	RP
WG 8790	1939	Leyland Tiger TS8	Alexander B39F	W Alexander & Sons	P573	RP
ETJ 108	1940	Leyland Tiger TS11	Roe -	Leigh Corporation	79	A
HF 9126	1940	Leyland Titan TD7	Metro Cammell	Wallasey Corporation	74	A
DSG 169	1942	Leyland Titan TD5	Alexander L27/26R	Scottish Motor Traction Co	J66	R
CDR 679	1943	Guy Arab II	Duple UH30/26R	Plymouth Corporation	249	R
JWS 594	1943	Guy Arab II	Duple/Nudd H31/24R	London Transport	G 77	R
BRS 37	1945	Daimler CWD6	Duple H30/26R	Aberdeen Corporation	155	R
AWG 623	1947	AEC Regal I O662	Alexander C31F	W Alexander & Sons	A36	R
AWG 639	1947	AEC Regal I O662	Alexander C35F	W Alexander & Sons	A52	R
HFO659	1947	Guy Arab III	(chassis only)	Blackburn Corporation	78	R
note o	1947	Albion Venturer CX19	Comeng H33/28R	DRTT of Sydney	1877	RP
XG 9304	1947	Leyland Titan PD1A	Northern Counties L27/26R	Middlesbrough Corporation	52	A
AWG 393	1948	Guy Arab III	Cravens H30/26R	W Alexander & Sons	RO607	R
BMS 405	1948	Daimler CVD6	Burlingham C33F	W Alexander & Sons	D10	A
BWG 39	1948	Bedford OB	Scottish Motor Traction C25F	W Alexander & Sons	W218	RP
ESG 652	1948	Guy Arab III	Metro Cammell B35R	Edinburgh Corporation	739	R
GGA 670	1948	Foden PVSC6	Plaxton FC35F	Scottish Co-operative Wholesale Society of Glasgow		A
FSC 182	1949	Daimler CVG6	Metro Cammell H31/25R	Edinburgh Corporation	135	R
CWG 283	1950	Leyland Tiger PS1	Alexander C35F	W Alexander & Sons	PA181	R
DCS 616	1950	Daimler CVD6	Massey O32/28RD	Hunter (A1) of Dreghorn	16A	R
EVA 324	1950	Guy Arab III	Guy B33R	Central SMT Co	K24	R
GVD 47	1950	Guy Arab III	Duple H31/26R	Hutchinson's Coaches of Overtown		R
SJ 1340	1950	Bedford OB	Duple C29F	Gordon of Lamlash		RP
SS 7486	1950	Bedford OB	Duple C29F	Stark's Motor Services of Dunbar		A
SS 7501	1950	Bedford OB	Duple C29F	Fairbairn of Haddington		R
AYJ 379	1951	Daimler CVD6	Croft H30/26R	Dundee Corporation	127	R
DGS 536	1951	Leyland Tiger PS1/1	McLennan C39F	A & C McLennan of Spittalfield		R
DGS 625	1951	Leyland Tiger PS1/1	McLennan C39F	A & C McLennan of Spittalfield		R
DMS 820	1951	Leyland Tiger OPS2/1	Alexander C35F	W Alexander & Sons	PB7	A
DMS 823	1951	Leyland Tiger OPS2/1	Alexander C35F	W Alexander & Sons	PB10	A
DWG 526	1951	Leyland Royal Tiger PSU1/15	Leyland C41F	W Alexander & Sons	PC30	A
MTE 639	1951	AEC Regent III 6812A	Weymann H33/26R	Morecambe & Heysham Corporation	77	R
BMS 222	1952	Leyland Royal Tiger PSU1/15	Alexander C41F	W Alexander & Sons	PC1	R
CYJ 252	1953	AEC Regent III 9613E	Alexander H32/26R	Dundee Corporation	137	R
FGS 59D	1953	Bedford SB	Mulliner B36F	Royal Navy		RP
NXP 506	1953	Bedford SB	Plaxton C33F	D Halley of Sauchie		R
CHG 541	1954	Leyland Tiger PS2/14	East Lancs B39F	Burnley Colne & Nelson	41	R

Registration	Date	Chassis	Body	New to	Fleet No	Status
GM 6384	1954	Leyland Titan PD2/10	Leyland L27/28R	Central SMT Co	L484	A
LFS 480	1954	Leyland Titan PD2/20	Metro Cammell H34/29R	Edinburgh Corporation	480	R
ETS 964	1955	Daimler CVG6	Metro Cammell H36/28R	Dundee Corporation	184	RP
FWG 846	1955	Bristol LS6G	ECW B45F	W Alexander & Sons	E11	RP
HRG 209	1955	AEC Regent V D2RV6G	Crossley H35/29R	Aberdeen Corporation	209	A
TYD 888	1955	AEC Reliance MU3RV	Duple C43F	Wakes of Sparkford		R
UFF 178	1955	AEC Regent V D2RV6G	Crossley H35/29R	Aberdeen Corporation	207	A
OFS 777	1957	Leyland Titan PD2/20	Metro Cammell H34/29R	Edinburgh Corporation	777	R
OFS 798	1957	Leyland Titan PD2/20	Metro Cammell H34/29R	Edinburgh Corporation	798	RP
OWS 620	1957	Bristol Lodekka LD6G	ECW H33/27R	Scottish Omnibuses	AA620	A
GM 9287	1958	Bristol Lodekka LD6G	ECW H-/-R	Central SMT Co	B87	RP
1252 EV	1959	Bristol MW5G	ECW DP41F	Eastern National Omnibus Co	488	R
FAS 982	1959	Albion Victor FT39KAN	Reading B35F	Jersey Motor Transport Co	5	R
SWS 671	1959	AEC Reliance 2MU3RV	Alexander C38F	Scottish Omnibuses	B671	A
SWS 715	1959	AEC Reliance 2MU3RV	Park Royal C41F	Scottish Omnibuses	B715	A
TFU 90	1959	Bedford SB1	Plaxton C41F	Paterson of Duffturn		RP
EDS 320A	1960	AEC Routemaster R2RH	Park Royal H36/28R	London Transport	RM 606	RP
NMS 366	1960	AEC Reliance 2MU3RV	Alexander C41F	W Alexander & Sons	AC155	RP
RAG 578	1960	Daimler CVG6LX	Northern Counties FH41/32F	T Hunter (A1) of Kilmarnock		R
VSC 86	1960	Leyland Tiger Cub PSUC1/3	Weymann B47F	Edinburgh Corporation	86	R
WAJ 112	1960	Albion Nimbus NS3N	Plaxton C29F	Watson of Huntingdon		A
XSL 945A	1960	Bristol MW6G	Alexander C41F	Western SMT Co	T1590	A
XSN 25A	1960	Bristol MW6G	Alexander C41F	Western SMT Co	T1591	A
EDS 288A	1961	AEC Routemaster R2RH	Park Royal H36/28R	London Transport	RM 910	R
JVS 541	1961	Leyland Tiger Cub PSUC1/2	Alexander C41F	Alexander (Fife)	FPD225	R
RAG 411	1961	Bristol Lodekka LD6G	ECW H33/27RD	Western SMT Co	1645	R
RCS 382	1961	Leyland Titan PD3A/3	Alexander L35/32RD	Western SMT Co	1684	R
YSG 101	1961	Leyland Leopard PSU3/2R	Alexander B33T	Edinburgh Corporation	101	R
YYJ 914	1961	Leyland Tiger Cub PSUC1/2	Alexander C41F	Stark's Motor Services of Dunbar	H8	A
7424 SP	1962	AEC Reliance 2MU3RV	Alexander C41F	W Alexander & Sons (Fife) Ltd	FAC4	R
LDS 201A	1962	AEC Routemaster R2RH	Park Royal H36/28R	London Transport	RM 1607	R
NSJ 502	1962	AEC Reliance 2MU3RV	Alexander C41F	W Alexander & Sons (Northern)	NAC205	R
UCS 659	1963	Albion Lowlander LR3	Northern Counties H40/31F	Western SMT Co	N1795	R
AFS 91B	1964	AEC Reliance 4MU3RA	Alexander B53F	Eastern Scottish	B91	R
ARG 17B	1964	AEC Reliance 2MU3RA	Alexander C41F	W Alexander & Sons (Northern) Ltd	NAC246	RP
ASC 665B	1964	Leyland Titan PD3/6	Alexander H41/29F	Edinburgh Corporation	665	R
AWA 124B	1964	Bedford SB13	Duple C41F	J O Andrew of Sheffield		R
BXA 452B	1964	Bristol Lodekka FS6G	ECW H33/27RD	W Alexander & Sons (Fife) Ltd	FRD187	R
BXA 464B	1964	Bristol Lodekka FS6G	ECW H33/27RD	W Alexander & Sons (Fife) Ltd	FRD199	R
CSG 29C	1965	Bristol Lodekka FLF6G	ECW -	Eastern Scottish		R
CSG 43C	1965	Bristol Lodekka FLF6G	ECW H38/32F	Scottish Omnibuses	AA43	RP
DMS 325C	1965	Leyland Leopard PSU3/3R	Alexander -	Alexander (Midland)	MPE40	R
DMS 359C	1965	Leyland Leopard PSU3/3R	Alexander -	Alexander (Midland)	MPE73	R
ESF 801C	1965	Leyland Atlantean PDR1/1	Alexander H43/31F	Edinburgh Corporation	801	R
LMG 952C	1965	Bedford VAL 14	Harrington C50F	Interline of London		A
EWS 130D	1966	AEC Reliance 2U3RA	Alexander C—F	Eastern Scottish	ZB130	A
EWS 168D	1966	Bristol RELH6G	Alexander C38Ft	Scottish Omnibuses (Eastern Scottish)	XA168	A
FFV 447D	1966	AEC Reliance 2U3RA	Plaxton C45F	J Abbott & Sons of Blackpool		R
WTE 155D	1966	Guy Arab V	Northern Counties H41/30F	Lancashire United Transport	232	R
GRS 343E	1967	Albion Viking VK43AL	Alexander DP40F	W Alexander & Sons (Northern) Ltd	NNV43	R
HDV 639E	1967	Bristol MW6G	ECW C39F	Western National Omnibus Co	1434	R
HGM 335E	1967	Bristol Lodekka FLF6G	ECW H44/34F	Central SMT Co	BL335	R
HGM 346E	1967	Bristol Lodekka FLF6G	ECW H44/34F	Central SMT Co	BL346	R
JSC 900E	1967	Leyland Atlantean PDR2/1	Alexander O47/35F	Edinburgh Corporation	900	R

Note: Please be aware that vehicles on display can vary from time to time as not all museums display their entire 'fleet'. Visitors wishing to see a particular vehicle should make enquiries prior to their visit.

54

Above left: **The minibus revolution of the 1980s/90s is now all but over. Some early combatants, such as Thames Transit 122 (D122 PTT), a Mellor-bodied Ford Transit 190D seen here are now in preservation. No122 is resident at the Oxford Bus Museum.** *Philip Lamb*

Left: **More traditional fayre at the Oxford Bus Museum includes long-term resident City of Oxford Motor Services 703 (NJO 703), an AEC Regal III with dual-purpose Willowbrook body, seen here in 2004 near Oxford Airport.** *Philip Lamb*

Above: **Manchester's last trolleybus BUT 9612T/Burlingham 1344 (ONE 744), having been at St Helens for many years was loaned by the North West Transport Museum Society in 2004 to the Black Country Museum, where it has been restored to working order.** *Philip Lamb*

Registration	Date	Chassis	Body	New to	Fleet No	Status
KPM 91E	1967	Bristol Lodekka FLF6G	ECW O32/28F	Brighton Hove & District	91	RP
LUS 524E	1967	AEC Reliance 2U3RA	Willowbrook C49F	David MacBrayne of Glasgow	150	R
NMY 636E	1967	AEC Routemaster	Park Royal H—/—F	British European Airways		R
KGM 664F	1968	Leyland Leopard PSU3/1R	Alexander B53F	Central SMT Co	T64	A
LFS 288F	1968	Bristol VRT/LL/6G	ECW O47/33F	Scottish Omnibuses	AA288	R
LFS 294F	1968	Bristol VRT/LL/6G	ECW H47/36F	Eastern Scottish	AA294	RP
LFS 303F	1968	Bristol VRT/LL/6G	ECW H-/-F	Scottish Omnibuses	AA303	RP
NTY 416F	1968	AEC Reliance 6MU3R	Plaxton C45F	J Rowell of Prudhoe		RP
VMP 8G	1968	Albion Viking VK43AL	Alexander DP40F	Road Transport Industry Training Board	16	RP
NAG 120G	1969	Bristol REMH6G	Alexander C42Ft	Western SMT Co	T2214	RP
XFM 42G	1969	Guy Arab V	Northern Counties H41/32F	Chester Corporation	42	R
SSF 237H	1970	Bedford VAL70	Duple C53F	Edinburgh Corporation	237	A
TMS 585H	1970	Leyland Leopard PSU3/1R	Alexander C49F	Road Transport Industry Training Board	84	A
TGM 214J	1971	Daimler Fleetline CRG6LX	ECW H43/34F	Central SMT Co	D14	R
XWS 165K	1971	Bedford J2	Plaxton C20F	Glass of Haddington		R
BFS 1L	1972	Leyland Atlantean AN68/1R	Alexander H45/30D	Edinburgh City Transport	1	R
BFS 471L	1972	Bedford YRQ	Alexander DP45F	Eastern Scottish	ZC471	A
BWG 833L	1972	Leyland Leopard PSU3/3R	Alexander B53F	W Alexander & Sons (Midland) Ltd	MPE133	A
BFS 463L	1973	Bedford YRQ	Alexander DP45F	Scottish Omnibuses (Eastern Scottish)	C463	A
BWS 105L	1973	Seddon Pennine IV-236	Seddon DP25F	Edinburgh Corporation	105	R
SCS 333M	1974	Leyland Leopard PSU3/3R	Alexander B53F	Western SMT Co	L2464	R
SCS 366M	1974	Leyland Leopard PSU3/3R	Alexander B53F	Western SMT Co	L2497	R
LSX 16P	1975	Volvo Ailsa B57	Alexander H44/35F	Alexander (Fife)	FRA16	A
MSF 750P	1976	Seddon Pennine VII	Alexander C42Ft	Scottish Omnibuses (Eastern Scottish)	XS750	R
NCS 16P	1976	Leyland Fleetline FE30AGR	Alexander H43/31F	Hill (A1) of Stevenston		A
ORS 60R	1977	Leyland Leopard PSU4C/4R	Alexander C45F	Grampian Regional Transport	60	R
OSJ 629R	1977	Leyland Leopard PSU3C/3R	Alexander B53F	Western SMT Co	L2629	RP
RRS 46R	1977	Leyland Leopard PSU3E/4R	Duple C49F	W Alexander & Sons (Northern)	NPE46	R
SMS 120P	1977	Daimler Fleetline CRG6LXB	Alexander H44/31F	W Alexander & Sons (Midland)	MRF120	RP
XMS 252R	1977	Leyland Leopard PSU3C/4R	Alexander B53F	W Alexander & Sons (Midland)	MPE252	A
CSG 773S	1978	Volvo Ailsa B55-10	Alexander H43/32F	Scottish Omnibuses (Eastern Scottish)	VV773	RP
CSG 792S	1978	Seddon Pennine VII	Plaxton C45F	Scottish Omnibuses (Eastern Scottish)	S792	A
JSF 928T	1978	Seddon Pennine VII	Alexander DP49F	Scottish Omnibuses	S928	RP
JTU 588T	1978	Leyland National 10351B/1R	Leyland National B—F	Crosville Motor Services	SNG588	RP
NDL 656R	1978	Bristol VRTSL3/6LXB	ECW H43/31F	Southern Vectis Omnibus Co	656	RP
XBO 121T	1978	Bristol VRT/SL3/6LXB	ECW O43/31F	National Welsh Omnibus Services		R
DSD 936V	1979	Seddon Pennine VII	Alexander C49F	Western SMT Co	S2936	RP
HLY 524V	1979	Leyland National 11351A/3R	Leyland National B—D	British Airways		R
JSX 595T	1979	Leyland Atlantean AN68A/1R	Alexander H45/30D	Lothian Regional Transport	595	R
LIL 9929	1979	Bedford VAS	Plaxton C29F	Blood Transfusion Service		RP
WTS 266T	1979	Volvo Ailsa B55-10	Alexander H44/31D	Tayside Regional Council	266	R
ESF 647W	1980	Guy Victory Mk 2	Alexander H60/24D	China Motor Bus	LV36	R
GSO 80V	1980	Leyland Leopard PSU3E/4R	Alexander C49F	Alexander (Northern)	NPE80	RP
LMS 374W	1980	Leyland Leopard PSU3F/4R	Alexander B53F	Alexander (Midland)	MPE374	A
RHS 400W	1980	Wales & Edwards	Wales & Edwards B12F	South of Scotland Electricity		R
SSX 602V	1980	Seddon Pennine VII	Alexander B53F	Scottish Omnibuses (Eastern Scottish)	S602	R
FES 831W	1981	Volvo B58-61	Duple B59F	Stagecoach of Perth		RP
GSC 658X	1981	Leyland Atlantean AN68A/1R	Alexander H45/30D	Lothian Regional Transport	658	A
HSC 173X	1981	Leyland Cub CU435	Duple B31F	Lothian Regional Transport	173	RP
GSC 667X	1982	Leyland Olympian ONTL11/1R	Alexander H47/28D	Lothian Regional Transport	667	R
KSX 102X	1982	Leyland National 2 NL116L11/2R	Leyland National B40D	Lothian Regional Transport	102	R
NFS 176Y	1982	Leyland Leopard PSU3G/4R	Alexander C49F	W Alexander & Sons (Fife)	FPE176	RP
ULS 716X	1982	Leyland Leopard PSU3G/4R	Alexander C49F	W Alexander & Sons (Midland)	MPE416	RP
ULS 717X	1982	Leyland Leopard PSU3G/4R	Alexander C49F	W Alexander & Sons (Midland)	MPE417	RP
B349 LSO	1985	Leyland Olympian ON5LXCT/1R	Alexander H45/32F	Alexander (Northern)	NLO49	A
C777 SFS	1985	Leyland Olympian ONTL11/2R	ECW H51/32D	Lothian Regional Transport	777	R

Notes:

CD 7045	Rebodied 1928. On loan from Stagecoach South East
SO 3740	Passed to W Alexander & Sons in 1930; numbered P63 in 1932 and rebodied in 1934
VD 3433	Rebodied 1945
WG 3260	Rebodied 1945
WG 8107	Breakdown Vehicle. Originally C35F.
ETJ 108	Breakdown Vehicle
HF 9126	Originally H28/26R; acquired by Lancashire County Constabulary in 1952 and converted for use as mobile control post
DSG 169	Alexander body to Leyland design; converted to open-top in 1959 and restored in 1980/1
JWS 594	Originally London Transport G77 (GLL 577); rebuilt and rebodied 1953
CDR 679	Orig Roe body converted to platform lorry in 1963. Present body from VV 9135.
note o	Not registered
HFO659	Originally registered ACB907. Breakdown Vehicle.
SS 7486	Passed to Scottish Omnibuses (C22) in 1964
DCS 616	Rebodied in 1958 as H32/28RD
GVD 47	Acquired by McGill's Bus Services of Barrhead in 1952
AYJ 379	On loan from Dundee Museums
FGS 59D	Originally registered 51 51 RN
UFF 178	Originally registered HRG 207
ETS 964	On loan from Travel Dundee
FAS 982	Originally registered J 1359
EDS 320A	Originally registered WLT 606; acquired by Kelvin Scottish Omnibuses (1919) in 1986
XSN 25A	Originally registered OCS 713
XSL 945A	Originally registered OCS 712
EDS 288A	Originally registered WLT 910; acquired by Kelvin Scottish Omnibuses (1929) in 1986
JVS 541	Originally registered RMS 714
YYJ 914	Originally registered ESS 989
NSJ 502	Originally registered SRS 117.
LDS 201A	Originally registered 607 DYE; acquired by Stagecoach at Perth in 1986
CSG 29C	Converted to breakdown vehicle
DMS 325C	Converted to Breakdown Vehicle
DMS 359C	Converted to Breakdown Vehicle
NMY 636E	Converted to mobile caravan
KPM 91E	Originally H38/32F; acquired by Scottish Omnibuses (AA971) in 1973 and converted to open-top (as OT2) in 1983
HDV 639E	First vehicle operated by Stagecoach
JSC 900E	Originally H47/35F
LFS 288F	Converted to open top
XBO 121T	Converted to open top by SVBM
NDL 656R	Acquired by Lowland Scottish Omnibuses (856) in 1991
LIL 9929	Originally registered CJU 998T
ESF 647W	Original Hong Kong registration was CH 9399
RHS 400W	Battery-electric bus
FES 831W	First new vehicle delivered to Stagecoach (as C50Ft)

Sheffield Bus Museum
Tinsley

Contact address: Tinsley Tram Sheds, Sheffield Road, Tinsley, Sheffield S9 2FY
Phone: 0114 255 3010
Website: www.sheffieldbusmuseum.com
Brief description: The display of over 25 vehicles is housed in part of a former tram shed.
Events planned: 12 June, 14 August, 11 September, 9 October, 11 December. Please see enthusiast press for details.
Opening days/times: Open days as advertised; also most Saturdays and Sundays (not Christmas) 12.00 to 16.00 (please telephone to check opening times before travelling especially to see specific vehicles).
Directions by car: From M1 Junction 34 take A6178
Directions by public transport: By Supertram to Carbrook (200yd from museum); also good bus links from Sheffield and Rotherham.
Charges: Adult £1.50, concession 75p, Family £3.
Facilities: A, B(e), D, F, H, G, S, R (open days)

Registration	Date	Chassis	Body	New to	Fleet No	Status
WG 9180	1940	Leyland Titan TD7	Leyland L27/26R	W Alexander & Sons	P266	R
GWJ 724	1941	AEC Regent O661	Sheffield Transport Department	Sheffield Corporation	G54	A
JWB 416	1947	Leyland Tiger PS1	Weymann B34R	Sheffield Corporation	216	A
HD 7905	1948	Leyland Tiger PS1	Brush B34F	Yorkshire Woollen District Transport Co	622	R
KWE 255	1948	AEC Regent III 9612E	Weymann	Sheffield Corporation	G55	RP
MHY 765	1950	Leyland Comet ECPO/1R	Duple C32F	Orient Coaches of Bristol		RP
OWE 116	1952	AEC Regent III 9613A	Roe H33/25R	Sheffield Joint Omnibus Committee	116	RP

Note: Please be aware that vehicles on display can vary from time to time as not all museums display their entire 'fleet'. Visitors wishing to see a particular vehicle should make enquiries prior to their visit.

Registration	Date	Chassis	Body	New to	Fleet No	Status
KET 220	1954	Daimler CVG6	Weymann H30/26R	Rotherham Corporation	220	RP
RWB 87	1954	Leyland Titan PD2/12	Weymann H32/26R	Sheffield Corporation	687	R
WRA 12	1955	AEC Monocoach MC3RV	Park Royal B45F	Booth & Fisher of Halfway		R
VDV 760	1958	Bristol Lodekka LD6G	ECW H33/27RD	Western National Omnibus Co	1943	R
TDK 322	1959	AEC Regent V D2RA	Weymann H33/28RD	Rochdale Corporation	322	R
TET 135	1959	Daimler CVG6-30	Roe	Rotherham Corporation		A
6330 WJ	1960	AEC Regent V 2D3RA	Roe H39/30RD	Sheffield Joint Omnibus Committee	1330	A
7874 WJ	1960	AEC Regent V 2D3RA	Alexander H37/32R	Sheffield Corporation	874	R
1322 WA	1961	AEC Reliance 2MU3RA	Plaxton C36F	Sheffield United Tours	322	A
GHD 765	1962	Leyland Titan PD3A/1	Metro Cammell H39/31F	Yorkshire Woollen District Transport Co	893	R
DWB 54H	1970	AEC Swift 5P2R	Park Royal B50F	Sheffield Transport	54	RP
LWB 388P	1976	Volvo Ailsa B55-10	Van Hool McArdle H44/31D	South Yorkshire PTE	388	RP
PSJ 825R	1976	Volvo Ailsa B55-10	Van Hool McArdle H44/31F	J Hunter (A1) of Kilmarnock		RP
UDT 189S	1978	Leyland Atlantean AN68A/1R	East Lancs H45/29D	South Yorkshire PTE	1589	A
CWG 756V	1979	Leyland Atlantean AN68A/1R	Roe H45/29D	South Yorkshire PTE	1756	A
C53 HDT	1985	Dennis Domino SDA1202	Optare B33F	South Yorkshire PTE	53	A

Notes:
GWJ 724 — Originally bus 462; converted to grit wagon
KWE 255 — Originally bus 255; converted to grit wagon
TET 135 — Originally H39/31F; converted to breakdown vehicle
PSJ 825R — Originally H44/31D

Tameside Transport Collection
Mossley

Contact address: Roaches Industrial Estate, Manchester Road, Mossley, Greater Manchester
Brief description: A working museum comprising a small but varied collection of vehicles ranging from 1929 to the 1960s. There is in addition a display of transport-related items.
Opening days/times: Last weekend of each month (except December), 10.00 to 15.00; visits at other times by prior appointment.
Directions by car: From Ashton-under-Lyne take A635 (Huddersfield) through Mossley. Museum is 1 mile on right-hand side, adjacent to Claybank Terrace.
Directions by public transport:
Bus service 355 from Ashton-under-Lyne or Oldham.
By rail to Mossley station (approximately 1 mile walk towards Greenfield).
Charges: No charge but donations welcome.
Facilities: D S R T
Other information: Car parking is limited.

Registration	Date	Chassis	Body	New to	Fleet No	Status
LG 2637	1929	Crossley Arrow	Crossley B32R	S Jackson & Sons of Crewe		A
DNF 204	1937	Crossley Mancunian	Metro Cammell/Crossley B32R	Manchester Corporation	129	RP
HG 9651	1948	Leyland Tiger PS1	Brush B35R	Burnley Colne & Nelson	10	R
DBN 978	1949	Crossley SD42/7	Crossley B32R	Bolton Corporation	8	R
JND 728	1950	Daimler CVG6	Metro Cammell H32/26R	Manchester Corporation	4127	RP
CRC 911	1951	Crossley DD42/8A	Brush H30/26R	Derby Corporation	111	R
FRJ 511	1951	Daimler CVG6	Metro Cammell H30/24R	Salford City Transport	511	R
422 CAX	1961	AEC Regent V MD3RV	Massey L31/28R	Bedwas & Machen UDC	5	R
105 UTU	1962	Leyland Titan PD2/37	Northern Counties H36/28F	SHMD Board	5	RP
7209 PW	1962	Bedford J2SZ2	Plaxton C20F	H & I Jarvis of Downham Market	4	R
BWO 585B	1964	AEC Regent V 2MD3RA	Massey L31/28R	Bedwas & Machen UDC	8	A
NMA 328D	1966	Daimler Fleetline CRG6LX	Northern Counties H-/-F	SHMD Board	28	RP

Notes:
LG 2637 — Passed to Crosville Motor Services (U2) in 1934
DNF 204 — Open rear platform
422 CAX — Converted to trainer by Rhumney Valley UDC 1976
BWO 585B — Last AEC to receive lowbridge body
NMA 328D — Used as exhibition bus 1983 to 1992

Transport Museum Society of Ireland
Howth

Contact address: Howth Castle Demesne, Howth, Dublin 13, Ireland
Phone: (00) 353 1 832 0427
Affiliation: NARTM
Brief description: The museum is run by a group of volunteers dedicated to the preservation and restoration of valuable road transport heritage. Exhibits include buses, trams and commercial, public utility, military, fire-appliance, electric and horse-drawn vehicles. Other displays include transport-associated memorabilia. The museum is a registered charity.
Opening days/times:
June to August: Monday to Saturday 10.00 to 17.00; Sunday 14.00 to 17.00.
September to May: Saturdays, Sundays and Bank Holidays 14.00 to 17.00.
Directions by car: Howth is 9 miles north of Dublin City Centre or 7 miles from the M1/M50 junction at Dublin Airport. Museum is located in grounds of Howth Castle Demesne.
Directions by public transport: Bus 31 from Dublin City Centre; Local DART rail service to Howth station, then short walk.
Charges: Please telephone for charges.
Facilities: E G P T
Other information: Limited access for disabled.
Note: No recent vehicle data received from this museum.

Registration	Date	Chassis	Body	New to	Fleet No	Status
TE 5110	1928	Leyland Lion PLSC3	(chassis only)	Colne Corporation	22	A
note i	1933	AEC Regal I	(chassis only)	(unknown)		A
ZI 9708	1933	Dennis Lancet I	Dublin United Tramways Co B32R	Dublin United Tramways Co	F21	A
ZC 714	1937	Leyland Titan TD4	Leyland H32/26R	Dublin United Tramways Co	R1	R
FRU 305	1945	Bristol K6A	Hants & Dorset FO31/28R	Hants & Dorset Motor Services	1108	A
GZ 7638	1947	Leyland Tiger PS1	Northern Ireland Road Transport Board B34R	Northern Ireland Road Transport Board	A8570	A
IY 1940	1948	AEC Regent III 9621E	Park Royal O33/26R	Morecambe & Heysham Corporation	58	A
ZD 7163	1948	Leyland Tiger OPS3	(chassis only)	CIE	P23	A
ZH 3926	1948	AEC Regal III O962	Park Royal C35R	Great Northern Railway (Ireland)	427	A
ZH 3937	1948	AEC Regent III 9612E	Park Royal H30/26RD	Great Northern Railway (Ireland)	438	R
ZH 4538	1948	Leyland Titan PD2/3	Leyland H33/27R	CIE	R389	R
LTU 869	1949	Commer Avenger I	Plaxton C33F	Thornley of Woodley		A
MZ 7396	1950	Guy Arab III	Harkness B31F	Belfast Corporation	298	A
ZL 2718	1950	GNR Gardner	Park Royal/GNR	Great Northern Railway (Ireland)	387	A
GUX 188	1951	Bedford OB	Duple B31F	Lloyd of Oswestry		A
IY 7384	1951	GNR Gardner	Park Royal/GNR DP33R	Great Northern Railway (Ireland)	390	RP
ZJ 5933	1951	Leyland Tiger OPS3	CIE	CIE	P193	A
OZ 6686	1953	Daimler CVG6	Harkness H30/26R	Belfast Corporation	432	A
ZL 6816	1953	Leyland Titan OPD2/1	CIE H37/31R	CIE	R506	A
ZO 6819	1953	Leyland Tiger PS2/14	CIE B39R	CIE	P309	A
ZO 6857	1953	Leyland Tiger PS2/14	CIE B39R	CIE	P347	R
ZO 6881	1954	Leyland Royal Tiger PSU1/15	CIE C34C	CIE	U10	A
ZO 6949	1954	Leyland Royal Tiger PSU1/15	CIE B39D	CIE	U78	A
ZY 79	1954	AEC Regal IV 9822E	Park Royal/GNR B45R	Great Northern Railway (Ireland)	274	A
ZU 9241	1955	Leyland Titan OPD2/1	CIE H37/31RD	CIE	R567	A
CYI 621	1958	Leyland Titan OPD2/2	CIE	CIE	R819	A
HZA 230	1960	Leyland Titan PD3/2	CIE H41/33R	CIE	RA105	RP
HZA 279	1961	AEC Regent V 2D2RA	CIE H41/28RD	CIE	AA2	A
404 RIU	1963	Albion Lowlander LR1	Alexander H41/31F	W Alexander & Sons (Midland) Ltd	MRE38	A
HZD 593	1963	Leyland Worldmaster ERT2/1	Van Hool DP53F	CIE	WVH13	A
NZE 598	1964	Leyland Leopard L2	CIE B45F	CIE	E170	A

Note: Please be aware that vehicles on display can vary from time to time as not all museums display their entire 'fleet'. Visitors wishing to see a particular vehicle should make enquiries prior to their visit.

Registration	Date	Chassis	Body	New to	Fleet No	Status
NZE 620	1964	Leyland Titan PD3A/6	Dundalk (Park Royal frame) H41/33R	CIE	R911	A
EZH 17	1965	Leyland Leopard PSU3/4R	CIE B45F	CIE	C17	A
EZH 64	1965	Leyland Leopard PSU3/4R	CIE/North East Health Board	CIE	C64	A
NZE 629	1965	Leyland Titan PD3A/3	Dundalk (Park Royal frame) O—/—R	CIE	R920	A
EZH 231	1966	Leyland Leopard PSU3/4R	CIE B53F	CIE	C231	A
VZL 179	1966	Bedford VAL14	Plaxton C53F	Wallace Arnold Tours of Leeds		A
EZL 1	1967	Bedford VAS5	CIE B33F	CIE	SS1	RP
VZI 44	1967	Leyland Atlantean PDR1/1	CIE H43/35F	CIE	D44	A
WZJ 724	1967	Bedford VAM 14	Duffy C45F	P O'Grady of Santry		A
DIV 83	1971	Daimler Fleetline CRG6LX	Alexander H45/32F	Trent Motor Traction Co	550	A
AIT 934	1972	Mercedes 406D	Asco Clubman	Flagline of Athlone		A
note j	1972	Bedford VAL 70	Duffy B40D	Aer Lingus	301	A
694 ZO	1975	Leyland Atlantean AN68/1R	Van Hool H45/29D	CIE	D694	A
GSI 353	1983	Bombardier	Bombardier H45/29D	CIE	KD 353	A
UZG 100	1984	Bombardier GAC	Bombardier B44D	CIE	KC100	A

Notes:
note i	Not registered	404 RIU	Originally registered VWG 376
FRU 305	Originally numbered TD774; renumbered in 1950 and rebodied 1952	EZH 64	Originally B45F; converted to mobile hospital
		NZE 629	Originally H41/33R
IY 1940	Originally H38/26R; registered KTF 587	VZL 179	Originally registered EUG 907D
ZL 2718	Ambulance conversion	DIV 83	Originally registered DRC 550J
ZJ 5933	Breakdown vehicle	note j	Not registered
CYI 621	Breakdown vehicle		

Sandtoft resident Doncaster 22 (MDT 222) is seen here in its hometown. No22 is a Roe-bodied AEC Regal III, one of three delivered in 1953. *Philip Lamb*

Trolleybus Museum at Sandtoft

Contact address: Belton Road, Sandtoft, Doncaster DN8 5SX
Phone: 01724 711391
E-mail: enquiries@sandtoft.org.uk
Web site: www.sandtoft.org.uk
Affiliation: NARTM
Brief description: Home of the nation's trolleybuses
Events planned: 26-28 March 2005 — Easter Weekend, 10 April 2005; 30 April, 1-2 May 2005 — May Day Bank Holiday, Southern Weekend; 28-30 May 2005 — Spring Bank Holiday Weekend, Wartime Weekend; 18-26 June 2005; 9/10 July 2005; 30/31 July 2005 — Gathering; 13/14 August 2005; 20/21August 2005 — North East Weekend; 27-29 August 2005 — August Bank Holiday, European Weekend; 24/25 September 2005 — 6-Wheel Weekend; 15/16 October 2005 — St Leger Rally; 13 November 2005; 10/11 December 2005 — Santa Days.
Opening days/times: 11.00 to 17.00 on the above dates.
Except: 30 July — 11.00-22.00; 31 July — 10.00-18.00; 10/11 December — 11.00-16.00
Directions by car: From M180 junction 2, take A161 southbound to Belton. Turn right and museum is 2 miles on right-hand side.
Directions by public transport: Free bus from Doncaster station at 13.30 on 24 April, 30 July, 28 August and 22 October (please telephone to check operation)
Charges: Adult £4.50, Child/Senior Citizen £2.50, Family £12.
Except: 30/31 July — Adult £6.00, Child/Senior Citizen £4.00.
  10/11 December — Adult £3.00, Child/Senior Citizen £4.50.
Facilities: A B(e) D E F G H L P R S T
Other information: Coach tours and private party visits can be accommodated at other times by prior arrangement

Registration	Date	Chassis	Body	New to	Fleet No	Status
KW 6052+	1929	English Electric A	English Electric B32F	Bradford Corporation	562	A
note t+	1929	Guy BTX	Ransomes B—C	Hastings Tramways Co		RP
TV 4484+	1931	Ransomes Sims & Jefferies D6	(chassis only)	Nottingham City Transport	346	R
1425 P+	1932	Fabrique Nationale	Fabrique Nationale B26SD	Liege (Belgium)	425	R
TV 9333+	1934	Karrier E6	Brush H64R	Nottingham City Transport	367	A
FW 8990+	1937	AEC 661T	Park Royal H30/26R	Cleethorpes Corporation	54	RP
FTO 614	1939	AEC Regent O661		Nottingham City Transport	802	R
964 H87+	1943	Vetra CB60	CTL B17D	Limoges (France)	5	R
GHN 574+	1944	Karrier W	East Lancs H39/31F	Bradford Corporation	792	R
GKP 511+	1944	Sunbeam W	Roe H34/28R	Maidstone Corporation	56	R
CDT 636+	1945	Karrier W	Roe H34/28R	Doncaster Corporation	375	RP
DKY 703+	1945	Karrier W	East Lancs H37/29F	Bradford Corporation	703	RP
DKY 706+	1945	Karrier W	East Lancs H37/29F	Bradford Corporation	706	R
GTV 666+	1945	Karrier W	Brush UH30/26R	Nottingham City Transport	466	RP
CVH 741+	1947	Karrier MS2	Park Royal H40/30R	Huddersfield Corporation	541	RP
EDT 703	1947	Leyland Titan PD2/1	Roe H34/28R	Doncaster Corporation	94	RP
HKR 11+	1947	Sunbeam W	Northern Coachbuilders H30/26R	Maidstone Corporation	72	R
JV 9901	1947	AEC Regent III O961 RT	Roe H31/25R	Grimsby Corporation	81	RP
JMN 727	1948	AEC Regent III O961	Northern Counties H30/26R	Douglas Corporation	63	R
KTV 493+	1948	BUT 9611T	Roe H31/25R	Nottingham City Transport	493	RP
BCK 939	1949	Leyland Titan PD1		Preston Corporation	6	RP
EKU 743+	1949	BUT 9611T	Roe H33/25R	Bradford Corporation	743	A
EKU 746+	1949	BUT 9611T	Roe H33/25R	Bradford Corporation	746	R
EKY 558	1949	Leyland Titan PD2/3	Leyland H33/26R	Bradford Corporation	558	RP
GDT 421	1949	Daimler CVD6	Roe L27/26R	Doncaster Corporation	112	A
LHN 784+	1949	BUT 9611T	East Lancs H37/29F	Bradford Corporation	834	R
ERD 152+	1950	Sunbeam S7	Park Royal H38/30RD	Reading Corporation	181	R
FET 618+	1950	Daimler CTE6	Roe H40/30R	Rotherham Corporation	44	R
GAJ 12+	1950	Sunbeam F4	Roe H35/26R	Tees-side Railless Traction Board	2	RP

Note: Please be aware that vehicles on display can vary from time to time as not all museums display their entire 'fleet'. Visitors wishing to see a particular vehicle should make enquiries prior to their visit.

Registration	Date	Chassis	Body	New to	Fleet No	Status
GFU 692+	1950	BUT 9611T	Northern Coachbuilders H38/26R	Cleethorpes Corporation	59	A
JWW 375+	1950	Sunbeam F4	East Lancs H37/29F	Bradford Corporation	845	RP
JWW 376+	1950	Sunbeam F4	East Lancs H37/29F	Bradford Corporation	846	A
JWW 377+	1950	Sunbeam F4	East Lancs H37/29F	Bradford Corporation	847	A
KTV 506+	1950	BUT 9641T	Brush H38/32R	Nottingham City Transport	506	R
BDJ 87+	1951	BUT 9611T	East Lancs H30/26R	St Helens Corporation	387	RP
FKU 758+	1951	BUT 9611T	Weymann H33/26R	Bradford Corporation	758	RP
KDT 393	1951	AEC Regent III 9613A	Roe H31/25R	Doncaster Corporation	122	R
LYR 542	1952	AEC Regent III O961 RT	Park Royal H30/26R	London Transport	RT 3323	RP
MDT 222	1953	AEC Regal III 9621A	Roe B39F	Doncaster Corporation	22	R
OTV 137	1953	AEC Regent III 9613E	Park Royal H30/26R	Nottingham City Transport	137	RP
JDN 668	1954	AEC Regent III 6812A	Roe H33/25RD	York Pullman Bus Co	64	R
KVH 219+	1956	BUT 9641T	East Lancs H40/32R	Huddersfield Corporation	619	R
XWX 795	1959	AEC Reliance 2MU3RV	Roe C—F	Felix Motors of Doncaster	40	RP
9629 WU	1960	AEC Reliance 2MU3RV	Roe DP41F	Felix Motors of Doncaster	41	R
VRD 193+	1961	Sunbeam F4A	Burlingham H38/30F	Reading Corporation	193	RP
657 BWB	1962	Leyland Atlantean PDR1/1	Park Royal H44/33F	Sheffield Joint Omnibus Committee	1357	R
433 MDT	1963	Leyland Tiger Cub PSUC1/11	Roe B45F	Doncaster Corporation	33	R
JTF 920B	1964	AEC Reliance 2MU3RV	East Lancs B—D	Reading Corporation	48	A
KDT 206D	1966	Daimler CVG6LX	Roe H34/28F	Doncaster Corporation	206	A
66+	1967	Lancia	Dalfa H43/25D	Oporto (Portugal)	140	R
UDT 455F	1968	Leyland Royal Tiger Cub RTC1/2	Roe B45D	Doncaster Corporation	55	R
WWJ 754M	1973	Daimler Fleetline CRG6LXB	Park Royal H43/27D	Sheffield Transport	754	R
C45 HDT+	1985	Dennis Dominator DTA1401	Alexander H47/33F	South Yorkshire PTE	2450	R

+ Trolleybus

Notes:

KW 6052	Caravan conversion to be restored.		BCK 939	Converted to breakdown vehicle
note t	Possibly Hastings 57 - not yet proven		FET 618	Rebodied 1957 (formerly single-decker)
FTO 614	Converted to tower wagon.		GAJ 12	Rebodied 1964
964 H87	French registration.		JWW 377	Rebodied 1962; chassis ex-Mexborough & Swinton
GHN 574	Originally single-decker; rebodied 1958		JWW 376	Rebodied 1962; chassis ex-Mexborough & Swinton
GKP 511	Rebodied 1960		JWW 375	Rebodied 1962; chassis ex-Mexborough & Swinton
DKY 703	Rebodied 1960		657 BWB	Rebodied 1968; renumbered 227 in 1970 following dissolution of JOC
CDT 636	Rebodied 1955			
DKY 706	Rebodied 1960		JTF 920B	Caravan conversion; originally registered 5148 DP
EDT 703	Originally Leyland body. Roe body 1955 ex-Trolleybus		66	Portugese registration.
HKR 11	On loan from Maidstone Borough Council		C45 HDT	Experimental vehicle; originally registered B450 CKW.
LHN 784	Rebodied 1962; chassis new to Darlington			

Ulster Folk & Transport Museum
Cultra

Contact address: Cultra, Holywood, Co Down, BT18 OEU
Phone: 028 9042 8428
Brief description: A unique collection of wheeled vehicles from cycles to trams, railways, buses and cars. Interpretive exhibitions show the development of road transport. Not all the vehicles listed are always on display. Please enquire before your visit.
Opening days/times: All the year round but closing for a few days at Christmas time. From 10.00 on weekdays and 11.00 on Sundays (please 'phone for details)
Directions by car: On A2 Belfast-Bangor road
Directions by public transport: On main Belfast-Bangor railway and bus routes
Charges: £6.50 (discounts for groups)
Facilities: A D E F G L P R T

Registration	Date	Chassis	Body	New to	Fleet No	Status
CZ 7013	1935	Dennis Lancet I	Harkness B31F	Belfast Corporation	102	R
FZ 7897+	1948	Guy BTX	Harkness H36/32R	Belfast Corporation	112	R
EOI 4857	1973	Daimler Fleetline CRG6LX-33	Alexander (Belfast) H49/37F	Belfast Corporation	857	R

+ Trolleybus

Notes:
EOI 4857 Passed to Citybus (2857) in 1973; rebodied 1976

Wirral Transport Museum
Birkenhead

Contact address: Pacific Road, Birkenhead, Merseyside, L41 5HN
Phone: 0151 666 2756
Affiliation: NARTM
Brief description: The museum houses a collection of buses, tramcars, motor cycles, cars and a few military vehicles. Some of the trams and buses are being restored by local enthusiast groups. Trams operate during weekends and some school holidays.
Opening days/times: Please telephone for details
Directions by car: Adjacent to Woodside ferry terminal
Directions by public transport: Bus or ferry to Woodside

Registration	Date	Chassis	Body	New to	Fleet No	Status
EAS 284	1940	AEC Matador	ECW -	Eastern National Omnibus Co		R
BG 8557	1944	Guy Arab II	Massey H31/26R	Birkenhead Corporation	242	RP
BG 9225	1946	Leyland Titan PD1A	Massey H30/26R	Birkenhead Corporation	105	RP
AHF 850	1951	Leyland Titan PD2/1	Metro Cammell H30/26R	Wallasey Corporation	54	R
GJB 279	1951	Bristol KSW6B	ECW L27/28R	Thames Valley Traction Co	641	R
GM 5875	1951	Leyland Titan PD2/10	Leyland	Central SMT Co	L475	A
RFM 641	1953	Guy Arab IV	Massey H30/26R	Chester Corporation	1	R
CHF 565	1956	Leyland Titan PD2/10	Burlingham H30/26R	Wallasey Corporation	106	RP
FBG 910	1958	Leyland Titan PD2/40	Massey H31/28R	Birkenhead Corporation	10	R
FHF 451	1958	Leyland Atlantean PDR1/1	Metro Cammell H44/33F	Wallasey Corporation	1	R
101 CLT	1962	AEC Routemaster R2RH	Park Royal H36/28R	London Transport	RM 1101	R
RCM 493	1964	Leyland Leopard L1	Massey B42D	Birkenhead Corporation	93	R
GCM 152E	1967	Leyland Titan PD2/37	Massey H36/30R	Birkenhead Corporation	152	R
UFM 52F	1968	Bristol RELL6G	ECW DP50F	Crosville Motor Services	ERG52	R
OFM 957K	1972	Daimler Fleetline CRG6LX-30	Northern Counties O43/29F	Chester Corporation	57	R
THM 692M	1973	Daimler Fleetline CRL6-30	MCW H34/10Dt	London Transport	DMS 1692	R
CWU 146T	1979	Leyland Fleetline FE30AGR	Roe H43/33F	West Yorkshire PTE	7146	R
XEM 898W	1981	Leyland Atlantean AN68B/1R	Alexander H43/32F	Merseyside PTE	1898	A
B926 KWM	1984	Leyland Atlantean AN68D/1R	Alexander H43/32F	Merseyside PTE	1070	R

Notes:
EAS 284 ECW Body ex-Queen Mary coach.
BG 8557 Rebodied in 1953. Original body was Park Royal utility.
GM 5875 Originally L27/26R; acquired by W Alexander & Sons (Midland) and converted to breakdown vehicle (ML245)
CHF 565 Carries 1949 body
FHF 451 First production Atlantean
FBG 910 Driver trainer 1974-81
RCM 493 Former road safety unit.
OFM 957K Originally H43/29F; rebodied 1984 and converted to open-top (renumbered 75) in 1998.
THM 692M Mobile classroom.
CWU 146T Promotional vehicle for The Hamilton Quarter. Currently H6/2FL.
B926 KWM Last production Atlantean

Note: Please be aware that vehicles on display can vary from time to time as not all museums display their entire 'fleet'. Visitors wishing to see a particular vehicle should make enquiries prior to their visit.

Left: **A very early recruit to the ranks of preserved buses was Southdown 813 (UF 4813), a Leyland Titan TD1 with Brush body. Originally preserved by its owner, the bus subsequently fell into Stagecoach hands and is currently on loan to Amberley Museum. It is seen here at Worthing in June 2004 celebrating the centenary of Worthing Motor Services, forerunner of Southdown Motor Services.** *Philip Lamb*

Below: **Also at Amberley is Leyland N Southdown 125 (CD 5125) with Shorts body.** *Philip Lamb*

Right: **Recently restored Leyland Titan PD2/12/Beadle Southdown 786 (RUF 186) is seen in Worthing in March 2004 recreating a working on its former owner's famous 31 Portsmouth-Brighton service. The bus is part of Eric Stobart's Classic Southdown Omnibuses fleet.**
Philip Lamb

Part 2

Other Collections of Preserved Buses & Coaches

Aldershot & District Bus Interest Group

Contact address: 111 Park Barn Drive, Guildford, Surrey, GU2 6ER
Web site: www.geocities.com/adbigweb
Affiliation: NARTM, FBHVC.
Brief description: The group was formed in 1994 to consolidate the collection of ex-Aldershot & District preserved vehicles and other artefacts which had been saved over the years. The vehicles range from 1920s Dennis E types to Dennis, AEC and Bristol buses which entered service in the 1960s and 1970s at the very end of the company's existence. The vehicles in the collection are in the care of members of an associated group which also welcomes the owners of other preserved Dennis buses and coaches.
Opening days/times: Running days are held from time to time at which many of the operational vehicles may be seen in service.
Other information: Regular working parties; new members welcome.

Registration	Date	Chassis	Body	New to	Fleet No	Status
OT 8283	1928	Dennis E	(chassis only)	Aldershot & District Traction Co	D210	A
OT 8592	1928	Dennis E	Strachan & Brown	Aldershot & District Traction Co	D217	A
OT 8898	1928	Dennis E	Strachan & Brown	Aldershot & District Traction Co	D226	A
OT 8902	1928	Dennis E	Dennis B32R	Aldershot & District Traction Co	D235	A
RT 4539	1928	Dennis 30cwt	(chassis only)	Green Coaches of Ashfield cum Thorpe		RP
CC 8671	1929	Dennis GL	Roberts T19	Llandudno UDC	2	R
CC 9424	1930	Dennis GL	Roberts T20	Llandudno UDC	3	A
MJ 4549	1932	Dennis Lancet I	Short B32F	Smith of Westoning		R
YD 9533	1934	Dennis Ace	Dennis B20F	Southern National Omnibus Co	3560	RP
JG 8720	1937	Dennis Lancet II	Park Royal B35R	East Kent Road Car Co		RP
GAA 580	1948	Dennis Lancet J3	Strachan B32R	Aldershot & District Traction Co	944	A
GAA 616	1948	Dennis Lancet J3	Strachan C32R	Aldershot & District Traction Co	980	RP
GOU 845	1950	Dennis Lance K3	East Lancs L25/26R	Aldershot & District Traction Co	145	A
HOU 904	1950	Dennis Lancet J10	Strachan B38R	Aldershot & District Traction Co	178	R
LAA 231	1953	Dennis Lancet J10C	Strachan FC38R	Aldershot & District Traction Co	196	RP
LOU 48	1954	Dennis Lance K4	East Lancs L28/28R	Aldershot & District Traction Co	220	R
MOR 581	1954	AEC Reliance MU3RV	Metro Cammell B40F	Aldershot & District Traction Co	543	R
POR 428	1956	Dennis Falcon P5	Strachan B30F	Aldershot & District Traction Co	282	RP
SOU 456	1958	Dennis Loline	East Lancs H37/31RD	Aldershot & District Traction Co	348	RP
SOU 465	1958	Dennis Loline	East Lancs H37/31RD	Aldershot & District Traction Co	357	R
XHO 370	1960	AEC Reliance 2MU3RV	Weymann DP40F	Aldershot & District Traction Co	370	R
462 EOT	1962	Dennis Loline III	Alexander H39/29F	Aldershot & District Traction Co	462	RP
488 KOT	1964	Dennis Loline III	Weymann H39/29F	Aldershot & District Traction Co	488	R
AAA 503C	1965	Dennis Loline III	Weymann H39/29F	Aldershot & District Traction Co	503	R
AAA 506C	1965	Dennis Loline III	Weymann H39/29F	Aldershot & District Traction Co	506	R
AAA 508C	1965	Dennis Loline III	Weymann H39/29F	Aldershot & District Traction Co	508	RP
CCG 296K	1971	Bristol RESL6G	ECW B40D	Aldershot & District Traction Co	651	RP
KCG 627L	1973	Leyland National 1151/1R/0402	Leyland National B49F	Thames Valley & Aldershot Omnibus Co	127	R
NPJ 472R	1976	Leyland National 11351A/1R	Leyland National B49F	Thames Valley & Aldershot Omnibus Co	251	R

Notes:
OT 8283	Originally Dennis F converted to E type
JG 8720	Rebodied 1949
MOR 581	Rebodied 1967

Aycliffe & District Bus Preservation Society

Contact address: 35 Lowther Drive, Newton Aycliffe, Co Durham, DL5 4UL
Affiliation: NARTM
Brief description: A collection of Darlington area service buses, the majority fully restored and in running order.
Opening days/times: Viewing by prior appointment only.

Registration	Date	Chassis	Body	New to	Fleet No	Status
GHN 189	1942	Bristol K5G	ECW L27/26R	United Automobile Services	BGL29	R
LHN 860	1950	Bristol L5G	ECW B35F	United Automobile Services	BG413	R
304 GHN	1958	Bristol LS6B	ECW C39F	United Automobile Services	BUC4	RP
AHN 451B	1964	Daimler CCG5	Roe H33/28R	Darlington Corporation	7	R
NDL 769G	1969	Bristol LHS6L	Marshall B35F	Southern Vectis Omnibus Co	833	R

Notes:

GHN 189	1949 body fitted in 1954	304 GHN	Now fitted with Gardner engine. Was C34F when new.
LHN 860	Converted to OMO c. 1957	NDL 769G	Acquired by United Automobile Services (1452) in 1977

Barrow Transport Group

Phone: 01229 870336
Web site: http://website.lineone.net/~barrow_transport
Brief Description: A brief collection of ex-Barrow in Furness vehicles. Restored examples can be seen at rallies. The group plans a museum in the future.

Registration	Date	Chassis	Body	New to	Fleet No	Status
EO 9051	1949	Leyland Titan PD2/3	Park Royal	Barrow in Furness Corporation	124	
EO 9177	1950	Leyland Titan PD2/3	Roe H31/28RD	Barrow in Furness Corporation	147	A
CEO 956	1958	Leyland Titan PD2/40	Park Royal H33/28R	Barrow in Furness Corporation	169	R
CEO 957	1958	Leyland Titan PD2/40	Park Royal H33/28R	Barrow in Furness Corporation	170	R
SEO 209M	1974	Leyland National 1151/1R	Leyland National B—F	Barrow in Furness Corporation	9	R
UEO 478T	1974	Leyland National	Leyland National B—F	Barrow in Furness Corporation	16	RP
CEO 720W	1981	Leyland National 2l	Leyland National B49F	Barrow in Furness Corporation	20	A
CEO 723W	1981	Leyland National 2	Leyland National B49F	Barrow in Furness Corporation	23	A
LEO 734Y	1983	Leyland Atlantean AN68	Northern Counties H43/32F	Barrow in Furness Corporation	104	RP
LEO 735Y	1983	Leyland Atlantean AN68	Northern Counties H43/32F	Barrow in Furness Corporation	105	A
E570 MAC	1988	Talbot Pullman	Talbot B20F	Barrow Borough Transport	99	RP

Notes:
EO 9051 Converted to recovery vehicle

Bohemia-Sachsen Transport Heritage Park

Contact address: PO Box 13, Zaluzany, 403 17 Chabarovice, Czech Republic
Phone: 00420 721 203 396

E-mail: transport.heritage.park@post.cz
Opening days/times: please enquire for details
Directions by car: From Chabarovice follow road to Roudniky. After Zalauzany rail crossing. Museum is on left
Directions by public transport: Bus 12 from Usti Nod Labem to Roudniky stops near museum site
Facilities: B, D, E, L, P, R, S, T

Registration	Date	Chassis	Body	New to	Fleet No	Status
NRH 802A	1961	AEC Routemaster	Park Royal H36/28R	London Transport	RM 798	R
AED 31B	1964	Leyland Titan PD2/40	East Lancs H37/28R	Warrington Corporation	149	A
LJF 31F	1968	Leyland Titan PD3A/12	MCW H41/31R	Leicester City Transport	31	RP
LHC 919P	1976	Bedford YLQ	Duple C45F	"Warrens Coaches, Ticehurst"	-	A
SDX 33R	1977	Leyland Atlantean AN68A/1R	Roe H43/29D	Ipswich Corporation	33	R
BTB 23T	1979	Leyland National 11351A/1R	Leyland National B52F	Halton Corporation	23	R
WYW 82T	1979	MCW Metrobus DR101/9	Metro Cammell H43/28D	London Transport	M 82	R
OTB 26W	1981	Leyland Atlantean AN68C/1R	East Lancs H45/33F	Warrington Corporation	26	R

Notes:
NRH 802A   Originally registered WLT 798

Bolton Bus Group

Contact address: 12 Arundale, Westhoughton, Bolton BL5 3YB
Brief description: A small group of enthusiasts formed to preserve examples of Bolton's buses. Some of the vehicles are displayed at Bury Transport Museum, which can be visited by prior arrangement.
Opening days/times: Please write to the above address to arrange a visit

Registration	Date	Chassis	Body	New to	Fleet No	Status
NBN 436	1959	Leyland Titan PD3/4	East Lancs H41/32F	Bolton Corporation	128	RP
UBN 902	1962	Leyland Titan PD3A/2	East Lancs FH41/32F	Bolton Corporation	169	R
UWH 185	1963	Leyland Atlantean PDR1/1	East Lancs H45/33F	Bolton Corporation	185	RP
FBN 232C	1965	Leyland Atlantean PDR1/1	East Lancs H45/33F	Bolton Corporation	232	R
KUS 607E	1967	Leyland Atlantean PDR1/1	Alexander H44/34F	Glasgow Corporation	LA352	RP
TWH 807K	1971	Leyland Atlantean PDR2/1	East Lancs H49/37F	SELNEC PTE	6807	A
TWH 809K	1971	Leyland Atlantean PDR2/1	East Lancs H49/37F	SELNEC PTE	6809	R

Notes:
TWH 807K   Playbus

Bournemouth Heritage Transport Collection

Phone: 01202 658333
Brief description: The collection comprises vehicles, mainly from Bournemouth Corporation or the Bournemouth area, built between the years 1928 and 1980. Most are owned by the Bournemouth Passenger Transport Association Ltd, which is a registered charity.
Events planned: Please see the enthusiast press for details
Opening days/times: Owing to storage relocation, the collection is not currently open to the public.

Registration	Date	Chassis	Body	New to	Fleet No	Status
RU 2266	1925	Shelvoke & Drewery Tramocar (chassis only)		Bournemouth Corporation	9	A
LJ 500	1929	Karrier WL6/1	Hall Lewis B40D	Bournemouth Corporation	33	RP
VH 6188	1934	AEC Regent O661	Hall Lewis H26/24R	Huddersfield Corporation	119	A

Registration	Date	Chassis	Body	New to	Fleet No	Status
VH 6217	1934	AEC Regent 661	Lee Motors -	Huddersfield Corporation	120	R
BOW 162	1938	Bristol L5G	Hants & Dorset -	Hants & Dorset Motor Services	9081	RP
DKY 712+	1944	Karrier W	East Lancs H37/29F	Bradford Corporation	712	A
FRU 224	1944	Guy Arab		Bournemouth Corporation	40	A
HLJ 44	1948	Bristol K6A	ECW L27/28R	Hants & Dorset Motor Services	TD895	RP
JLJ 403	1949	Leyland Tiger PS2/3	Burlingham FDP35F	Bournemouth Corporation	46	R
KEL 110	1949	Leyland Titan PD2/3	Weymann FH33/25D	Bournemouth Corporation	110	R
NNU 234+	1949	BUT 9611T	Weymann H32/26R	Nottinghamshire & Derbyshire Traction Co	353	RP
KEL 133	1950	Leyland Titan PD2/3	Weymann FH27/21D	Bournemouth Corporation	247	R
KLJ 346+	1950	BUT 9641T	Weymann H31/25D	Bournemouth Corporation	212	R
MOD 978	1952	Bristol LS6G	ECW C41F	Southern National Omnibus Co (Royal Blue)	1291	A
NLJ 268	1953	Leyland Royal Tiger PSU1/13	Burlingham B42F	Bournemouth Corporation	258	R
NLJ 272	1953	Leyland Royal Tiger PSU1/13	Burlingham B42F	Bournemouth Corporation	262	R
RRU 901	1955	Leyland Tiger Cub PSUC1/1	Park Royal B42F	Bournemouth Corporation	264	R
RRU 904	1955	Leyland Tiger Cub PSUC1/1	Park Royal B42F	Bournemouth Corporation	267	R
YLJ 147	1959	Leyland Titan PD3/1	Weymann H37/25D	Bournemouth Corporation	147	R
8154 EL	1960	Leyland Titan PD3/1	Weymann H37/25D	Bournemouth Corporation	154	R
8156 EL	1960	Leyland Titan PD3/1	Weymann O37/25D	Bournemouth Corporation	156	R
NMR 345	1960	Leyland Titan PD3/1	Weymann H37/25D	Bournemouth Corporation	155	RP
297 LJ+	1962	Sunbeam MF2B	Weymann H37/28D	Bournemouth Corporation	297	R
6167 RU	1963	Leyland Titan PD3A/1	Weymann H39/30F	Bournemouth Corporation	167	R
AEL 170B	1964	Leyland Atlantean PDR1/1	Weymann H43/31F	Bournemouth Corporation	170	R
ALJ 340B	1964	Daimler Fleetline CRG6LX	M H Cars H44/33F	Bournemouth Corporation	40	R
CRU 103C	1965	Leyland Leopard PSU3/2R	Weymann DP45F	Bournemouth Corporation	103	R
CRU 180C	1965	Daimler Fleetline CRG6LX	Weymann CO43/31F	Bournemouth Corporation	180	R
CRU 187C	1965	Daimler Fleetline CRG6LX	Weymann CO43/31F	Bournemouth Corporation	187	R
CRU 197C	1965	Daimler Fleetline CRG6LX	Weymann H43/31F	Bournemouth Corporation	197	R
ERV 252D	1966	Leyland Atlantean PDR1/1	MCW O43/33F	Portsmouth Corporation	252	R
KRU 55F	1967	Daimler Roadliner SRC6	Willowbrook B49F	Bournemouth Corporation	55	R
ORU 230G	1969	Leyland Atlantean PDR1A/1	Alexander H43/31F	Bournemouth Corporation	230	R
VRU 124J	1971	Daimler Fleetline CRG6LXB	Roe H43/31F	Hants & Dorset Motor Services	1901	R
DLJ 111L	1972	Daimler Fleetline CRL6	Alexander O43/31F	Bournemouth Corporation	111	R
XRU 277K	1972	Leyland Atlantean PDR1A/1	Alexander H43/31F	Bournemouth Corporation	277	RP
FEL 105L	1973	Leyland Leopard PSU3B/4R	Plaxton C47F	Bournemouth Corporation	105	RP
FEL 209V	1979	Dodge KCSK6055	Rootes B18F	Bournemouth Corporation	M9	A

+ Trolleybus

Notes:

RU 2266	Believed only chassis & axles are from RU 2266
VH 6217	Converted to tower wagon in 1948
VH 6188	Chassis new 1934 fitted with 1928 body
BOW 162	New with Beadle body; converted to breakdown vehicle
FRU 224	Converted to breakdown vehicle.
DKY 712	Rebodied 1960
NLJ 268	Originally B42F; used as canteen at Chesterfield 1970-81. Now mobile museum display vehicle.
NMR 345	Originally registered 8155 EL. For sale.
8156 EL	Converted to open top in 1991
DLJ 111L	Originally H43/31F
FEL 209V	Battery powered bus

Bristol Omnibus Vehicle Collection

Contact address: 'Combe Barton', High Street, Dinder, Wells BA5 3PL
e-mail: drmichaelwalker@hotmail.com
Brief description: A collection of former of Bristol Omnibus Company vehicles.
Events planned: The vehicles will be attending rallies during the season

Registration	Date	Chassis	Body	New to	Fleet No	Status
JHT 802	1946	Bristol K6A	ECW H30/26R	Bristol Tramways	C3386	A
LHY 976	1949	Bristol L5G	ECW B33D	Bristol Omnibus Co	C2736	R
NHU 2	1950	Bristol LSX5G	ECW B42D	Bristol Tramways	2800	R
OHY 938	1952	Bristol KSW6B	ECW L27/28RD	Bristol Tramways	L8089	R
UHY 360	1955	Bristol KSW6B	ECW H32/28R	Bristol Omnibus Co	C8320	R
UHY 384	1955	Bristol KSW6G	ECW H32/28RD	Bristol Tramways	8336	R
924 AHY	1958	Bristol MW5G	ECW B45F	Bristol Omnibus Co	2934	R
969 EHW	1959	Bristol Lodekka LD6G	ECW H33/25RD	Bristol Omnibus Co	L8515	R
972 EHW	1959	Bristol Lodekka LD6B	ECW H33/25R	Bristol Omnibus Co	LC8518	RP
869 NHT	1961	Bristol Lodekka FS6G	ECW CO33/27RD	Bristol Omnibus Co	L8579	RP
BHU 92C	1965	Bristol MW6G	ECW C39F	Bristol Omnibus Co	2138	R
HHW 920L	1973	Bristol RELL6L	ECW B44D	Bristol Omnibus Co	1307	A
OAE 954M	1973	Bristol RELL6L	ECW B50F	Bristol Omnibus Co	1332	A
AFB 592V	1980	Bristol LH6L	ECW B43F	Bristol Omnibus Co	461	R

Notes:
JHT 802 1949 body fitted in 1957
NHU 2 Prototype Bristol LS.

Bristol Vintage Bus Group

Contact address: 74 Ridgeway Lane, Whitchurch, Bristol BS14 9PJ
Location: Unit G, Flowers Hill Road, Brislington, Bristol
Affiliation: NARTM
Brief description: A small group of enthusiasts formed to preserve examples of Bristol's buses.
Events planned: Please see enthusiast press for details
Opening days/times: At any time by prior arrangement if someone is available
Directions by car: Flowers Hill Road is off the A4 Bath road, right on the City boundary near the Park & Ride
Directions by public transport: Main bus service to Bath from the Bus Station and Temple Meads railway station stops near Flowers Hill
Charges: No admission charge for viewing or special events

Registration	Date	Chassis	Body	New to	Fleet No	Status
AHU 803	1934	Bristol J5G	Brislington Body Works B35R	Bristol Tramways	2355	R
GHT 154	1940	Bristol K5G	Brislington Body Works H30/26R	Bristol Tramways	C3336	R
GHT 127	1941	Bristol K5G	ECW O30/26R	Bristol Tramways	C3315	R
FTT 704	1945	Bristol K6A	ECW L27/28R	Western National Omnibus Co	353	R
LAE 13	1948	Leyland Titan PD1A	ECW H30/26R	Bristol Tramways	C4044	R
YHY 80	1957	Bristol LS6G	ECW B43F	Bristol Omnibus Co	3004	RP
CWN 629C	1965	Bristol MW6G	ECW B45F	United Welsh Services	134	A

Notes:
AHU 803 Rebodied 1947. Originally a petrol engined coach.
GHT 127 Restored in Brighton Hove & District livery
FTT 704 Original Strachans body replaced in 1955.
YHY 80 Rebodied 1972.

British Trolleybus Society

Contact address: 8 Riding Lane, Hildenborough, Tonbridge, Kent, TN11 9HX
Affiliation: NARTM

Brief description: The British Trolleybus Society is a contributor society to the Trolleybus Museum at Sandtoft. Vehicles from the collection of trolleybuses can be seen from time to time at Sandtoft on display.
Events planned: Details given in the section on Sandtoft Transport Centre

Registration	Date	Chassis	Body	New to	Fleet No	Status
note h	1902	Rob Blackwell & Co	Horse-drawn tower wagon	Reading Corporation	'William'	A
WW 4688+	1927	Garrett O type	Garrett B32C	Mexborough & Swinton Traction Co	34	A
ALJ 973+	1935	Sunbeam MS2	Park Royal H31/25D	Bournemouth Corporation	99	R
RD 7127	1935	AEC Regent O661	Park Royal L26/26R	Reading Corporation	47	R
CU 3593+	1937	Karrier E4	Weymann H29/26R	South Shields Corporation	204	RP
ARD 676+	1939	AEC 661T	Park Royal H30/26R	Reading Corporation	113	R
CKG 193+	1942	AEC 664T	Northern Counties H38/32R	Cardiff Corporation	203	R
HYM 812+	1948	BUT 9641T	Metro Cammell H40/30R	London Transport	1812	R
NDH 959+	1951	Sunbeam F4	Brush H34/31R	Walsall Corporation	342	R
AC-L 379+	1956	Henschel 562E	Ludewig RB17/44T	Aachen (Germany)	22	R
XDH 72+	1956	Sunbeam F4A	Willowbrook H36/34RD	Walsall Corporation	872	RP
FYS 839+	1958	BUT 9613T	Crossley H37/34R	Glasgow Corporation	TB78	R
PVH 931+	1959	Sunbeam S7A	East Lancs H40/32R	Huddersfield Corporation	631	R

+ Trolleybus

Notes:
note h	Unregistered wooden bodied tower wagon	XDH 72	Last Walsall trolleybus; on display at Aston Manor Road Transport Museum.
NDH 959	Rebuilt/lengthened 1965		
AC-L 379	German registration		

Cardiff & South Wales Trolleybus Project

Contact address: 211 Hillrise, Llanedeyrn, Cardiff CF23 6UQ
Affiliation: NARTM
Brief description: The only trolleybus preservation group in the principality of Wales. A regular newsletter is issued, and new members are always welcome.

Registration	Date	Chassis	Body	New to	Fleet No	Status
DKY 704+	1945	Karrier W	East Lancs H37/29F	Bradford Corporation	704	RP
EBO 919+	1949	BUT 9641T	Bruce H38/29D	Cardiff Corporation	262	RP
KBO 961+	1955	BUT 9641T	East Lancs B40R	Cardiff Corporation	243	RP
DHW 293K	1972	Bristol LH6L	ECW B42F	Bristol Omnibus Co	353	R

+ Trolleybus

Notes:
DKY 704	Rebodied 1959
EBO 919	Body built on East Lancs frames
DHW 293K	Support vehicle

Chelveston Preservation Society

Contact address: 36 Moor Road, Rushden, Northants, NN10 9SP
Affiliation: NARTM
Brief description: A private collection owned by a few members has evolved to represent most types of Bristol chassis from a range of former Tilling group companies.

Registration	Date	Chassis	Body	New to	Fleet No	Status
VV 5696	1937	Bristol JO5G	ECW B35R	United Counties Omnibus Co	450	R
MPU 21	1948	Bristol K6B	ECW L27/28R	Eastern National Omnibus Co	3960	RP
FRP 692	1950	Bristol KS5G	ECW L27/28R	United Counties Omnibus Co	692	R
FRP 828	1950	Bristol LL5G	ECW B39R	United Counties Omnibus Co	828	A
NAE 3	1950	Bristol L6B	ECW FC31F	Bristol Tramways	2467	RP
CNH 860	1952	Bristol LWL6B	ECW B39R	United Counties Omnibus Co	426	R
CNH 862	1952	Bristol LWL6B	ECW DP33R	United Counties Omnibus Co	428	R
HWV 294	1952	Bristol KSW5G	ECW L27/28R	Wilts & Dorset Motor Services	365	A
JBD 975	1953	Bristol KSW6B	ECW L27/28R	United Counties Omnibus Co	938	A
KNV 337	1954	Bristol KSW6B	ECW L27/28R	United Counties Omnibus Co	964	R
RFM 408	1954	Bristol Lodekka LD6B	ECW H33/25R	Crosville Motor Services	ML663	A
TUO 497	1956	Bristol LS6G	ECW B45F	Southern National Omnibus Co	1781	RP
604 JPU	1957	Bristol SC4LK	ECW B35F	Eastern National Omnibus Co	427	A
ONU 425	1957	Bristol SC4LK	ECW B35F	United Counties Omnibus Co	125	RP
RFU 689	1958	Bristol SC4LK	ECW DP33F	Lincolnshire Road Car Co	2611	R
TFF 251	1958	Bristol MW6G	ECW -	Crosville Motor Services	G341	A
566 JFM	1959	Bristol SC4LK	ECW B35F	Crosville Motor Services	SSG626	A
980 DAE	1959	Bristol MW5G	ECW B45F	Bristol Omnibus Co	2960	A
675 COD	1960	Bristol SUS4A	ECW B30F	Western National Omnibus Co	603	A
264 KTA	1962	Bristol MW6G	ECW C39F	Western National Omnibus Co	1395	A
268 KTA	1962	Bristol SUL4A	ECW C37F	Western National Omnibus Co	434	A
675 AAM	1962	Bristol MW6G	ECW C34F	Wilts & Dorset Motor Services		A
891 XFM	1962	Bristol FS5G	ECW H36/26F	Crosville Motor Services	DF981	A
375 GWN	1964	Bristol RELL6G	ECW C47F	United Welsh Services	52	RP
ABD 253B	1964	Bristol RELH6G	ECW C47F	United Counties Omnibus Co	253	A
CHY 419C	1965	Bristol Lodekka FLF6G	ECW H38/32F	Bristol Omnibus Co	C7201	RP
GAX 2C	1965	Bristol RELL6G	ECW B54F	Red & White Services	R2 65	RP
EDV 555D	1966	Bristol SUL4A	ECW B36F	Southern National Omnibus Co	692	RP
HFM 561D	1966	Bristol MW6G	ECW C39F	Crosville Motor Services	CMG561	R
OWC 182D	1966	Bristol MW6G	ECW C34F	Tillings Transport	182	R
UFM 53F	1968	Bristol RELL6G	ECW DP50F	Crosville Motor Services	ERG53	RP
MMW 354G	1969	Bristol RELL6G	ECW B45D	Wilts & Dorset Motor Services	824	R
TBD 279G	1969	Bristol RELH6G	ECW DP49F	United Counties Omnibus Co	279	A
HAH 537L	1972	Bristol LH6P	ECW B45F	Eastern Counties Omnibus Co	LH537	RP
YFM 283L	1973	Bristol RELL6G	ECW DP50F	Crosville Motor Services	ERG283	R
JFJ 506N	1975	Bristol LH6L	Plaxton C43F	Greenslades Tours	326	A
HBD 919T	1977	Bristol VRTSL6G	ECW H66F	United Counties Omnibus Co	919	R
ARP 601X	1981	Leyland Olympian ONLXB/1R	ECW H45/32F	United Counties Omnibus Co	601	R

Notes:

VV 5696	Rebodied 1949
CNH 860	Renumbered 426 in 1952; Gardner 5LW engine fitted 1956
CNH 862	Gardner 5LW engine fitted in 1956. Reverted to Bristol AVW in 1996.
RFM 408	Eighth production Lodekka. Currently has no engine or gearbox
TFF 251	Converted to towing vehicle
OWC 182D	Passed to Eastern National (392) in 1968 and to Tilling's Travel (9392) in 1971

Cherwell Bus Preservation Group

Contact address: 32 Mill Street, Kidlington OX5 2EF
Brief description: A collection of mainly ex-City of Oxford vehicles housed under cover.
Events planned: The operational vehicles will attend a few events during the rally season.

Registration	Date	Chassis	Body	New to	Fleet No	Status
OJO 727	1950	AEC Regal III 9621A	Willowbrook B32F	City of Oxford Motor Services	727	R
191 AWL	1956	AEC Regent V MD3RV	Weymann L30/26R	City of Oxford Motor Services	L191	R
975 CWL	1958	AEC Regent V LD3RA	Park Royal H37/28R	City of Oxford Motor Services	H975	RP
312 MFC	1961	AEC Bridgemaster 2B3RA	Park Royal H43/29F	City of Oxford Motor Services	312	R
332 RJO	1963	AEC Renown 3B3RA	Park Royal H38/27F	City of Oxford Motor Services	332	R
OFC 902H	1970	Bristol VRTSL2/6LX	ECW H39/31F	City of Oxford Motor Services	902	RP
AUD 310J	1971	Leyland Leopard PSU3B/4R	Plaxton C51F	O A Slatter & Sons of Long Hanborough	40	A
TJO 56K	1971	AEC Reliance 6MU4R	Marshall DP49F	City of Oxford Motor Services	56	A
YWL 134K	1972	Leyland Leopard PSU3B/4R	Plaxton C53F	R Jarvis & Sons of Middle Barton		A
NUD 105L	1973	Bristol VRTSL2/6LX	ECW CH41/27F	City of Oxford Motor Services	105	A
RBW 87M	1974	Bristol RELH6L	ECW DP49F	City of Oxford Motor Services	87	A
PWL 999W	1980	Leyland Olympian B45 ONTL11/2R	Alexander H50/32D	Leyland (prototype)	999	A
VJO 201X	1982	Leyland Olympian ONLXB/1R	ECW H47/28D	City of Oxford Motor Services	201	A
VUD 30X	1982	Leyland Leopard PSU3G/4R	ECW C49F	City of Oxford Motor Services	30	R
C729 JJO	1986	Ford Transit 190D	Carlyle DP20F	City of Oxford Motor Services	729	RP

Notes:
PWL 999W   Prototype operated by Singapore Bus registered SBS5396B. Acquired by COMS in 1987.

City of Portsmouth Preserved Transport Depot

Contact address: Please see enthusiast press or contact web site for location and contact information.
E-mail: friends@cpptd.freeserve.co.uk
Web site: www.cpptd.freeserve.co.uk
Affiliation: NARTM, WOMP
Brief description: A collection comprising a range of veteran and vintage buses, trams and trolleybuses, most of which spent their working lives in the South of England. Museum is currently being relocated following closure of the Broad Street site. Please see the enthusiast press or contact the web site for the latest developments.

Registration	Date	Chassis	Body	New to	Fleet No	Status
BK 2986	1919	Thornycroft J	Dodson O18/16R	Portsmouth Corporation	10	R
RV 3411	1933	Leyland Titan TD2	English Electric/ Portsmouth Corporation	Portsmouth Corporation	17	R
RV 4649+	1934	AEC 661T	English Electric H26/24R	Portsmouth Corporation	201	RP
RV 6368	1935	Leyland Titan TD4	English Electric O26/24R	Portsmouth Corporation	8	R
CTP 200	1944	Bedford OWB	Duple (replica) UB32F	Portsmouth Corporation	170	R
DTP 823	1947	Leyland Titan PD1	Weymann H30/26R	Portsmouth Corporation	189	RP
AHC 442	1951	AEC Regent III 9613A	Bruce H30/26R	Eastbourne Corporation	42	R
EHV 65	1951	Bedford OB	Duple B29F	East Ham Borough Council		R
LRV 996	1956	Leyland Titan PD2/12	Metro Cammell O33/26R	Portsmouth Corporation	4	R
ORV 989	1958	Leyland Titan PD2/40	Metro Cammell H30/26R	Portsmouth Corporation	112	RP
BBK 236B	1964	Leyland Atlantean PDR1/1	Metro Cammell H43/33F	Portsmouth Corporation	236	R
GTP 175F	1967	Leyland Panther Cub PSURC1	MCW B42D	Portsmouth Corporation	175	R
TBK 190K	1971	Leyland Atlantean PDR2/1	Seddon Pennine B40D	Portsmouth Corporation	190	R
XTP 287L	1973	Leyland Atlantean AN68/1R	Alexander H45/30D	Portsmouth Corporation	287	RP

+ Trolleybus

Notes:
BK 2986   Body is c.1910 ex-LGOC B-type. Currently loaned by Portsmouth City Museum to Milestones Museum Basingstoke
RV 3411   Converted to Tower Wagon in 1955. Currently loaned by Portsmouth City Museum to Milestones Museum Basingstoke
RV 4649   Currently loaned by Portsmouth City Museum to Milestones Museum Basingstoke
RV 6368   Originally H26/24R. Currently loaned by Portsmouth City Museum to Milestones Museum Basingstoke
CTP 200   Replica body; wartime livery
EHV 65   Preserved in Hants & Sussex livery
LRV 996   Originally H33/26R

Above: **One of a growing number of vehicles with the Glasgow Vintage Vehicle Trust is one-time Abbeyways of Halifax Duple Bella Vega-bodied Bedford VAS2 BJX 848C. The VAS spent most of its service life with Jamiesons of Cullivoe in the Shetlands, and following withdrawal it was stored undercover by the operator for many years.** *Philip Lamb*

Below: **The annual Friends of King Alfred Buses Running day on 1 January is a major event on the rally calendar. Seen taking part in 2002 is King Alfred AEC Renown/Park Royal 596 LCG.** *Philip Lamb*

Above: **Seen with East Lancs-bodied Leyland Atlantean Oldham 163 (OBU 163F) at the Manchester Museum of Transport is the Lincolnshire Vintage Vehicle Society's rare Roberts-bodied Daimler CVD6 Colchester 4.** *Philip Lamb*

Below: **The Lancastrian Transport Trust's Massey-bodied Leyland PD2A/27 Lytham 70 (CTF 627B) is on long-term loan from St Helens Transport Museum.** *Philip Lamb*

Classic Southdown Omnibuses

Contact address: Dormy Cottage, 2 Alan Road, Wimbledon Village, London SW19 7PT
Affiliation: NARTM
Brief description: One of the largest single privately owned collections of Southdown Vehicles in the country, ranging from 1939 Leyland Titan TD4 to the last Bristol VR delivered new to Southdown.
Events planned: The operational vehicles will attend events in the south of England during the rally season as well as being used for private hire work.

Registration	Date	Chassis	Body	New to	Fleet No	Status
GCD 48	1939	Leyland Titan TD5	Park Royal H28/26R	Southdown Motor Services	248	R
RUF 186	1956	Leyland Titan PD2/12	Beadle H33/26R	Southdown Motor Services	786	R
410 DCD	1964	Leyland Titan PD3/4	Northern Counties FCO39/30F	Southdown Motor Services	410	R
422 DCD	1964	Leyland Titan PD3/4	Northern Counties FCO39/30F	Southdown Motor Services	422	R
HCD 347E	1967	Leyland Titan PD3/4	Northern Counties FH39/30F	Southdown Motor Services	347	R
UUF 110J	1971	Bristol VRTSL6LX	ECW H39/31F	Southdown Motor Services	510	RP
JWV 976W	1980	Bristol VRTSL3/6LXB	ECW H43/31F	Southdown Motor Services	276	R

Notes:
GCD 48   Rebodied 1950   RUF 186   Body built on Park Royal frames

The Devon General Society

Contact address: Membership Secretary, Greenfields, The Rowe, Stableford, Newcastle-under-Lyme, Staffs ST5 4EN
Web site: www.devongeneral.org.uk
Brief description: The Devon General Society was formed in 1982 to promote interest in the former Devon General company and its successors, also to stimulate the preservation of all aspects of the company's past for the benefit of future generations. Approximately 35 former Devon General vehicles are currently preserved privately by society members, The society actively assists them and regularly stages events in Devon whereby these vehicles can be enjoyed.
Events planned: Please see web site

Registration	Date	Chassis	Body	New to	Fleet No	Status
OD 7497	1934	AEC Regent O661	Short O31/24R	Devon General	DR210	RP
HTT 487	1946	AEC Regal I O662	Weymann B35F	Devon General	SR487	R
KOD 585	1949	AEC Regent III 9612E	Weymann H30/26R	Devon General	DR585	RP
NTT 661	1952	AEC Regent III 9613A	Weymann H30/26R	Devon General	DR661	R
NTT 679	1952	AEC Regent III 9613S	Weymann H30/26R	Devon General	DR679	R
UFJ 296	1957	Guy Arab IV	Park Royal H31/26R	Exeter City Transport	56	R
VDV 798	1957	AEC Reliance MU3RA	Weymann B41F	Devon General	SR798	A
XTA 839	1958	Albion Nimbus NS3N	Willowbrook B31F	Devon General	SN839	RP
XUO 721	1958	Bristol MW6G	ECW B41F	Western National Omnibus Co (Royal Blue)	2238	R
872 ATA	1959	Leyland Atlantean PDR1/1	Metro Cammell H44/32F	Devon General	DL872	RP
913 DTT	1960	Leyland Atlantean PDR1/1	Roe H43/31F	Devon General	DL913	A
931 GTA	1961	Leyland Atlantean PDR1/1	Metro Cammell CO44/31F	Devon General	DL931	R
932 GTA	1961	Leyland Atlantean PDR1/1	Metro Cammell CO44/31F	Devon General	DL932	R
935 GTA	1961	AEC Reliance 2MU3RV	Willowbrook C41F	Devon General (Grey Cars)	TCR935	R
960 HTT	1962	AEC Reliance 2MU3RV	Willowbrook C41F	Devon General (Grey Cars)	TCR960	R
503 RUO	1964	AEC Regent V 2D3RA	Willowbrook H39/30F	Devon General	503	RP
9 RDV	1964	AEC Reliance 2U3RA	Marshall B49F	Devon General	9	R
CTT 23C	1965	AEC Reliance 2MU3RA	Park Royal B39F	Devon General	23	R

Registration	Date	Chassis	Body	New to	Fleet No	Status
NDV 537G	1968	Leyland Atlantean PDR1/2	MCW H44/31F	Devon General	537	R
TUO 74J	1970	AEC Reliance 6MU3R	Willowbrook B41F	Devon General	74	RP
VOD 550K	1971	Bristol VRTSL2/6LX	ECW H43/31F	Western National (Devon General)	550	RP
FDV 829V	1979	Leyland National II NL116L/1R	Leyland National B50F	Western National (Devon General)	2883	R
C519 FFJ	1985	Ford Transit 160D	Carlyle B16F	Devon General (Bayline) Ltd	519	R

Notes:
OD 7497 Converted to open top in 1955
XUO 721 Originally C39F Royal Blue coach. Rebuilt 1973 as bus numbered 2902 in Devon General fleet.
FDV 829V First production National 2 to enter service in UK

Dewsbury Bus Museum

Contact address: 5 Oakenshaw Street, Agbrigg, Wakefield WF1 5BT
Phone: 01924 258314
Affiliation: NARTM
Brief description: The group was formed in the early 1970s and concentrated on ex-West Riding vehicles. By 1989 the collection had grown and, to provide covered accommodation, a new, 14-vehicle shed was erected. Vehicles can be seen at local events, or on site by appointment.
Opening days/times: Open only on rally days and when work is being done on vehicles (please enquire before visiting).
Transport Collectors Fairs 13 March and 13 November 2004.
8 May 2005 — museum open day in association with West Yorkshire Transport Society spring rally in Dewsbury town centre.
Other information: Other events are being planned — please see enthusiast press for details.

Registration	Date	Chassis	Body	New to	Fleet No	Status
TY 9608	1932	AEC Regal 662	Strachan C28R	Orange Bros of Bedlington	42	A
DHN 475	1939	Bristol L5G	ECW B35R	United Automobile Services	BLO 11	A
BHL 682	1948	Leyland Titan PD2/1	Leyland L27/26R	West Riding Automobile Co	640	RP
TWY 8	1950	Albion CX39N	Roe L27/26RD	South Yorkshire Motors	81	RP
EHL 344	1952	Leyland Tiger PS2/12A	Roe B39F	West Riding Automobile Co	733	R
OWX 167	1955	Bristol Lodekka LD6B	ECW H33/27RD	West Yorkshire Road Car Co	DX23	RP
JHL 708	1956	AEC Reliance MU3RV	Roe B44F	West Riding Automobile Co	808	RP
JHL 983	1957	AEC Reliance MU3RV	Roe C41C	West Riding Automobile Co	803	R
KHL 855	1957	Guy Arab IV	Roe L29/26RD	West Riding Automobile Co	855	RP
TWT 123	1958	Bristol MW5G	ECW DP41F	West Yorkshire Road Car Co	EUG 71	RP
LEN 101	1960	Guy Wulfrunian	(chassis only)	Bury Corporation	101	A
574 CNW	1962	Daimler CVG6	Roe H39/31F	Leeds City Transport	574	RP
PJX 35	1962	Leyland Leopard L1	Weymann B44F	Halifax Corporation	35	R
827 BWY	1963	Bristol MW6G	ECW B45F	West Yorkshire Road Car Co	SMG19	RP
WHL 970	1963	Guy Wulfrunian	Roe H43/32F	West Riding Automobile Co	970	RP
CUV 208C	1965	AEC Routemaster R2RH	Park Royal H36/28R	London Transport	RM 2208	R
EHT 108C	1965	Bristol Lodekka FLF6G	ECW H38/32F	Bristol Omnibus Co	C7219	RP
MWW 114D	1966	Bristol Lodekka FS6B	ECW H33/27RD	York - West Yorkshire	YDX233	RP
LHL 164F	1967	Leyland Panther PSUR1/1	Roe B51F	West Riding Automobile Co	164	R
NWW 89E	1967	Leyland Leopard L1	Willowbrook B45F	Todmorden Joint Omnibus Committee	9	R
XWW 474G	1968	Bristol VRTSL6G	ECW H39/31F	West Yorkshire Road Car Co	VR4	A
THL 261H	1970	Bristol RELL6G	ECW B53F	West Riding Automobile Co	261	RP
MCK 229J	1971	Leyland Panther PSUR1B/1R	Pennine B47D	Preston Corporation	229	RP
OWY 750K	1972	Bristol RESL6G	ECW B47F	Keighley-West Yorkshire Services	2109	RP
WEX 685M	1973	AEC Swift 3MP2R	ECW B43D	Great Yarmouth Corporation	85	R
MUA 865P	1976	Leyland Atlantean AN68/1R	Roe H43/30F	Yorkshire Woollen District Transport Co	768	R
OWW 905P	1976	Bristol VRT/SL3	ECW H43/31F	West Riding Automobile Co	761	RP
XUA 73X	1982	Leyland National II NL116AL11/1R	Leyland National B49F	West Riding Automobile Co	73	RP

Notes:

DHN 475	Rebodied 1947 with 1938 body	OWY 750K	Originally B44F.
TWY 8	New in 1950 registered JWT 112; rebodied and reregistered in 1958	MUA 865P	Rebodied 1981
MWW 114D	Latterly driver trainer 4068	XUA 73X	Gardner engine fitted c. 12/87

East Kent Road Car Heritage Trust

Contact address: 33 Alfred Road, Dover, Kent, CT16 2AD
Phone/Fax: 01304 204612
Brief Description: Between the trust and Friends of the East Kent members have around 18 former East Kent vehicles, based at various locations. A museum is planned but until then, the vehicles are taken to the public at various locatons and some are avaiable for stage carriage and hire work

Registration	Date	Chassis	Body	New to	Fleet No	Status
EFN 592	1950	Dennis Lancet J3	Park Royal C32F	East Kent Road Car Co		R
FFN 399	1951	Guy Arab III	Park Royal H32/26R	East Kent Road Car Co		R
GFN 273	1952	Leyland Titan TD5	Beadle C35F	East Kent Road Car Co		R
KFN 239	1955	AEC Reliance MU3RV	Weymann DP41F	East Kent Road Car Co		RP
MFN 898	1956	Guy Arab IV	Park Royal H33/28RD	East Kent Road Car Co		RP
6801 FN	1961	AEC Regent V 2D3RA	Park Royal H40/32F	East Kent Road Car Co		R
YJG 807	1962	AEC Bridgemaster 2B3RA	Park Royal H43/29F	East Kent Road Car Co		R
AFN 780B	1963	AEC Regent V 2D3RA	Park Royal H40/30F	East Kent Road Car Co		R
AFN 488B	1964	AEC Reliance 2MU4RA	Duple C34F	East Kent Road Car Co		RP
DJG 619C	1965	AEC Reliance 2U3RA	Park Royal C49F	East Kent Road Car Co		A
GJG 739D	1966	AEC Regent V 2D3RA	Park Royal H40/32F	East Kent Road Car Co		RP
OFN 721F	1968	AEC Reliance 6U3ZR	Marshall B53F	East Kent Road Car Co		RP
RFN 953G	1969	Daimler Fleetline CRG6LX	Park Royal H39/33F	East Kent Road Car Co		R
VJG 187J	1970	AEC Swift 5P2R	Marshall B51F	East Kent Road Car Co		R
EFN 178L	1973	Leyland National 1151/1R	Leyland National B49F	East Kent Road Car Co		RP
PFN 788M	1974	AEC Reliance 6U3ZR	Duple C42F	East Kent Road Car Co		A
JJG 1P	1976	Leyland Atlantean AN68/1R	ECW H43/30F	East Kent Road Car Co		RP
NFN 84R	1977	Leyland National 11351A/1R	Leyland National DP48F	East Kent Road Car Co		RP
TFN 980T	1978	Bristol VRT/SL3/6LXB	Willowbrook H43/31F	East Kent Road Car Co	7980	RP

Notes:

GFN 273	Running units are ex-AJG30 1939 Leyland TD5
EFN 178L	Fitted with a wheelchair lift

Eastern Transport Collection Society
Attleborough

Phone: 01603 744794 or 891284
Affiliation: NARTM
Brief description: The collection includes a number of vehicles owned by the society and members, together with a range of bus memorabilia bequeathed by the late Tony Powell together with other items added by the society. Viewing is by appointment only.
Events planned: Norwich Bus Rally - please see enthusiast press for date.
Opening days/times: By appointment only.
Charges: Free admission but donations welcome.

Registration	Date	Chassis	Body	New to	Fleet No	Status
KNG 718	1950	Bristol LL5G	ECW B39F	Eastern Counties Omnibus Co	LL718	R
NAH 941	1952	Bristol KSW5G	ECW H32/28R	Eastern Counties Omnibus Co	LKH341	RP
MXX 481	1953	AEC Regal IV 9821 LT RF	Metro Cammell B41F	London Transport	RF 504	R
OVF 229	1954	Bristol Lodekka LD5G	ECW H33/25RD	Eastern Counties Omnibus Co	LKD229	R
KDB 696	1957	Leyland Tiger Cub PSUC1/1	Weymann B44F	North Western Road Car Co	696	RP
5789 AH	1959	Bristol MW5G	ECW C39F	Eastern Counties Omnibus Co	LS789	R
675 OCV	1962	Bedford SB3	Duple C41F	Crimson Tours		R
MOO 177	1962	Bristol MW6G	ECW B45F	Eastern National Omnibus Co	556	RP
KVF 658E	1967	Bristol RESL6G	ECW B46F	Eastern Counties Omnibus Co	RS658	R
PBJ 2F	1967	Leyland Titan PD2/47	Massey H34/28R	Lowestoft Corporation	12	RP
NAH 135P	1976	Bristol VRT/SL3/501	ECW H43/31F	Eastern Counties Omnibus Co	VR172	RP
RGS 598R	1976	Bedford YMT	Duple C57F	Eagre Coaches		RP
WAD 640S	1978	Ford R1114	Plaxton C53F	Ladvale of Dursley		RP
H74 ANG	1990	Dennis Condor DD1810	Duple Metsec H69/41D + 32	China Motor Bus	DM17	R

Friends of King Alfred Buses

Contact address: 27 White Dirt Lane, Catherington, Waterlooville, Hampshire, PO8 0NB
E-mail: info@fokab.org.uk
Web site: www.fokab.org.uk
Affiliation: NARTM
Brief description: The collection includes 12 former King Alfred Motor Services vehicles that have been rescued from around the world and restored. A charitable trust, FoKAB aims eventually to establish a museum. In the meantime, the vehicles can be viewed at the annual running day and other events.
Events planned:
1 Jan 2006 — Annual running day at Winchester.

Registration	Date	Chassis	Body	New to	Fleet No	Status
OU 9286	1931	Dennis 30cwt	Short B18F	King Alfred Motor Services		R
JAA 708	1950	Leyland Olympic HR40	Weymann B40F	King Alfred Motor Services		RP
POU 494	1956	Leyland Titan PD2/24	East Lancs L27/28R	King Alfred Motor Services		R
WCG 104	1959	Leyland Tiger Cub PSUC1/1	Weymann B45F	King Alfred Motor Services		R
326 CAA	1961	Bedford SB3	Harrington C41F	King Alfred Motor Services		R
595 LCG	1964	AEC Renown 3B2RA	Park Royal H43/31F	King Alfred Motor Services		R
596 LCG	1964	AEC Renown 3B2RA	Park Royal H43/31F	King Alfred Motor Services		R
CCG 704C	1965	Bedford VAL14	Plaxton C49F	King Alfred Motor Services		R
HOR 590E	1967	Leyland Atlantean PDR1/2	Roe O43/31F	King Alfred Motor Services		R
HOR 592E	1967	Leyland Atlantean PDR1/2	Roe H43/33F	King Alfred Motor Services		R
UOU 417H	1970	Leyland Panther PSUR1A/1R	Plaxton B52F	King Alfred Motor Services		RP
UOU 419H	1970	Leyland Panther PSUR1A/1R	Plaxton B52F	King Alfred Motor Services		R
NKJ 849P	1976	Commer Karrier KC6055	Rootes B22F	Enham Village Disabled Transport		R

Notes:
POU 494 Repatriated from the USA in 1993
596 LCG Repatriated from the USA in 1988
CCG 704C Restoration involved body-swap.
HOR 590E Originally H43/33F; acquired by Bristol Omnibus Co (8602) and converted to open-top in 1979
HOR 592E Acquired by Bristol Omnibus Co (8600) and converted to open-top in 1979; restored using roof from vehicle HOR591E
NKJ 849P Mobile display vehicle.

Glasgow Vintage Vehicle Trust

Contact address: 17 Balmedie, Erskine, PA8 6EW
Museum address: Fordneuk Street, Glasgow G40 3AH
Phone: 0141 587 0418
E-mail: info@gvvt.org
Affiliation: NARTM
Brief description: Established in a former Glasgow Corporation bus depot.
Opening days/times: Telephone for access information. Prior arrangement only.
Directions by car: From City centre follow London Road eastbound.
Directions by public transport: First Glasgow 43 or 64 from City centre. SPT rail network to Bridgeton station
Events planned: Please see enthusiast press or telephone for details
Facilities: B(e), D, T

Registration	Date	Chassis	Body	New to	Fleet No	Status
DBY 001	1932	Fordson ET7	Barbara B31F	Malta		RP
WG 2373	1934	Leyland Lion LT5B	Burlingham B35F	W Alexander & Sons (Midland)	P169	R
WG 4445	1937	Leyland Tiger TS7	Alexander C35F	Alexander	P331	A
HGG 359	1950	Thornycroft HF/ER4	Croft B20F	MacBrayne	149	R
6769	1955	Albion Victor FT39AN	Heaver B35F	Guernsey Railway Co	55	RP
NSF 757	1956	Leyland Titan PD2/20	Metro Cammell H34/29R	Edinburgh Corporation	757	A
KAG 856	1957	Leyland Titan PD2/20	Alexander L31/23R	Western SMT	D1375	RP
TVS 367	1958	Bristol Lodekka LD6G	ECW H33/27R	Central SMT Co	B87	A
MSD 408	1959	Leyland Titan PD3/3	Alexander L35/32RD	Western SMT Co	D1544	RP
NMS 358	1960	AEC Reliance 2MU3RV	Alexander C41F	Alexander	AC147	R
YYS 174	1960	Bedford C5Z1	Duple C21FM	David MacBrayne of Glasgow	54	R
198 CUS	1961	AEC Reliance 2MU3RA	Duple C41F	MacBrayne	63	RP
RAG 400	1961	Bristol Lodekka LD6G	ECW H33/27RD	Western SMT Co	B1634	A
TCK 821	1963	Leyland Titan PD3/5	Metro Cammell FH41/31F	Ribble Motor Services	1821	R
828 SHW	1964	Bristol Lodekka FLF6B	ECW H38/32F	Bristol Omnibus Co	C7135	A
NGE 172P	1964	AEC Reliance 2U3RA	Plaxton C46F	World Wide of Lanark		A
BJX 848C	1965	Bedford VAS 2	Duple C29F	Abbeyways of Halifax		A
CUV 121C	1965	AEC Routemaster	Park Royal H36/28R	London Transport	RM 2121	R
GYS 896D	1966	Leyland Atlantean PDR1/1	Alexander H44/34F	Glasgow Corporation	LA320	R
HGA 983D	1966	Leyland VAS 1	Willowbrook B24FM	David MacBrayne of Glasgow	210	R
GRS 334E	1967	Albion Viking VK43AL	Alexander DP40F	Alexander (Northern)	NNV34	A
HFR 501E	1967	Leyland Titan PD3A/1	MCW H41/30R	Blackpool Corporation	501	A
JMS 452E	1967	Albion Viking VK43AL	Alexander DP40F	Alexander (Midland)	MNV37	RP
NRG 26H	1969	AEC Swift 2MP2R	Alexander B43D	Aberdeen Corporation	26	A
VMP 10G	1969	AEC Reliance 6U3ZR	Alexander B57F	Road Transport Industry Training Board	24	R
XTC 530H	1970	Bedford VAL 70	Plaxton			A
WSD 756K	1972	Leyland Leopard PSU3/3R	Alexander -	Western SMT Co	L2366	R
XGM 450L	1972	Leyland Leopard PSU3/3R	Alexander B53F	Central SMT Co	T150	R
KRH 411P	1975	Scania Metropolitan BR111DH	Metro Cammell H44/29F	Kingston upon Hull Corporation	411	A
MSF 122P	1975	Leyland Leopard PSU3C/4R	Alexander C49F	Lothian Regional Transport	122	A
MSF 465P	1976	Leyland Atlantean AN68A/1R	Abbott H-/-D	Lothian Regional Transport	465	RP
PRA 109R	1976	Leyland Leopard PSU3C/4R	Alexander C49F	Trent Motor Traction Co		A
OJD 903R	1977	Leyland National 10351A/1R	Leyland National B36D	London Transport	LS 103	R
PAU 204R	1977	Daimler Fleetline CRG6LX	Northern Counties H-/-D	Nottingham City Transport	204	RP
RSD 973R	1977	Seddon Pennine VII	Alexander C49F	Western SMT Co	S2670	RP
SSN 248S	1977	Volvo Ailsa B55-10	Alexander H44/35F	Tayside Regional Council	248	RP
XUS 575S	1977	Leyland Atlantean AN68A/1R	Alexander H-/-F	Greater Glasgow PTE	LA1204	R
TSJ 47S	1978	Leyland Leopard PSU3D/4R	Alexander B53F	Western SMT Co	L2747	RP
VHB 678S	1978	Bristol VRT/SL3/501	ECW O43/31F	National Welsh Omnibus Services	HR4378	A
LHS 748V	1979	Volvo Ailsa B55-10	Alexander H44/35F	Central SMT Co	AH24	RP
WTS 270T	1979	Volvo Ailsa B55-10	Alexander H44/31D	Tayside Regional Council	270	RP

Registration	Date	Chassis	Body	New to	Fleet No	Status
DDW 431V	1980	Leyland National 10351A/1R	Leyland National B41F	Cynon Valley	31	A
EMS 362V	1980	Leyland Leopard PSU3E/4R	Alexander C49F	Alexander (Midland)	MPE362	A
LMS 168W	1980	Leyland Fleetline FE30AGR	Alexander H44/31F	Alexander (Midland)	MRF168	RP
RSG 825O	1980	Leyland National 2 NL116L11/1R	Leyland National B52F	Alexander (Fife)	FPN25	RP
UHG 141V	1980	Leyland Atlantean AN68A/2R	Alexander H49/36F	Preston Bus	141	R
RMS 400W	1981	Leyland Leopard PSU3F/4R	Alexander C49F	Alexander (Midland)	MPE400	R
RRM 386X	1981	Leyland National NL116AL11/1R	Leyland National B52F	Cumberland Motor Services	386	RP
SSA 5X	1981	Leyland Olympian ONLXB/1R	Alexander H45/32R	Alexander (Northern)	NL05	A
FLD 447Y	1982	Bedford YMP	Plaxton C35F			A
TMS 403X	1982	Leyland Leopard PSU3G/4R	Alexander DP49F	Alexander (Midland)	MPE403	RP
ALS 102Y	1983	Leyland Tiger TRCTL11/2R	Alexander C49F	Alexander (Midland)	MPT102	RP
MNS 10Y	1983	Leyland Tiger TRBTL11/2R	Alexander C49F	Central SMT Co	LT10	A
XMS 422Y	1983	Leyland Leopard PSU3G/4R	Alexander B53F	Alexander (Midland)	MPE422	RP
47638	1984	Ford R1015	Wadham Stringer B45F	Jersey Motor Transport Co	23	RP
B177 FFS	1985	Volvo Citybus B10M-50	Alexander H47/37F	Alexander (Fife)	977	A
F300 SSX	1989	Renault G10	Wadham Stringer DP29F	Blood Transfusion Service		A

Notes:

6769	Guernsey registration		WSD 756K	Converted to recovery vehicle 1982
WG 2373	Rebodied 1947.		XUS 575S	Exhibition unit
WG 4445	Rebodied 1949		VHB 678S	Converted to open top
NGE 172P	Chassis originally registered AAG 651B. Rebodied and reregistered 1976		FLD 447Y	Originally registered BAC 551Y
			47638	Original registration Jersey J43063. Currently carries Guernsey registration.
VMP 10G	Restored in Baxters livery			

Golcar Transport Collection

Contact address: 45 Cowlersley Lane, Cowlersley, Huddersfield HD4 5TZ
Affiliation: NARTM
Brief description: A unique collection of Karrier vehicles, most of which are long-term restoration projects. The collection includes two WL6 six-wheeled saloons.
Opening days/times: Collection opens to coincide with craft weekends at the Colne Valley Museum; can be opened at other times by prior arrangement.

Registration	Date	Chassis	Body	New to	Fleet No	Status
note v	1922	Karrier	(unknown) B20F	(unknown)		A
WT 9156	1925	Karrier JH	Strachan & Brown B26F	Premier Transport of Keighley		RP
DY 5029	1928	Karrier JKL	London Lorries C26D	A Timpson & Son of Catford	117	A
KD 3185	1928	Karrier WL6	Liverpool Corporation B38R	Liverpool Corporation		A
TE 5780	1928	Karrier WL6	English Electric B32F	Ashton-under-Lyne Corporation	8	RP
VH 2088	1929	Karrier ZA	(unknown) B14F			RP
RB 4757	1932	Commer Centaur	Reeve & Kenning B14D	H G Fox of Alfreton		R
JC 5313	1938	Guy Wolf	Waveney C20F	Llandudno UDC		R
14 PKR	1961	Karrier BFD	Plaxton C14F	W Davis & Sons of Sevenoaks		A

Notes:

note v	Unregistered solid-tyred disc-wheeled chassis.
WT 9156	Body originally on EH 4960
VH 2088	Period body acquired from Anglesey
RB 4757	Carries 1929 body from Ford AA chassis

Halifax Bus Museum

Contact address: 1 Vicar Park Road, Norton Tower, Halifax HX2 ONL
Brief description: A collection of privately-owned vehicles, most of which operated originally in West Yorkshire.
Events planned: Please see enthusiast press for details.
Opening days/times: The collection is not normally open to the public, but an appointment to view can be arranged by contacting the above address.

Registration	Date	Chassis	Body	New to	Fleet No	Status
JUB 29	1932	Leyland Titan TD2	Eastern Counties L27/26R	Keighley-West Yorkshire Services	K451	A
JX 7046	1939	AEC Regent O661	Park Royal H30/26R	Halifax Corporation	80	A
JX 9106	1946	AEC Regal O662	Weymann	Hebble Motor Services	181	A
GTJ 694	1947	AEC Regent II O661	Park Royal	Morecambe & Heysham Corporation	10	RP
HHP 755	1948	Maudslay Regal III	Duple FC33F	Greenslades Tours of Exeter		A
AJX 369	1949	AEC Regent III 9612E	Park Royal H33/26R	Halifax Joint Omnibus Committee	243	A
ECX 425	1949	AEC Regent III 9612E	Northern Coachbuilders L29/26R	Huddersfield Joint Omnibus Committee	225	RP
BCP 671	1950	AEC Regent III 9612E	Park Royal H33/26R	Halifax Joint Omnibus Committee	277	R
LTF 254	1950	AEC Regent III 9612E	Park Royal H33/26R	Morecambe & Heysham Corporation	69	R
ODK 705	1956	AEC Regent V D2RA6G	Weymann H33/28R	Rochdale Corporation	305	
ROD 765	1956	AEC Regent V MD3RV	Metro Cammell H33/26RD	Devon General	DRD765	R
TTT 781	1956	AEC Regent V MD3RV	Metro Cammell H33/26RD	Devon General	DRD781	RP
UTV 229	1956	AEC Regent V D3RV	Park Royal H33/28R	Nottingham City Transport	229	RP
3916 UB	1959	AEC Regent V 2D3RA	Metro Cammell H38/32R	Leeds City Transport	916	R
LJX 198	1959	AEC Regent V 2D3RA	Metro Cammell H39/32F	Hebble Motor Services	307	R
LJX 215	1960	AEC Regent V 2D3RA	Metro Cammell H40/32F	Halifax Joint Omnibus Committee	215	RP
1925 WA	1961	AEC Bridgemaster 2B3RA	Park Royal H43/29F	Sheffield Corporation	525	R
214 CLT	1962	AEC Routemaster R2RH	Park Royal H36/28R	London Transport	RM 1214	R
TSJ 272	1962	AEC Bridgemaster 2B3RA	Park Royal	East Yorkshire Motor Services	725	RP
CTT 518C	1965	AEC Regent V 2MD3RA	Willowbrook H33/28F	Devon General	518	RP

Notes:

JUB 29	Rebodied in 1951 using 1932 body	HHP 755	Exhibited at the 1948 Commercial Motor Show
JX 9106	Converted to tow lorry in 1956 and renumbered L4	TSJ 272	Originally registered 9725 AT
GTJ 694	Breakdown Vehicle	214 CLT	In Halifax Joint Omnibus livery.

Huddersfield District Transport Museum Society

Contact address: 20 Alma Drive, Dalton, Huddersfield HD5 9EF
Affiliation: NARTM
Brief description: The collection is based in Huddersfield and comprises nearly 20 vehicles, including commercial vehicles and trams.
Opening days/times: Please contact the above address for an appointment to view.

Registration	Date	Chassis	Body	New to	Fleet No	Status
LHN 785+	1949	BUT 9611T	East Lancs H37/29F	Bradford Corporation	835	R
EFV 300	1951	Leyland Titan PD2/5	Burlingham FH29/23C	Blackpool Corporation	300	RP
ODE 182	1952	Sentinel STC6	Sentinel B44F	Edwards Bros of Crymych		RP
JVH 373	1955	AEC Regent III 9613E	East Lancs L30/28R	Huddersfield Corporation	243	R
JVH 378	1955	AEC Regent III	East Lancs H33/28R	Huddersfield Joint Omnibus Committee	178	R
GHD 215	1961	Ford 570E	Duple C41F	Yorkshire Woollen District Transport Co	871	R
SHL 917	1961	AEC Reliance 2MU3RV	Plaxton C41C	West Riding Automobile Co	917	R
HVH 472D	1966	Daimler CVG6LX-30	East Lancs H41/29F	Huddersfield Corporation	472	R

Registration	Date	Chassis	Body	New to	Fleet No	Status
RWU 534R + Trolleybus	1977	Leyland Leopard PSU4D/4R	Plaxton DP43F	West Yorkshire PTE	8534	R

Notes:
LHN 785   Rebodied 1962. Chassis originally Darlington

Irish Transport Trust

Contact address: 3 Donegall Drive, Whitehead, Co Antrim, Northern Ireland BT38 9LT
Affiliation: NARTM
Website: www.irishtransporttrust.freeserve.co.uk
Brief description: Formed in 1969, the Trust provides for the preservation, recording and information exchange on all aspects pertaining to road transport history, current and future matters. A number of vehicles both pre- and postwar have been restored by Trust members and the Trust itself has six vehicles from more recent times which are under-represented in preservation. It is planned to seek charitable status, with a view to eventually establishing a museum.
Events planned: 23 April 2005. Annual bus and coach rally at Cultra, Co Down, at the site of the Ulster Folk & Transport Museum. For other events, please refer to the enthusiast press.

Registration	Date	Chassis	Body	New to	Fleet No	Status
FOI 1629	1973	Bristol LH6L	Alexander (Belfast) B45F	Ulsterbus	1629	R
OSJ 620R	1977	Leyland Leopard PSU3C/4R	Alexander (Belfast) B53F	Western SMT Co	1886	R
SOI 3591	1978	Leyland Leopard PSU3A/4R	Alexander (Belfast) B53F	Ulsterbus	1591	R
VOI 8415	1980	Bristol RELL6G	Alexander (Belfast) B43D	Belfast Citybus	2415	R
AXI 2259	1982	Leyland Leopard PSU3E/4R	Wright C49F	Ulsterbus	259	R
BXI 2583	1982	Bristol RELL6G	Alexander (Belfast) B51F	Ulsterbus	2583	RP

John Shearman Collection
Tunbridge Wells

Phone: 01892 534067
Brief description: A private collection which includes vehicles representing traditional British double deckers designed for export markets.
Opening days/times: Vehicles attend rallies every summer.

Registration	Date	Chassis	Body	New to	Fleet No	Status
LEV 917	1946	Leyland Titan PD1/1	Alexander O33/26R	City Coach Company of Brentwood	LD1	R
KSV 102	1954	AEC Regent III 9631E	Weymann H37/28R	Carris of Lisbon	255	R
AD 7156	1966	AEC Regent V 2D2RA	Metal Sections H51/39D	Kowloon Motor Bus	A165	R

Notes:
LEV 917   Converted to open top by Eastern National in 1958. Originally H30/26R. Restored as EN 2102 with the support of the Springhill Vehicle Preservation Group.
KSV 102   Left hand drive. Portugese registration GB-21-07. Originally H32/26R. Restored with support of Carris AEC Preservation Group.
AD 7156   34ft 3in long. Hong Kong registration. Originally H50/28D. On display at the Oxford Bus Museum. Restored with support from KMB.

Above: **The Leicester Corporation Bus Owners Group maintains a number of vehicles of local origin including this 1972 Metro-Scania. Former Leicester 225 (ARY 225K) is seen in its home city in 2002.** *Philip Lamb*

Above right: **The Peter Stanier Collection is home to very rare Leyland Lioness LTB1 DM 6228. New to Brookes Bros (White Rose) of Rhyl, this fine coach is fitted with Burlingham coachwork.** *Philip Lamb*

Right: **Seen 'on service' between Kirkby Stephen and Brough in 2002 is Saro-bodied Leyland Tiger Cub PSUC1/1T Ribble 452 (FCK 884). No452 is part of the Ribble Vehicle Preservation Trust collection.** *Philip Lamb*

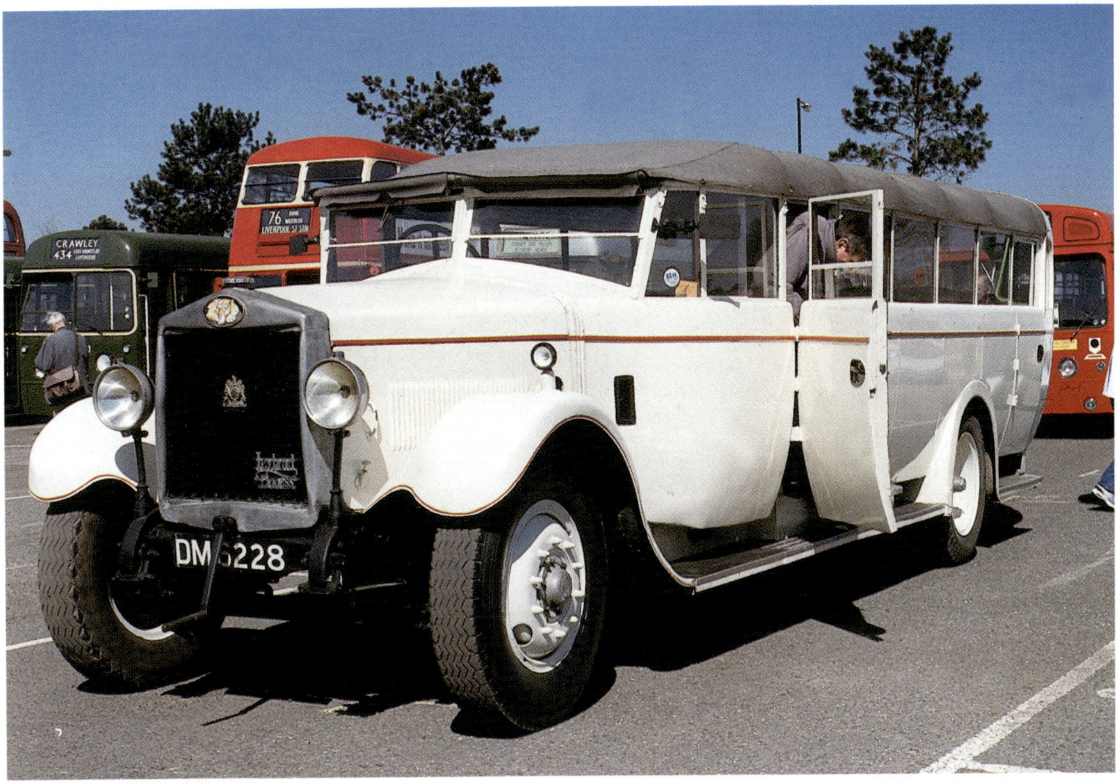
CRAWLEY
434
76

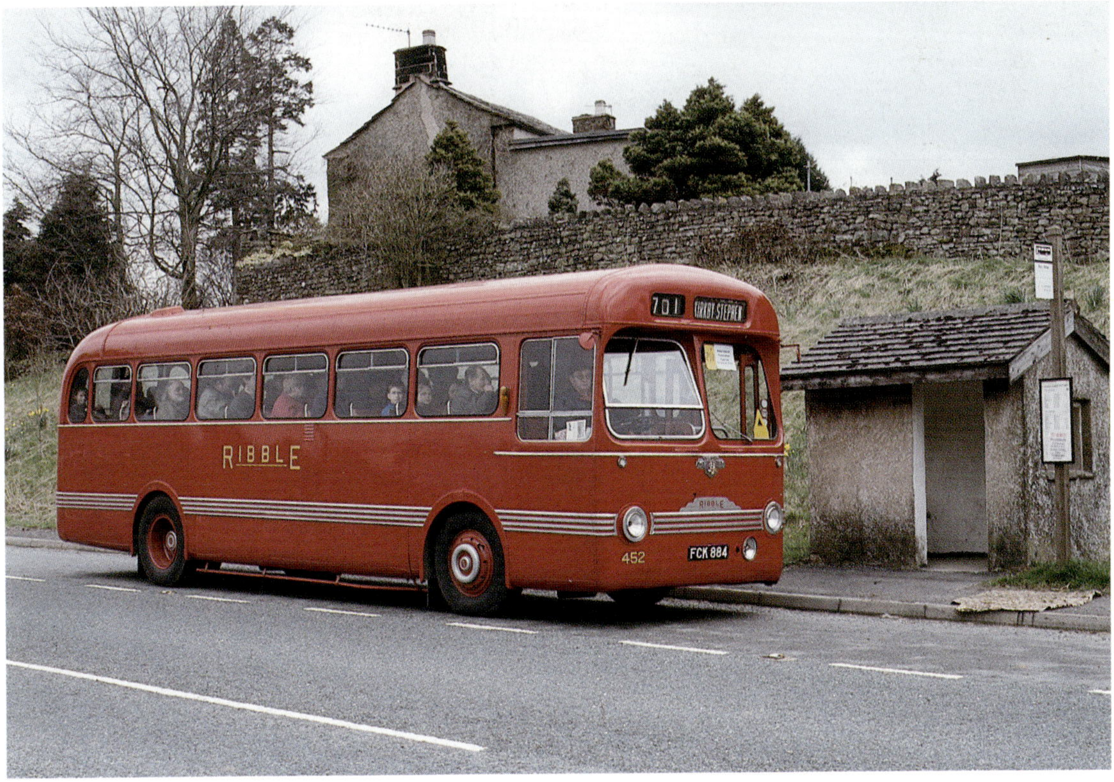
701
KIRKBY STEPHEN
RIBBLE
452
FCK 884

Kelvin Amos Collection

Contact address: 30 Blandford Close, Nailsea, Bristol BS48 2QQ
Brief description: The vehicles in the collection are regularly shown and run on free bus services.

Registration	Date	Chassis	Body	New to	Fleet No	Status
LHT 911	1948	Bristol L5G	Brislington Body Works B35R	Bristol Tramways	2388	R
KED 546F	1968	Leyland Panther Cub PSURC1	East Lancs B41D	Warrington Corporation	92	R
PWS 492S	1977	Leyland Leopard PSU3E/4R	Plaxton C49F	Bristol Omnibus Co	2098	R

Notes:
LHT 911 Rebodied 1958 with 1950 body
PWS 492S Rebodied 1983 with Paramount body after a fire

Lancastrian Transport Trust

Contact address: 1 Beverley Grove, South Shore, Blackpool, Lancashire FY4 2BG
E-mail: philip@ltt.org.uk
Web site: www.ltt.org.uk
Brief description: The Trust is dedicated to preserving historic buses from Lancashire. Vehicles can often be seen at local rallies and other events.
Membership details: Support organisation is TransSupport with a £10 annual membership fee. Quarterly magazine published *In Trust*.

Registration	Date	Chassis	Body	New to	Fleet No	Status
GTB 903	1946	Leyland Titan PD1	Leyland H30/26R	Lytham St Annes Corporation	19	R
CCK 663	1949	Leyland Titan PD2/3	Brush L27/26R	Ribble Motor Services	2687	A
DFV 146	1949	Leyland Titan PD2/5	Burlingham FH31/23C	Blackpool Corporation	246	A
JCK 530	1956	Leyland Titan PD2/12	Burlingham H33/28RD	Ribble Motor Services	1455	R
760 CTD	1957	Leyland Titan PD2/20	Northern Counties H30/28R	Lytham St Annes Corporation	61	A
534 RTB	1961	Guy Arab IV	Metro Cammell H41/32R	Lancashire United Transport	43	R
561 TD	1962	Daimler Fleetline CRG6LX	Northern Counties H43/33F	Lancashire United Transport	97	R
583 CLT	1962	AEC Routemaster 2R2RH	Park Royal H36/28R	London Transport	RM 1583	R
RRN 405	1962	Leyland Atlantean PDR1/1	Weymann L38/33F	Ribble Motor Services	1805	R
YFR 351	1962	Leyland Titan PD3/1	Metro Cammell FH41/32R	Blackpool Corporation	351	A
AAO 771A	1963	Leyland Titan PD3/5	Metro Cammell FH41/31F	Ribble Motor Services	1841	R
CTF 627B	1964	Leyland Titan PD2A/27	Massey H37/27F	Lytham St Annes Corporation	70	R
HFR 512E	1967	Leyland Titan PD3A/1	MCW H41/30R	Blackpool Corporation	512	R
HFR 516E	1967	Leyland Titan PD3A/1	MCW H41/30R	Blackpool Corporation	516	R
LFR 529F	1968	Leyland Titan PD3/11	MCW H41/30R	Blackpool Corporation	529	RP
LFR 540G	1968	Leyland Titan PD3/11	MCW H41/30R	Blackpool Corporation	540	A
PFR 554H	1970	AEC Swift MP2R	Marshall B47D	Blackpool Corporation	554	R
ATD 281J	1971	Leyland Atlantean PDR1A/1	Northern Counties H44/33F	Lytham St Annes Corporation	77	R
OCK 997K	1972	Bristol VRTSL6G	ECW H43/31F	Ribble Motor Services	1997	A
RTJ 422L	1972	Daimler Fleetline CRG6LXB-33	Northern Counties H47/32F	Lancashire United Transport	394	A
STJ 847L	1972	Seddon RU	Pennine B51F	Lytham St Annes Corporation	47	A
OFR 970M	1974	AEC Swift 3MP2R	Marshall B47D	Blackpool Corporation	570	R
HRN 99N	1975	Leyland Atlantean AN68	Northern Counties H43/31F	Fylde Borough Transport	79	A
OJI 4371	1977	Leyland Atlantean	Northern Counties H74F	Fylde Borough Transport	71	R
AHG 334V	1980	Leyland Atlantean AN68	East Lancs H50/36F	Blackpool Transport	331	A
F575 RCW	1988	Volkeswagen LT55	Optare City Pacer B21F	Blackpool Transport	575	R

Notes:

583 CLT	Restored to Blackpool livery
AAO 771A	Driver training vehicle 1981-1998. Originally registered TCK 841
CTF 627B	On loan from St Helens Transport Museum
HFR 516E	Preserved as driver training bus
OJI 4371	Originally registered EBV 85S

Legionnaire Group

Contact address: 66 Montfort Road, Strood, Rochester, Kent ME2 3EX
E-mail: bob.wingrove@btinternet.com
Brief description: The group aims to restore at least one of each combination of chassis/Legionnaire so that Harrington's last body style is represented in preservation.

Registration	Date	Chassis	Body	New to	Fleet No	Status
SPU 985	1951	Leyland Olympic HR44	Weymann DP44F	Jennings Coaches of Ashen		RP
72 MMJ	1964	Bedford VAL14	Harrington C52F	Reliance Coaches of Meppershall	72	RP
CDK 409C	1965	Bedford VAL14	Harrington C52F	Yelloway Motor Services of Rochdale		A
JNK 681C	1965	Ford Thames 36 676E	Harrington C52F	SP Coaches of Sutton		RP

Notes:
JNK 681C — Used as Harrington demonstrator when new

Leicester Corporation Bus Owners Group

Phone: 01872 552616
Affiliation: NARTM
Brief description: Formed in 2002, the group has been set up to bring together those owning buses formerly operated by 'The Corpo'. Vehicles are mostly stored in the Leicester area and may be viewed by appointment.
Opening days/times: By appointment only.
Charges: Free admission but donations welcome.

Registration	Date	Chassis	Body	New to	Fleet No	Status
OJF 191	1956	Leyland Tiger Cub PSUC1/1	Weymann B44F	Leicester City Transport	191	RP
217 AJF	1961	AEC Bridgemaster B3RA	Park Royal H76R	Leicester City Transport	217	RP
90 HBC	1964	Leyland Totan PD3A/1	East Lancs H41/33R	Leicester City Tramsport	90	RP
DBC 190C	1965	AEC Renown 3B3RA	East Lancs H44/31F	Leicester City Transport	190	R
FJF 40D	1966	AEC Renown 3B3RA	East Lancs H43/31R	Leicester City Transport	40	RP
GRY 48D	1966	Leyland Titan PD3A/1	MCW H41/33R	Leicester City Transport	48	A
PBC 98G	1968	Leyland Atlantean PDR1A/1	ECW H43/31F	Leicester City Transport	98	RP
PBC 113G	1969	Leyland Atlantean PDR1A/1	Park Royal H43/31F	Leicester City Transport	113	RP
TRY 122H	1969	Bristol RELL6L	ECW B47D	Leicester City Transport	122	RP
ARY 225K	1972	Scania BR111MH	MCW B46D	Leicester City Transport	225	R
GJF 301N	1975	Scania BR111DH	MCW H45/28D	Leicester City Transport	301	R
UFP 233S	1977	Dennis Dominator DD101	East Lancs H43/31F	Leicester City Transport	233	RP

Notes:
ARY 225K — Exhibited Earls Court 1972.

Medstead Depot Omnibus Group

Contact Address: 20 Budd's Close, Basingstoke, RG21 8XJ.
Affiliation: NARTM, WOMP, Aldershot & District Bus Interest Group, Friends of King Alfred Buses, Southampton & District Transport Heritage Trust.
Brief Description: Vehicles from the Medstead Depot Omnibus Group are regularly to be seen at shows and rallies throughout the season. In addition to the vehicles listed, others belonging to members of the Aldershot & District Bus Interest Group, Friends of King Alfred Buses and the Southampton & District Transport Heritage Trust are associated with the Group. There is an open day once per year, the next being on Sunday, 17 July 2005.
Events Planned: Free bus services between Medstead & Four Marks Station and Alton Station operate on the first Sunday of each month between May and September.

Registration	Date	Chassis	Body	New to	Fleet No	Status
JRX 823	1955	Bristol KSW6B	ECW L27/28R	Thames Valley Traction Co	748	R
TDL 998	1960	Bristol Lodekka FS6G	ECW H33/27R	Southern Vectis Omnibus Co	565	R
RCP 237	1962	AEC Regent V 2D3RA	Northern Counties H39/32F	Hebble Motor Services	619	RP
YDL 315	1962	Bristol Lodekka FS6G	ECW H33/27RD	Southern Vectis Omnibus Co	570	R
KHC 367	1963	AEC Regent V 2D3RV	East Lancs H32/28R	Eastbourne Corporation	67	R

Merseyside Transport Trust

Contact address: 88 Hawthorne Road, Bootle, Merseyside, L20 9JX
E-mail: mpnw31374@blueyonder.co.uk
Web site: www.mttrust.co.uk
Affiliation: AEC Society; Leyland Society
Brief description: A collection of vehicles, mostly from the Merseyside area but including others of special interest.

Registration	Date	Chassis	Body	New to	Fleet No	Status
NKD 536	1953	AEC Regent III 9613S	Crossley H30/26R	Liverpool Corporation	A36	RP
NKD 540	1954	AEC Regent III 9613S	Saunders Roe H32/26R	Liverpool Corporation	A40	RP
VKB 711	1956	Leyland Titan PD2/20	Crossley H33/29R	Liverpool Corporation	L255	RP
501 KD	1962	Leyland Atlantean PDR1/1	Metro Cammell H43/35F	Liverpool Corporation	L501	R
FKF 933G	1968	Leyland Panther PSUR1A/1R	MCW B47D	Liverpool City Transport	1054	RP
SKB 695G	1969	Bristol RELL6G	Park Royal B45D	Liverpool City Transport	2025	R
UKA 562H	1969	Leyland Atlantean PDR2/1	Alexander H47/32D	Liverpool City Transport	1111	R
MAN 1378	1971	Leyland Atlantean PDR2/1	Alexander H47/32D	Merseyside PTE	1162	RP
WWM 904W	1980	Dennis Dominator DD120B	Willowbrook H45/33F	Merseyside PTE	0027	RP
A101 HLV	1984	Leyland Atlantean AN68D/1R	Alexander H43/32F	Merseyside PTE	1021	R
A112 HLV	1984	Leyland Atlantean AN68D/1R	Alexander H43/32F	Merseyside PTE	1032	R

The Mike Sutcliffe Collection

Phone: 01525 221676
E-mail: sutcliffes@valleyforge.fslife.co.uk
Affiliation: NARTM; Leyland Society member; HCVS member

Brief description: A collection of 16 vehicles, mainly buses of Leyland manufacture from the period 1908 to 1934, this is the most significant collection of of early motorbuses in the world, and includes the oldest British-built motorbus. Mike Sutcliffe was recently awarded the MBE 'for his services to Motor Heritage'.

Opening days/times: Viewing can be arranged by prior appointment only. There is no charge, but donations are welcome.

Registration	Date	Chassis	Body	New to	Fleet No	Status
LN 7270	1908	Leyland X2	Thomas Tilling O18/16RO	London Central Motor Omnibus Co	14	R
HE 12	1913	Leyland S3.30.T	Brush B27F	Barnsley & District Electric Traction Co	5	RP
LF 9967	1913	Leyland S3.30.T	Birch O20/16RO	Wellingborough Motor Omnibus Co	H	R
CC 1087	1914	Leyland S4.36.T3	Leyland Ch32	London & North Western Railway	59	R
BD 209	1921	Leyland G7	Dodson Ch/B32D	United Counties Omnibus Co	B15	R
C 2367	1921	Leyland G	Phoenix O23/20RO	Todmorden Corporation	14	R
DM 2583	1923	Leyland SG7	Leyland FB40D	Brookes Bros ('White Rose') of Rhyl	27	R
XU 7498	1924	Leyland LB5	Dodson O26/22RO	Chocolate Express Omnibus Co	B6	R
PW 8605	1926	ADC 415	United B35F	United Automobile Services	E61	A
CK 4518	1931	Leyland Lion LT2	Leyland B30F	Ribble Motor Services	1161	A
YG 7831	1934	Leyland Tiger TS6	Northern Counties B36R	Todmorden Joint Omnibus Committee	15	A

Notes:

LN 7270	Body new 1906. Bought by LCMOC 1908. Orig on Milnes Daimler chassis of Thomas Tilling
LF 9967	On loan to British Commercial Vehicle Museum at Leyland
CC 1087	Registered by War Office in 1915. Re-registered XA 8086 in 1919; reverted to CC 1087 in 1980
C 2367	On loan to Manchester Museum of Transport
BD 209	Formerly a Dodson demonstrator and Olympia Commercial Motor Show exhibit 1921
YG 7831	Rebuilt to recovery vehicle; to be restored back to a bus

North East Bus Preservation Trust Ltd

Contact address: THe Secretary. 8 Seaburn Hill, Sunderland SR6 8BS
Phone: 0191 548 7369
E-mail: northbritish@supanet.com
Affiliation: NARTM
Brief description: The collection is displayed at an 1820 former locomotive shed on the Bowes Railway, Gateshead. This accommodates up to 10 vehicles, and so vehicles rotate between this and other locations. If you wish to view a particular vehicle, you will need to mention this when making arrangements to view.
Opening days/times: Viewing by prior arrangement only.

Registration	Date	Chassis	Body	New to	Fleet No	Status
CN 4740	1931	SOS IM4	Short B34F	Northern General Transport Co	540	A
WG 1620	1933	Gilford Hera L176S	(chassis only)	Alexander	Y49	A
BTN 113	1934	Daimler COS4	Northern Coachbuilders B34R	Newcastle Corporation	173	A
CN 6100	1934	Northern General Transport SE6 (LSE4)	Short B44F	Northern General Transport Co	604	RP
DPT 848	1939	Leyland Tiger TS8	Roe B32F	Sunderland District	159	R
EF 7380	1942	Leyland Titan TD7	Roe H26/22C	West Hartlepool Corporation	36	R
AHL 694	1947	Leyland Tiger PS1/1	Barnaby C33F	J Bullock & Sons of Featherstone	284	R
HHN 202	1947	Bristol L5G	ECW B35R	Bells of Westerhope		R
JRA 635	1947	Leyland Tiger PS1	Crossley B35R	Chesterfield Corporation	48	R
KTJ 502	1947	Leyland Tiger PS1	Burlingham B35F	Haslingden Corporation	2	R
HUP 236	1948	Albion Valiant CX39N	ACB C33F	Economic Bus Services of Whitburn	W7	R
JPT 544	1948	Daimler CVD6	Willowbrook B35F	Venture Transport Co of Consett	156	R
LVK 123	1948	Leyland Titan PD2/1	Leyland H30/26R	Newcastle Corporation	123	RP
ABR 433	1949	Crossley DD42/7C	Crossley H56R	Sunderland Corporation	100	RP
CFK 340	1949	AEC Regal III 6821A	Burlingham C33F	H & E Burnham of Worcester		R
NVK 341	1950	AEC Regent III 9612A	Northern Coachbuilders H30/26R	Newcastle Corporation	341	R

Registration	Date	Chassis	Body	New to	Fleet No	Status
LYM 729	1951	AEC Regal IV	ECW C—F	Tillings Transport		RP
CBR 539	1952	Guy Arab III	Roe H33/25R	Sunderland Corporation	139	RP
PHN 831	1952	Bristol LS5G	ECW B45F	United Automobile Services	BU2	A
SHN 301	1952	AEC Regal IV 9821E	Burlingham C41C	Scotts Greys of Darlington	5	R
DCN 83	1953	AEC Beadle	Beadle C35F	Northern General Transport Co	1483	A
TUG 20	1954	AEC Reliance MU3RV	Roe C41C	Roe Demonstrator		RP
SPT 65	1955	Guy Arab LUF	Weymann B44F	Northern General Transport Co	1665	RP
UUA 212	1955	Leyland Titan PD2/11	Roe H33/25R	Leeds City Transport	212	R
JHL 701	1956	Bedford SBG	Plaxton C41F	Swan of Berwick		RP
TUP 859	1956	AEC Regent V MD3RV	Roe H35/28R	Hartlepool Corporation	4	RP
UFJ 292	1957	Guy Arab IV	Massey H30/26R	Exeter Corporation	52	R
VUP 328	1957	Leyland Tiger Cub PSUC1/1	Crossley B44F	Economic Bus Services of Whitburn	A2	A
WTS 708A	1957	Bristol LS5G	ECW B45F	United Automobile Services	BU250	A
AFT 930	1958	Leyland Titan PD3/4	Metro Cammell H41/32R	Tynemouth & District	230	RP
OSK 831	1958	Karrier BFD3023	Plaxton C14F	Brocksbank of Leeds		RP
RSL 905	1958	AEC Reliance MU3RV	Roe C41C	Essex County Coaches of Stratford		R
YPT 796	1958	AEC Reliance MU3RV	Roe C41C	Economic Bus Services of Whitburn	W3	R
TCO 537	1960	Leyland Atlantean	Metro Cammell H44/33F	Plymouth Corporation	137	R
221 JVK	1962	Leyland Atlantean PDR1/1	Alexander H44/34F	Newcastle Corporation	221	R
WNL 259A	1962	AEC Reliance 4MU3RA	Plaxton B55F	Economic Bus Services of Whitburn	W5	R
6249 UP	1963	Leyland Leopard PSU3/3RT	Alexander DP51F	Venture Transport Co of Consett	249	R
ACU 304B	1963	Leyland Leopard PSU3/3R	Plaxton B55F	Stanhope Motor Services		R
EUP 405B	1964	AEC Routemaster 3R2RH	Park Royal H41/31F	Northern General Transport Co	2105	R
PCN 762	1964	AEC Routemaster 3R2RH	Park Royal H41/31F	Northern General Transport Co	2099	R
WBR 248	1964	Atkinson Alpha PM746HL	Marshall B45D	Sunderland Corporation	48	R
FBR 53D	1966	Leyland Panther PSUR1/1R	Strachan B47D	Sunderland Corporation	53	R
ECU 201E	1967	Bristol RESL6L	ECW B45D	South Shields Corporation	1	R
WHN 411G	1969	Bristol VRTSL6LX	ECW H39/31F	United Automobile Services	601	A
VTY 543J	1970	Leyland Leopard PSU3A/4R	Plaxton C45F	Tyne Valley of Acomb		A
WHA 237H	1970	Leyland Leopard PSU3A/4R	Plaxton C49F	BMMO ('Midland Red')	6237	RP
GAN 744J	1971	Leyland Leopard PSU5/4RT	Plaxton C57F	Banfield Coaches		RP
PCW 203J	1971	Bristol RESL6L	Pennine B45F	Burnley Colne & Nelson	103	R
SWV 155J	1971	Daimler Fleetline CRG6LX	Northern Counties			RP
GBB 524K	1972	Leyland Atlantean PDR2/1	Alexander H48/30D	Tyne & Wear PTE	688	RP
MCN 30K	1972	Leyland/NGT Tynesider	Weymann/Northern General H39/29F	Northern General Transport Co	3000	R
NHN 250K	1972	Daimler Fleetline SRG6LX-36	Roe B48D	Darlington Corporation	50	R
E901 DRG	1973	Bedford YRQ	Plaxton C45F	Smith of Durham		RP
GGR 103N	1974	Leyland Atlantean AN68/2R	Northern Counties H47/36F	OK Motor Services		RP
E903 DRG	1975	Ford R1114	Plaxton C53F	Smith of Durham		RP
GUP 907N	1975	Bristol LH6L	ECW B43F	United Automobile Services	1623	R
KGG 184N	1975	Bedford YRQ	Plaxton C45F	Earnside Coaches of Perth		R
TUP 329R	1976	Bristol VRTSL3/501	ECW H43/31F	Northern General Transport Co	3329	RP
OCU 769R	1977	Scania BR111DH	MCW H45/29D	Tyne & Wear PTE	769	RP
OCU 807R	1977	Leyland Fleetline FE30AGR	Alexander H44/30F	Tyne & Wear PTE	807	RP
RCU 588S	1977	Leyland Atlantean AN68/2R	Willowbrook H48/34F	Tyne & Wear PTE	588	RP
VPT 598R	1977	Leyland National 11351A/1R	Leyland National B49F	Northern General Transport Co	4598	RP
JPT 901T	1978	Bristol VRT/SL3/501	ECW H43/31F	Northern General Transport Co	3401	R
JPT 906T	1978	Bristol VRT/SL3/501	ECW H43/31F	Northern General Transport Co	3406	RP
RCU 838S	1978	Daimler Fleetline FE30AGR	Alexander H44/30F	Tyne & Wear PTE	838	R
PAJ 829X	1981	Bristol VRT/SL3/6LXB	ECW H43/31F	United Automobile Services	829	RP
JFT 413X	1982	Scania BR112DH	Alexander H47/31F	Tyne & Wear PTE	413	RP
VCW 597Y	1982	Dennis Lancet SD505	Marshall B51F	Blackpool Transport	597	A
UTN 501Y	1983	MCW Metrobus DR102/31	MCW H46/31F	Northern General Transport Co	3501	RP

Notes:
HHN 202 Rebodied 1957 with 1946 body; passed to Durham District Services (DB216) in 1959
ABR 433 Fitted with Gardner 5LW engine
WTS 708A Originally registered 650 CHN.
RSL 905 Originally registered MJD 759
OSK 831 Originally registered 6666 U.
WNL 259A Originally registered 8031 PT

ACU 304B	Originally registered 6MPT		E901 DRG	Built 1973 stored until 1988
PCN 762	Originally registered RCN 699		E903 DRG	Built 1975 stored until 1988
WHA 237H	Towing vehicle		RCU 838S	Originally H44/27D
MCN 30K	Rebuilt from 1958 Leyland Titan PD3/4 new to Tyneside Tramways & Tramroads Co (49) registered NNL 49			

Peter Stanier Collection

Phone: 01474 814476
Brief description: A collection of preserved Leyland petrol-engined vehicles with their origins in the island of Jersey
Opening days/times: Not normally open for viewing. Arrangements to visit can be made, strictly by appointment, telephoning first for details

Registration	Date	Chassis	Body	New to	Fleet No	Status
DM 6228	1929	Leyland Lioness LTB1	Burlingham C26D	Brooks Bros of Rhyl	7	R
SV 6107	1929	Leyland Titan TD1	Leyland L24/24R	Jersey Motor Transport Co	24	R

Notes:
SV 6107   1931 body fitted in 1934. Chassis new to Jersey originally registered J 1199

Ribble Vehicle Preservation Trust

Contact address: 6 Crompton Road, Lostock, Bolton BL6 4LP
Affiliation: NARTM
Brief description: The Trust promotes the preservation and restoration of vehicles from Ribble and associated companies.

Registration	Date	Chassis	Body	New to	Fleet No	Status
CK 4474	1931	Leyland Tiger TS3	Leyland C26F	Ribble Motor Services	1117	A
RN 7588	1935	Leyland Tiger TS7	Burlingham B35F	Ribble Motor Services	209	R
TJ 6760	1935	Leyland Lion LT5A	Leyland B32R	Lytham St Annes Corporation	24	RP
BTF 25	1937	Leyland Titan TD4c	Leyland FH30/24R	Lytham St Annes Corporation	45	A
ACK 796	1944	Guy Arab II	Northern Counties / Bond UL27/26R	Ribble Motor Services	2413	A
ACB 904	1947	Guy Arab II	Northern Counties	Blackburn Corporation	502	A
CRG 811	1947	Daimler CVD6	Alexander C35F	Aberdeen Corporation	41	A
CCK 359	1948	Leyland Titan PD2/3	Leyland L27/26R	Ribble Motor Services	2584	A
CRS 834	1948	Daimler CVD6	Walker / Aberdeen CT C31F	Aberdeen Corporation	44	A
DRN 289	1950	Leyland Titan PD2/3	Leyland L27/26RD	Ribble Motor Services	1349	A
MTC 540	1950	AEC Regent III 9613E	Park Royal H30/26R	Morecambe & Heysham Corporation	72	RP
ECK 934	1952	Leyland Titan PD2/12	Leyland L27/26RD	Ribble Motor Services	1364	A
ERN 700	1952	Leyland Royal Tiger PSU1/13	Leyland B44F	Ribble Motor Services	377	R
FCK 884	1954	Leyland Tiger Cub PSUC1/1T	Saunders Roe B44F	Ribble Motor Services	452	R
HRN 31	1955	Leyland Titan PD2/13	Metro Cammell H33/28RD	Ribble Motor Services	1391	A
HRN 39	1955	Leyland Titan PD2/13	Metro Cammell H33/28RD	Ribble Motor Services	1399	A
JFV 527	1955	Commer TS3	Harrington C41C	Abbott of Blackpool		RP
JCK 542	1956	Leyland Titan PD2/12	Burlingham H33/28RD	Ribble Motor Services	1467	RP
JRN 41	1956	Leyland Tiger Cub PSUC1/2T	Burlingham C41F	Ribble Motor Services	975	A
528 CTF	1957	Leyland Titan PD2/40	Weymann L29/28RD	J Fishwick & Sons of Leyland	5	R
881 BTF	1958	Leyland Titan PD2/41	East Lancs H35/28R	Lancaster City Transport	881	A

Above: **Preservationist Roger Burdett has amassed a large collection of vehicles, mostly of Midlands or West Country origin. Former Southern National (Royal Blue) 2380 (OTA 640G) is smartly presented in National Bus Company 'National Express' livery.** *Philip Lamb*

Below: **Greater Manchester 3001 (ANA 1Y), a Northern Counties-bodied Leyland Olympian is the SELNEC Preservation Society's latest restoration.** *Philip Lamb*

Above: **St Margaret's School in Aigburth, Liverpool has a long history of bus preservation. Alexander PA133 (CMS 201), an Alexander-bodied Leyland PS1 was completed in 2001.** *Philip Lamb*

Below: **Back on the road last year was Southampton 402 (KOW 910F). This mighty AEC Regent V with Neepsend coachwork is part of the collection of local buses maintained by the Southampton & District Transport Heritage Trust.** *Philip Lamb*

Registration	Date	Chassis	Body	New to	Fleet No	Status
KCK 869	1958	Leyland Titan PD3/4	Burlingham FH41/31F	Ribble Motor Services	1523	A
KCK 914	1958	Leyland Titan PD3/4	Burlingham FH41/31F	Ribble Motor Services	1553	A
MBN 177	1958	Leyland Titan PD3/5	East Lancs H41/33R	Bolton Corporation	122	RP
NRN 586	1960	Leyland Atlantean PDR1/1	Metro Cammell H44/33F	Ribble Motor Services	1686	R
SFV 421	1960	Leyland Atlantean PDR1/1	Weymann CH34/16Ft	W C Standerwick	25	A
PCK 618	1961	Leyland Leopard L2	Harrington C32F	Ribble Motor Services	1036	R
PRN 145	1961	Leyland Atlantean PDR1/1	Metro Cammell H44/33F	Scout Motor Services of Preston	5	RP
PRN 906	1961	Leyland Titan PD3/4	Metro Cammell H39/31F	Preston Corporation	14	RP
RRN 428	1962	Leyland Atlantean PDR1/1	Weymann CH39/20F	Ribble Motor Services	1279	R
TCK 465	1963	Leyland Leopard PSU3/1R	Marshall B53F	Ribble Motor Services	465	A
TCK 494	1963	Leyland Leopard PSU3/1R	Marshall B53F	Ribble Motor Services	494	A
TCK 726	1963	Leyland Leopard PSU3/3RT	Harrington C49F	Ribble Motor Services	726	RP
ARN 811C	1965	Leyland Leopard PSU3/3RT	Weymann DP49F	Ribble Motor Services	811	RP
DJP 468E	1967	Leyland Panther Cub PSRC1/1	Massey B43D	Wigan Corporation	20	RP
FPT 6G	1969	Leyland Leopard PSU3/3RT	Plaxton C51F	Weardale Motor Services of Frosterley		A
HRN 249G	1969	Bristol RELL6G	ECW B41D	Ribble Motor Services	249	A
LRN 321J	1970	Bristol RESL6L	Marshall B47F	Ribble Motor Services	321	A
NCK 338J	1971	Bristol RESL6L	ECW B47F	Ribble Motor Services	338	R
PRN 79K	1972	Bristol VRL/LLH/6L	ECW CH42/18Ct	W C Standerwick	S79	A
PTF 718L	1972	Leyland National 1151/2R/0401	Leyland National B48D	Ribble Motor Services	372	RP
PTF 727L	1972	Leyland National 1151/2R	Leyland National B48D	Ribble Motor Services	386	R
UTF 732M	1974	Leyland Leopard PSU3B/4R	Duple C49F	Ribble Motor Services	1052	A
MFR 306P	1976	Leyland Leopard PSU3C/2R	Alexander B53F	Lancaster City Transport	306	R
XCW 955R	1978	Leyland National 11351A/1R	Leyland National B49F	J Fishwick & Sons of Leyland	24	R
TRN 481V	1979	Leyland Atlantean AN68A/1R	ECW H43/31F	Ribble Motor Services	1481	R
DBV 100W	1980	Leyland Olympian B45	ECW H45/33F	Ribble Motor Services	2100	R

Notes:

RN 7588	Rebodied 1949		ERN 700	Originally B44F
CRG 811	Rebodied 1958		SFV 421	Gay Hostess double deck motorway coach
ACB 904	Breakdown Vehicle		TCK 694	Possible source of parts
CRS 834	Body rebuilt 1962		PTF 727L	Used as exhibition bus

The Roger Burdett Collection

Contact Address: 2 Pennyfields Boulevard, Long Eaton, NG10 3QS
E-mail: rogerrbctc@aol.com
Affiliation: NARTM
Brief Description: A collection of distinctive coaches supplemented by four double deckers of interest to the collection owner. All vehicles with the exception of the Bristol RE are either unique or one of a small number of survivors.
Opening days/times: Vehicles regularly attend rallies and events and the collection can be viewed by appointment. Please write to the address given.

Registration	Date	Chassis	Body	New to	Fleet No	Status
VG 5541	1933	Bristol GJW	Weymann O28/26R	Norwich Electric Tramways		RP
JYC 855	1948	Leyland Tiger PS1	Harrington C33F	Scarlet Motors of Minehead		R
GOU 732	1949	Tilling Stevens K6LA7	Scottish Aviation C33F	Altonian Coaches of Alton		R
GKV 94	1950	Daimler CVA6	Metro Cammell H31/29R	Coventry City Transport	94	RP
LTA 813	1950	Bristol KS5G	ECW L27/28R	Western National Omnibus Co	994	R
NTU 125	1951	Foden PVRF6	Metalcraft C41C	Hollinshead of Biddulph		RP
NXL 874	1953	AEC Regal III	Duple C39F	Eastern Belle of Bow London		R
OTT 43	1953	Bristol LS6G	ECW C39F	Western National Omnibus Co (Royal Blue)	2200	R
WKJ 787	1956	Beadle-Commer	Beadle C41C	Beadle Demonstrator		R

Registration	Date	Chassis	Body	New to	Fleet No	Status
780 GHA	1959	BMMO C5	BMMO C41F	BMMO ('Midland Red')	4780	RP
56 GUO	1961	Bristol MW6G	ECW C39F	Western National Omnibus Co (Royal Blue)	2267	RP
5056 HA	1962	BMMO S15	BMMO B40F	BMMO ('Midland Red')	5056	R
EHA 424D	1966	BMMO D9	BMMO/Willowbrook H40/32RD	BMMO ('Midland Red')	5424	R
OTA 640G	1969	Bristol RELH6G	ECW C45F	Southern National Omnibus Co (Royal Blue)	2380	R

Notes:
VG 5541   Converted to Diesel 1938 and open top 1950

Rotherham Trolleybus Group

Contact address: 113 Tinker Lane, Walkley, Sheffield S6 5EA
Phone: 0114 266 3173
Affiliation: Trolleybus Museum at Sandtoft
Brief description: This group is open to all with an interest in Rotherham area trolleys, the vehicles and the system. Active restoration of the vehicles takes place and the group works closely with the Trolleybus Museum at Sandtoft. A video *Remember the Trackless* is sold to raise funds for restoration. Vehicles can be viewed by contacting the group.

Registration	Date	Chassis	Body	New to	Fleet No	Status
CET 613+	1942	Sunbeam MS2c	East Lancs B39C	Rotherham Corporation	88	RP
FET 617+	1950	Daimler CTE6	Roe H40/30R	Rotherham Corporation	37	R
+ Trolleybus						

Notes:
FET 617   Rebodied 1956 (formerly single-decker). On display at Sandtoft

RTW Bus Group

Contact address: 7 Oldbury Close, St Mary Cray BR5 3TH
Affiliation: RT/RF Register, Cobham Bus Museum, HCVS
Brief description: The group was formed in 1999 and comprises the owners of the preserved RTW vehicles and those interested in the type. The vehicles appear at rallies from time to time. A video on the history of the RTW is available from the group.

Registration	Date	Chassis	Body	New to	Fleet No	Status
KGK 529	1949	Leyland Titan 6RT	Leyland H30/26R	London Transport	RTW 29	R
KGK 575	1949	Leyland Titan 6RT	Leyland H30/26R	London Transport	RTW 75	R
KLB 908	1949	Leyland Titan 6RT	Leyland H30/26RD	London Transport	RTW 178	R
KLB 915	1949	Leyland Titan 6RT	Leyland H30/26R	London Transport	RTW 185	R
KXW 435	1949	Leyland Titan 6RT	Leyland H30/26RD	London Transport	RTW 335	RP
LLU 957	1950	Leyland Titan 6RT	Leyland H30/26R	London Transport	RTW 467	R
LLU 987	1950	Leyland Titan 6RT	Leyland H30/26R	London Transport	RTW 497	R

Notes:
KGK 575   Operates as PSV for Blue Triangle
KLB 908   Originally H30/26R. Acquired by Stevensons of Spath in 1966 and fitted with platform doors and saloon heaters

St Margaret's Transport Society

Contact Information: St Margaret's High School, Aigburth Raod, Liverpool L17 6AB
Telephone: 01263 834829
Affiliation: NARTM
Brief Description: Formed in 1979, the Society specialises in single deck half-cabs from the 1940s and 1950s. Meetings are held regularly to carry out restoration of the vehicles. Visitors are welcome but prior appointment is essential. Please contact the address given.

Registration	Date	Chassis	Body	New to	Fleet No	Status
CMS 201	1949	Leyland Tiger PS1	Alexander C35F	Alexander	PA133	RO5
GWM 816	1951	Crossley SD42/7	Crossley B32F	Southport Corporation	116	RP

SELNEC Preservation Society

Contact address: 16 Thurleigh Road, Didsbury, Manchester M20 2DF
Affiliation: NARTM
Brief description: A collection of buses from the SELNEC era including SELNEC Standards, the trail-blazing 'Mancunian' and other vehicles from the Greater Manchester area.
Events planned: The operational vehicles will appear at a range of local rallies and shows.

Registration	Date	Chassis	Body	New to	Fleet No	Status
EN 9965	1950	Leyland Titan PD2/4	Weymann	Bury Corporation	165	RP
DNF 708C	1965	Daimler Fleetline CRG6LX	Metro Cammell O43/29C	Manchester Corporation	4708	A
END 832D	1966	Leyland Atlantean PDR1/2	Metro Cammell H43/32F	Manchester Corporation	3832	RP
GNB 518D	1966	Bedford VAL 14	Plaxton C47F	Manchester Corporation	205	A
LNA 166G	1968	Leyland Atlantean PDR2/1	Park Royal H26/7D	Manchester City Transport	1066	R
NNB 547H	1969	Leyland Atlantean PDR2/1	East Lancs H47/32F	Manchester City Transport	1142	A
NNB 589H	1970	Daimler Fleetline CRG6LXB	Park Royal H47/28D	SELNEC PTE	2130	A
ONF 865H	1970	Leyland Atlantean PDR2/1	Park Royal H47/28D	SELNEC PTE	1177	A
PNF 941J	1971	Leyland Atlantean PDR1A/1	Northern Counties H43/32F	SELNEC PTE	EX1	R
RNA 220J	1971	Daimler Fleetline CRG6LXB	Park Royal H47/29D	SELNEC PTE	2220	A
TNB 759K	1972	Daimler Fleetline CRG6LXB	Northern Counties H45/27D	SELNEC PTE	EX19	A
VNB 132L	1972	Leyland Atlantean AN68/1R	Park Royal O43/32F	SELNEC PTE	7032	R
VNB 173L	1972	Leyland Atlantean AN68/1R	Northern Counties H43/32F	SELNEC PTE	7147	A
VNB 177L	1972	Daimler Fleetline CRG6LXB	Northern Counties H45/27D	SELNEC PTE	7206	R
VNB 203L	1972	Daimler Fleetline CRG6LXB	Northern Counties H31/4D	SELNEC PTE	7232	R
WBN 955L	1972	Leyland Atlantean AN68/1R	Park Royal O43/32F	SELNEC PTE	7077	R
YDB 453L	1972	Seddon Pennine IV-236	Seddon DP25F	SELNEC PTE	1700	RP
AJA 408L	1973	Bristol VRTSL2/6LXB	ECW H43/32F	SELNEC Cheshire Bus Co	408	R
WWH 43L	1973	Daimler Fleetline CRG6LXB	Park Royal H43/32F	SELNEC PTE	7185	R
XJA 534L	1973	Leyland Atlantean AN68/1R	Park Royal H43/32F	SELNEC PTE	7143	A
XVU 341M	1973	Seddon Pennine IV-236	Seddon B23F	SELNEC PTE	1711	A
YNA 321M	1973	Daimler Fleetline CRG6LXB	Northern Counties H43/32F	SELNEC PTE	7366	A
BNE 729N	1974	Seddon Pennine IV-236	Seddon B19F	Greater Manchester PTE	1735	A
BNE 751N	1974	Leyland Atlantean AN68/1R	Northern Counties H43/32F	Greater Manchester PTE	7501	A
BNE 764N	1974	Bristol LH6L	ECW B43F	Greater Manchester PTE	1321	A
XVU 363M	1974	Seddon Pennine IV-236	Seddon B19F	Greater Manchester PTE	1733	A
HJA 121N	1975	Seddon Pennine IV-236	Seddon B19F	Greater Manchester PTE	1737	A
HNB 24N	1975	Leyland National 10351/1R	Leyland National B41F	Greater Manchester PTE	105	R
OBN 502R	1977	Leyland Fleetline FE30GR	Northern Counties H43/32F	Lancashire United Transport	485	A

Registration	Date	Chassis	Body	New to	Fleet No	Status
PTD 640S	1977	Leyland Fleetline FE30GR	Northern Counties H43/32F	Lancashire United Transport	496	A
UNA 848S	1977	Leyland Atlantean AN68A/1R	Park Royal H43/32F	Greater Manchester Transport	7848	A
XBU 1S	1978	Leyland Fleetline FE30GR	Northern Counties H43/32F	Greater Manchester PTE	8001	R
BNC 960T	1979	Leyland Atlantean AN68A/1R	Park Royal H43/32F	Greater Manchester PTE	7960	A
GBU 1V	1979	MCW Metrobus DR101/6	MCW H43/30F	Greater Manchester PTE	5001	R
YTE 587V	1979	Leyland Fleetline FE30GR	Northern Counties H43/32F	Lancashire United Transport	573	A
GNF 15V	1980	Leyland Titan TNTL11/1RF	Park Royal H47/26F	Greater Manchester PTE	4015	A
GNF 16V	1980	Leyland Fleetline FE30GR	Northern Counties H43/32F	Greater Manchester PTE	8141	RP
NJA 568W	1980	Bristol Olympian B45/TL11/1R	Northern Counties H43/30F	Greater Manchester PTE	1451	RP
DWH 706W	1981	Leyland Fleetline FE30GR	Northern Counties H43/32F	Lancashire United Transport	613	R
SND 455X	1981	Leyland Atlantean AN68B/1R	Northern Counties H43/32F	Greater Manchester PTE	8455	A
SND 460X	1981	Leyland Atlantean AN68B/1R	Northern Counties H43/32F	Greater Manchester PTE	8460	R
ANA 1Y	1982	Leyland Olympian ONTL11/1R	Northern Counties H43/30F	Greater Manchester PTE	3001	R
ANA 601Y	1983	Leyland Atlantean AN68A/1R	Northern Counties H43/32F	Greater Manchester Transport	8601	A
ANA 645Y	1983	Leyland Atlantean AN68D/1R	Northern Counties H43/32F	Greater Manchester PTE	8645	RP
FWH 461Y	1983	Scania BR112DH	Northern Counties H43/32F	Greater Manchester Transport	1461	A
A30 ORJ	1984	Leyland Olympian ONLXB/1R	Northern Counties H43/30F	Greater Manchester Transport	3030	A
A472 HNC	1984	Dennis Falcon V DD405	Northern Counties H43/37F	Greater Manchester PTE	1472	A
A765 NNA	1984	Leyland Atlantean AN68D/1R	Northern Counties H43/32F	Greater Manchester PTE	8765	RP
B901 TVR	1985	Dennis Dominator DDA1003	Northern Counties H43/32F	Greater Manchester PTE	2001	RP
C751 YBA	1985	Dennis Domino SDA 1201	Northern Counties B24F	Greater Manchester PTE	1751	R
C823 CBU	1986	Dodge S 56	Northern Counties B18F	Greater Manchester PTE	1823	RP
D320 LNB	1987	MCW Metrobus DR102/51	Northern Counties CH43/29F	Greater Manchester Buses	5320	RP
D509 MJA	1987	Iveco 49-10	Robin Hood B21F	Greater Manchester Buses	1509	A

Notes:

EN 9965	Converted to Breakdown vehicle
DNF 708C	Originally H43/32F
LNA 166G	Originally H47/29D; converted by Greater Manchester PTE for use as 'Exhibus' exhibition vehicle - restored in this condition
NNB 547H	Mancunian
NNB 589H	Mancunian
ONF 865H	Mancunian
RNA 220J	Mancunian
PNF 941J	Exhibited at 1970 Commercial Motor Show as prototype SELNEC Standard
VNB 177L	Exhibited at 1972 Commercial Motor Show
VNB 203L	Originally H45/27D. Used as exhibition vehice.
VNB 132L	Converted to open top.
WBN 955L	Converted to open top.
PTD 640S	Rebodied 1983. Passed to GMPTE in 1981 as 6912.
OBN 502R	Passed to Greater Manchester PTE (6901) in 1981
XBU 1S	First GMT Leyand Fleetline Standard
BNC 960T	Last Park Royal Bodied Standard
GBU 1V	Greater Manchester's first Metrobus
NJA 568W	Exhibited at 1980 Commercial Motor Show. GM First Olympian
GNF 15V	Greater Manchester's last Titan
SND 455X	Seating reduced - converted to driver training vehicle
DWH 706W	Passed to Greater Manchester PTE (6990) in 1981. Greater Manchester's last Fleetline
ANA 1Y	Exhibited at 1982 Commercial Motor Show
A472 HNC	One of only 6 built
A765 NNA	Greater Manchester's last Atlantean
C751 YBA	Exhibited at 1984 Commercial Motor Show
D320 LNB	Greater Manchester's last Metrobus

Southampton & District Transport Heritage Trust

Contact address: 104 Oak Tree Road,, Southampton SO18 1PH
Affiliation: NARTM; WOMP
Brief description: The collection includes a selection of Southampton's fleet from the early 1970s. The small membership carries out restoration work. Several of the vehicles are privately owned by Trust members.

Registration	Date	Chassis	Body	New to	Fleet No	Status
FTR 511	1949	Guy Arab III	Park Royal O30/26R	Southampton Corporation	64	R
LOW 217	1954	Guy Arab III	Park Royal H30/26R	Southampton Corporation	71	R
JOW 928	1955	Guy Arab UF	Park Royal B39F	Southampton Corporation	255	RP
318 AOW	1962	AEC Regent V 2D3RA	Park Royal H37/29R	Southampton Corporation	318	RP
335 AOW	1963	Leyland Titan PD2A/27	Park Royal H37/29R	Southampton Corporation	335	RP
370 FCR	1963	AEC Regent V 2D3RA	East Lancs H37/29R	Southampton Corporation	350	R
BTR 361B	1964	AEC Regent V 2D3RA	East Lancs Neepsend H37/29R	Southampton Corporation	361	R
BOW 507C	1965	AEC Regent V 2D3RA	East Lancs Neepsend H37/29R	Southampton Corporation	371	RP
JOW 499E	1967	AEC Swift MP2R	Strachan B47D	Southampton Corporation	1	RP
KOW 909F	1967	AEC Regent V 3D2RA	East Lancs Neepsend H40/30R	Southampton Corporation	401	RP
KOW 910F	1967	AEC Regent V 3D2RA	East Lancs Neepsend H40/30R	Southampton Corporation	402	RP
PCG 888G	1968	AEC Reliance 6U3ZR	Plaxton C55F	Coliseum Coaches of Southampton		A
PCG 889G	1968	AEC Reliance 6MU3R	Plaxton C45F	Coliseum Coaches of Southampton		A
TTR 167H	1970	Leyland Atlantean PDR1A/1	East Lancs H45/31F	Southampton Corporation	133	RP
HNP 989J	1971	Leyland Atlantean PDR1A/1	East Lancs O45/31F	Southampton Corporation	139	RP
BCR 379K	1972	Seddon Pennine RU	Pennine B44F	Southampton Corporation	15	RP

Notes:
FTR 511	Converted to Open Top. Owned by Southampton City Museums.
LOW 217	Owned by Southampton City Museums.
JOW 928	Originally B36D
BOW 507C	Owned by Southampton City Museums.
PCG 888G	Originally C57F
HNP 989J	Preserved in Guide Friday livery. Originally registered WOW 531J.

Southdown Historic Vehicle Group

Contact address: 73 Cuckfield Crescent, Worthing, West Sussex
E-mail: pd3@btinternet.com
Website: http://home.fastnet.co.uk/gerrycork/worthingbusrally/worthingbusrally.htm
Brief description: A private collection of vehicles, most of which operated for Southdown Motor Services or which have south coast connections or have taken our fancy. The collection is not on public view but vehicles are rallied and often appear in service at running days.

Registration	Date	Chassis	Body	New to	Fleet No	Status
EHO 869	1943	Guy Arab II	Reading CO30/26R	Gosport & Fareham Omnibus Co	57	RP
GUF 191	1945	Guy Arab II	Northern Counties O30/26R	Southdown Motor Services	451	A
XUF 141	1960	Leyland Tiger Cub PSUC1/2	Weymann C41F	Southdown Motor Services	1141	R
70 AUF	1962	Commer Avenger IV	Harrington C—F	Southdown Motor Services	70	A
416 DCD	1964	Leyland Titan PD3/4	Northern Counties FCO39/30F	Southdown Motor Services	416	R
419 DCD	1964	Leyland Titan PD3/4	Northern Counties FCO39/30F	Southdown Motor Services	419	R
972 CUF	1964	Leyland Titan PD3/4	Northern Counties FH39/30F	Southdown Motor Services	972	RP
AOR 158B	1964	Leyland Titan PD3/4	Northern Counties FCO39/30F	Southdown Motor Services	412	R
PRX 187B	1964	Leyland Titan PD3/4	Northern Counties FCO39/30F	Southdown Motor Services	415	RP
PRX 200B	1964	Leyland Titan PD3/4	Northern Counties FCO39/30F	Southdown Motor Services	418	R
PRX 206B	1964	Leyland Titan PD3/4	Northern Counties FCO39/30F	Southdown Motor Services	401	R

Registration	Date	Chassis	Body	New to	Fleet No	Status
BUF 122C	1965	Leyland Leopard PSU3/1RT	Marshall B45F	Southdown Motor Services	122	RP
BUF 260C	1965	Leyland Titan PD3/4	Northern Counties FC39/30F	Southdown Motor Services	260	R
BUF 277C	1965	Leyland Titan PD3/4	Northern Counties FC39/30F	Southdown Motor Services	277	R
BUF 426C	1965	Leyland Titan PD3/4	Northern Counties FCO39/30F	Southdown Motor Services	426	R
BJK 672D	1966	Leyland Titan PD2A/30	East Lancs H32/28R	Eastbourne Corporation	72	RP
FCD 294D	1966	Leyland Titan PD3/4	Northern Counties FH39/29F	Southdown Motor Services	294	R
DHC 784E	1967	Leyland Titan PD2A/30	East Lancs O32/28R	Eastbourne Corporation	84	R
KUF 199F	1968	Leyland Leopard PSU3/1RT	Willowbrook B45F	Southdown Motor Services	199	R
LFS 296F	1968	Bristol VRT/LL/6G	ECW O41/36F	Scottish Omnibuses (Eastern Scottish)	AA296	R
SYK 569F	1968	Leyland Leopard PSU4/4R	Duple C41F	Grey Green Coaches of London		A
PUF 165H	1969	Leyland Leopard PSU3/1RT	Northern Counties DP49F	Southdown Motor Services	465	R
TCD 374J	1970	Daimler Fleetline CRG6LX	Northern Counties H-/-F	Southdown Motor Services	374	RP
TCD 383J	1970	Daimler Fleetline CRG6LX	Northern Counties H-/-F	Southdown Motor Services	383	RP
TCD 490J	1970	Bristol RESL6L	Marshall B45F	Southdown Motor Services	490	RP
BHH 83J	1971	Leyland Leopard PSU3B/4RT	Plaxton C47F	Southdown Motor Services	1835	RP
UUF 116J	1971	Bristol VRTSL6LX	ECW PO-/-F	Southdown Motor Services	516	RP
UUF 328J	1971	Leyland Leopard PSU3B/4RT	Plaxton C53F	Southdown Motor Services	1828	R
SCD 731N	1974	Leyland Atlantean AN68/1R	Park Royal - Roe H43/30F	Southdown Motor Services	731	R
RUF 37R	1977	Leyland National 11351A/2R	Leyland National B44D	Southdown Motor Services	37	R
ANJ 306T	1978	Leyland Leopard PSU3E/4RT	Plaxton C53F	Southdown Motor Services	1306	A
HNP 154S	1978	Leyland Atlantean AN68A/1R	East Lancs O43/31F	Brighton Corporation	3	R
TYJ 4S	1978	Leyland Atlantean AN68A/1R	East Lancs H43/31F	Brighton Corporation	4	R
KAZ 6703	1979	Leyland Leopard PSU5C/4R	Duple C53F	Southdown Motor Services	1339	RP
OPV 821	1979	Leyland Leopard PSU3E/4RT	Plaxton C48F	Southdown Motor Services	1321	RP
USV 324	1979	Leyland Leopard PSU3E/4RT	Plaxton C48F	Southdown Motor Services	1320	RP
MAP 340W	1981	Leyland Leopard PSU3F/4R	Plaxton C48F	Southdown Motor Services	1340	R

Notes:

EHO 869	Rebodied in 1953		UUF 116J	Originally H39/31F
PRX 206B	Originally registered 401 DCD		BHH 83J	Originally registered UUF 335J
AOR 158B	Originally registered 412 DCD		HNP 154S	Originally H43/31F registered TYJ 3S
PRX 187B	Originally registered 415 DCD		USV 324	Originally registered BYJ 920T
PRX 200B	Originally registered 418 DCD		OPV 821	Originally registered EAP 921V
LFS 296F	Originally H47/32F.		KAZ 6703	Originally registered EAP 939V

Telford Bus Group

Contact address: 65 Sandbach Road, Rode Heath, Cheshire, ST7 3RW
Brief description: The Telford Bus Group has a collection of privately-owned buses and coaches in various parts of England.
The Group has become known for its Bedford VALs of which 12 examples are preserved, with examples of several body types. Other vehicles include Daimler Fleetline 'Mancunian', Seddon Pennine VI, Commer Avenger and Leyland Leopard 'Midland Red S27 type'.
Not all vehicles are restored and some are long term projects.

Registration	Date	Chassis	Body	New to	Fleet No	Status
386 DD	1961	Bedford J2	Plaxton C20F	Talbott of Moreton-in-Marsh		RP
3190 UN	1962	Commer Avenger IV	Plaxton C41F	Wright of Penycae		RP
9797 DP	1964	Bedford VAL 14	Duple C52F	Smiths of Reading		RP
EHL 472D	1966	Bedford VAL 14	Plaxton C52F	West Riding Automobile Co	3	R
JTH 100F	1968	Bedford VAM 14	Duple C45F	Davies of Pencader		RP
UWX 981F	1968	Bedford VAL 70	Plaxton C52F	Mosley of Barugh Green		R
RBC 345G	1969	Bedford VAL 70	Duple C52F	Cook of Dunstable		RP
WWY 115G	1969	Bedford VAL 70	Plaxton C53F	Abbey Coachways of Selby		R
FYG 663J	1970	Bedford VAL 70	Willowbrook B56F	Wigmore of Dinnington		RP

Registration	Date	Chassis	Body	New to	Fleet No	Status
VBD 310H	1970	Bedford VAL 70	Plaxton C48F	Coales of Woolaston		R
BHO 670J	1971	Bedford VAL 70	Duple C53F	Castle Coaches of Waterlooville		R
RAR 690J	1971	Bedford VAL 70	Van Hool C51F	All Seasons of London		R
RNA 236J	1971	Daimler Fleetline CRG6LXB-33	Park Royal H47/29D	SELNEC PTE	2236	A
CDC 166K	1972	Seddon Pennine VI	Plaxton C45F	Bob's of Middlesbrough	26	RP
CDC 168K	1972	Seddon Pennine VI	Plaxton C41F	Bob's of Middlesbrough	28	RP
FAR 724K	1972	Bedford VAL 70	Duple C53F	Langley Coaches of Slough		A
JHA 227L	1973	Leyland Leopard PSU3B/2R	Marshall DP49F	Midland Red Omnibus Co	227	RP

Notes:
RNA 236J   Mancunian

TH Collection

Contact Information: Telephone 01263 834829
E-mail: nick@topolino.demon.co.uk
Affiliation: NARTM
Brief Description: A private collection representing coachwork built by Thomas Harrington of Hove. It is believed the vehicles are now all unique examples of the chassis and body combination.
Opening days/times: The collection is not on public view and all vehicles are at varying stages of restoration. Arrangements to visit can be made, strictly by appointment, telephoning first for details.

Registration	Date	Chassis	Body	New to	Fleet No	Status
KD 5296	1928	Leyland Tiger TS2	Harrington C31F	Imperial Motor Services of Liverpool		A
VRF 372	1951	Foden PVRF6	Harrington C41C	Bassett's Coaches of Tittensor		RP
JAP 698	1954	Harrington Contender	Harrington C41C	Audawn Coaches of Corringham		RP
YYB 118	1957	Dennis Lancet UF	Harrington B42F	Hutchings & Cornelius Services of South Petherton		A
PFR 747	1959	Bedford SB3	Harrington C41F	Abbotts of Blackpool		A

Notes:
JAP 698   Former Harrington demonstrator

Three Counties Bus and Commercial Vehicle Museum

Contact address: 83 Millwright Way, Flitwick, Beds MK45 1BQ
Phone: 01525 712091
E-mail: nick.doolan@btopenworld.com
Web site: www.3cbcvm.org.uk
Affiliation: NARTM
Brief description: Established to provide a focus for the preservation, and historical record of buses in Bedfordshire, Buckinghamshire and Hertfordshire. Seeks to ensure a long-term future for the vehicles.
Events planned: Please see enthusiast press for planned Operating Days. Operational vehicles frequently attend local rallies

Registration	Date	Chassis	Body	New to	Fleet No	Status
FXT 122	1939	Leyland Cub REC	LPTB B20F	London Transport	CR 16	RP
DBL 154	1946	Bristol K6A	ECW L27/28R	Thames Valley Traction Co	446	R
CFN 104	1947	Leyland Tiger PS1/1	Park Royal C32R	East Kent Road Car Co		R

Registration	Date	Chassis	Body	New to	Fleet No	Status
JWU 307	1950	Bedford OB	Duple C29F	Lunn of Rothwell		RP
LYR 915	1952	AEC Regent III O961 RT	Weymann H30/26R	London Transport	RT 3496	R
MXX 434	1952	AEC Regal IV 9821LT RF	Metro Cammell B39F	London Transport	RF 457	R
MXX 332	1953	Guy Special NLLVP	ECW B26F	London Transport	GS 32	R
MXX 489	1953	AEC Regal IV 9821LT RF	Metro Cammell B39F	London Transport	RF 512	RP
RSJ 747	1956	Albion Victor FT39AN	Heaver C27F	Guernsey Motor Co	69	R
VYO 767	1959	Bristol MW6G	ECW C41F	Tilling		RP
OVL 473	1960	Bristol Lodekka FS5G	ECW H33/27RD	Lincolnshire Road Car Co	2378	R
EFM 631C	1965	Bristol Lodekka FS6G	ECW H33/27RD	Crosville Motor Services	DFG182	R
DEK 3D	1966	Leyland Titan PD2/37	Massey H37/27F	Wigan Corporation	140	R
KBD 712D	1966	Bristol Lodekka FS6G	ECW H33/27RD	United Counties Omnibus Co	712	R
KBD 715D	1966	Bristol Lodekka FS6G	ECW H60RD	United Counties Omnibus Co	715	RP
NBD 311F	1967	Bristol RELL6G	ECW B53F	United Counties Omnibus Co	311	RP
RBD 319G	1968	Bristol RELL6G	ECW B53F	United Counties Omnibus Co	319	RP
UXD 129G	1968	Bristol RELL6L	ECW B48D	Luton Corporation	129	RP
UBD 757H	1969	Bristol VRTSL6LX	ECW H39/31F	United Counties Omnibus Co	757	A
VLW 444G	1969	AEC Merlin 4P2R	MCW B25D	London Transport	MBS 444	A
VMO 234H	1969	Bristol LH6L	ECW B41F	Thames Valley Traction Co	214	RP
ANV 775J	1971	Bristol VRTSL2/6G	ECW H39/31F	United Counties Omnibus Co	775	R
WRP 767J	1971	Bristol VRTSL6G	ECW H39/31F	United Counties Omnibus Co	767	RP
JPL 153K	1972	Leyland Atlantean PDR1A/1	Park Royal H43/29D	London Country Bus Services	AN53	RP
GPD 313N	1974	Bristol LHS6L	ECW B35F	London Country Bus Services	BN45	RP
RBD 111M	1974	Bedford YRT	Willowbrook B53F	United Counties Omnibus Co	111	A
UPE 203M	1974	Leyland National 10351/1R	Leyland National B41F	London Country Bus Services	SNB 103	A
HPF 318N	1975	Leyland National 10351/1R/SC	Leyland National DP39F	London Country Bus Services	SNC 168	R
SBD 525R	1977	Leyland National 11351A/1R	Leyland National B49F	United Counties Omnibus Co	525	RP
SOA 674S	1977	Leyland Leopard PSU3E/4R	Plaxton C49F	Midland Red Omnibus Co	674	R
UPB 312S	1977	Leyland National 10351A/1R	Leyland National B41F	London Country Bus Services	SNB 312	R
GCK 279S	1978	Bedford YLQ	Plaxton C46F	Battersbys Silver Grey Coaches		RP
XPK 51T	1978	AEC Reliance 6U2R	Duple C53F	London Country Bus Services	RB51	R
BPL 469T	1979	Leyland National 10351B/1R	Leyland National B41F	London Country Bus Services	SNB 469	RP
EPM 134V	1979	AEC Reliance 6U2R	Duple C49F	London Country Bus Services	RB 134	A
SVV 587W	1980	Leyland National 2 NL116L11/1R	Leyland National II B49F	United Counties Omnibus Co	587	R
GUW 443W	1981	Leyland National 2 NL106AL11/2R	East Lancs National Greenway B25D	London Transport	GLS 443	A
GUW 444W	1981	Leyland National 2 NL106AL11/2R	Leyland National II DP43F	London Transport	LS 444	RP
TPD 109X	1982	Leyland Olympian ONTL11/1R	Roe H43/29F	London Country Bus Services	LR 9	A
C24 NVV	1985	Ford Transit	Carlyle B16F	United Counties Omnibus Co	24	A

Notes:
RSJ 747   Original Guernsey registration was 1529

Wealdstone & District Vintage Vehicle Collection

Contact address: 91 Graham Road, Wealdstone, Middx HA3 5RE
E-mail: oldbusgarage@sftt.co.uk
Web site: www.sftt.co.uk/busgarage
Affiliation: NARTM
Brief description: A small collection of mainly London buses from the 1950s, examples of which regularly attend rallies. Anyone wishing to visit or assist with the vehicles is welcome. Please write to the address given.

Registration	Date	Chassis	Body	New to	Fleet No	Status
DL 9706	1935	Dennis Lancet	ECW B36R	Southern Vectis Omnibus Co	516	RP
KYY 622	1950	AEC Regent III O961 RT	Park Royal H30/26R	London Transport	RT 1784	R
MLL 817	1952	AEC Regal IV 9821LT RF	Metro Cammell B37F	London Transport	RF 280	R

Registration	Date	Chassis	Body	New to	Fleet No	Status
MXX 410	1953	AEC Regal IV 9821LT RF	Metro Cammell B41F	London Transport	RF 433	R
MXX 430	1953	AEC Regal IV 9821LT RF	Metro Cammell B39F	London Transport	RF 453	R
NLE 939	1953	AEC Regent III O961 RT	Park Royal H30/26R	London Transport	RT 4275	RP

Notes:
DL 9706   Rebodied 1944

The West Country Historic Omnibus & Transport Trust

Contact address: The Secretary, 33 Broad View, Broadclyst, Exeter EX5 3HA
Web site: www.busmuseum.org.uk
Affiliation: NARTM
Brief description: An Historic Bus, Coach and Lorry Rally is held annually on the third Sunday in September at the Westpoint Showground, Clyst St Mary, near Exeter (junction 30, M5). The Trust plans to establish a museum and archive of West Country commercial road transport at this location in the near future.

Registration	Date	Chassis	Body	New to	Fleet No	Status
TDV 217J	1970	Leyland Panther PSUR1B/1R	Marshall B—D	Devon General	217	R
AFJ 727T	1979	Bristol LH6L	Plaxton C41F	Western National Omnibus Co	3307	RP
AFJ 764T	1979	Bristol VRT/SL3/6LXB	ECW H43/31F	Western National Omnibus Co	115	RP
A927 MDV	1983	Ford Transit 160D	Carlyle B16F	Devon General	7	R
C801 FRL	1985	Mercedes L608D	Reeve Burgess B20F	Western National Ltd	104	RP
L929 CTT	1994	Iveco 59-12	Mellor B21D	Devon General	1000	R
M627 HDV	1994	Iveco	Wadham Stringer B21D	Devon General	1029	A

Notes:
TDV217J   Ordered by Exeter City Transport. Prev B47D. Converted to publicity vehicle in 1980.

West Midlands Bus Preservation Society

Contact address: Secretary, 22 Beaumont Way, Norton Canes, Cannock WS11 9FQ
Brief description: The main core of the collection is of vehicles from the West Midlands PTE in the period 1969 to 1986. Other artefacts are being collected for inclusion in a planned transport museum.
Opening days/times: Vehicles can be viewed by special arrangement, contact secretary.

Registration	Date	Chassis	Body	New to	Fleet No	Status
DUK 278	1946	Guy Arab II 5LW	Roe H31/25R	Wolverhampton Corporation	378	RP
UHY 362	1955	Bristol KSW6B	ECW H32/28R	Bristol Tramways	8322	R
436 KOV	1964	Daimler Fleetline CRG6LX	Park Royal H43/33F	Birmingham City Transport	3436	A
NOV 880G	1969	Daimler Fleetline CRG6LX	Park Royal H43/29D	Birmingham City Transport	3880	RP
TOB 997H	1970	Daimler Fleetline CRG6LX-33	Park Royal H47/33D	West Midlands PTE	3997	A
JOV 738P	1976	Volvo Ailsa B55-10	Alexander H44/35F	West Midlands PTE	4738	R
JOV 741P	1976	Volvo Ailsa B55-10	Alexander H44/35F	West Midlands PTE	4741	A
NOC 600R	1976	Leyland Fleetline FE30AGR	Park Royal H43/33F	West Midlands PTE	6600	A
TRR 814R	1977	Volvo Ailsa B55-20	Alexander H43/34F	Derby	71	R
WDA 835T	1978	MCW Metrobus DR102/1	MCW H43/30F	West Midlands PTE	6835	RP
WDA 956T	1979	Leyland Fleetline FE30AGR	MCW B37F	West Midlands PTE	1956	A

Notes:

DUK 278	Body built 1952	WDA 835T	Exhibited at 1978 Commercial Motor Show
TOB 997H	Gardner 6LXB engine fitted after acquisition by C J Partridge & Son of Hadleigh	WDA 956T	Originally double deck bus (H43/33F) 6956; rebuilt as single-decker in 1994
TRR 814R	Originally registered RTO 1R		

West of England Transport Collection

Contact address: 15 Land Park, Chulmleigh, Devon, EX18 7BH
Affiliation: NARTM
Brief description: A large private collection of vehicles, mainly from West Country major operators. The collection includes buses, coaches and transport memorabilia.
Events planned: 2 October 2005 — Annual WETC Open Day
Opening days/times: Viewing at other times by prior arrangement with C. T. Shears, tel: 01769 580811.

Registration	Date	Chassis	Body	New to	Fleet No	Status
UO 2331	1927	Austin 20 5PL	Tiverton B13F	Sidmouth Motor Co		A
JY 124	1932	Tilling Stevens B10A2 Express	Beadle B—R	Western National Omnibus Co	3379	RP
OD 5489	1933	Vauxhall Cadet VY	Mount Pleasant B7	Davis of Rockbeare		R
OD 5868	1933	Leyland Lion LT5	Weymann B31F	Devon General	68	A
OD 7500	1934	AEC Regent O661	Brush H30/26R	Devon General	DR213	R
ADV 128	1935	Bristol JO5G	Beadle B—R	Western National Omnibus Co	222	RP
ATT 922	1935	Bristol JJW6A	Beadle B35R	Western National Omnibus Co	172	RP
AUO 74	1935	Leyland Lion LT5A	(chassis only) -	Devon General	SL79	A
FV 5737	1936	Leyland Tiger TS7	Duple C31F	Ribble Motor Services	753	R
ADR 813	1938	Leyland Titan TD5c	Leyland L27/26R	Plymouth Corporation	141	R
BOW 169	1938	Bristol L5G	-	Hants & Dorset Motor Services	TS676	A
EFJ 241	1938	Leyland Titan TD5	Leyland H30/26R	Exeter Corporation	26	A
EFJ 666	1938	Leyland Tiger TS8	Cravens B32R	Exeter Corporation	66	R
ETT 946	1938	Bristol L5G	Beadle B36R	Southern National Omnibus Co	280	A
DOD 474	1940	AEC Regal O662	Weymann B35F	Devon General	SR474	RP
GTA 395	1941	Bristol LL5G	Brislington Body Works B39R	Southern National Omnibus Co	373	RP
DDR 414	1947	Leyland Titan PD1	Weymann L27/26R	Plymouth Corporation	114	R
KHU 624	1947	Bristol K6	ECW H30/26R	Bristol Omnibus Co	3705	A
GLJ 957	1948	Leyland Titan PD1A	ECW L27/26R	Hants & Dorset Motor Services	PD959	A
JFJ 606	1949	Daimler CVD6	Brush H30/26R	Exeter Corporation	43	R
LTV 702	1951	AEC Regal III	East Lancs B35R	Nottingham City Transport	702	R
WRL 16	1956	Rowe Hillmaster	Reading B42F	Millbrook Steamboat & Trading Co		A
VDV 817	1957	AEC Regent V MD3RV	Metro Cammell H33/26R	Devon General	DR817	R
974 AFJ	1960	Guy Arab IV	Massey H31/26R	Exeter Corporation	74	R
484 EFJ	1962	Leyland Titan PD2A/30	Massey H31/26R	Exeter City Transport	84	A
373 FCR	1963	AEC Regent V	East Lancs H-/-R	Southampton Corporation	353	A
532 DWW	1963	Bedford SB5	Plaxton C41F	Barnsley British Co-op		A
815 KDV	1963	Bristol Lodekka FLF6B	ECW H38/30F	Western National Omnibus Co	2010	A
991 MDV	1963	AEC Reliance 2MU3RV	Marshall B41F	Devon General	991	A
CTT 513C	1965	AEC Regent V 2D3RA	Park Royal H40/29F	Devon General	513	R
EDG 250L	1972	Leyland Leopard PSU3B/4R	Plaxton C51F	Castleways of Winchcombe		R
VOD 88K	1972	Bristol LHS6L	Marshall B33F	Western National Omnibus Co	88	A
OAE 957M	1973	Bristol RELL6L	ECW B—F	Bristol Omnibus Co	1335	A
31909	1975	Bristol LH6L	Plaxton C45F	Greenslades Tours	318	A
GNM 235N	1975	Bristol LHL6L	Plaxton C51F	Caroline Seagull of Great Yarmouth		R
JFJ 500N	1975	Bristol LH6L	Plaxton C45F	Greenslades Tours	320	A
KTT 42P	1975	Bristol LH6L	ECW B43F	Western National Omnibus Co	112	A
MUN 942R	1976	AEC Reliance 6U3ZR	Plaxton C51F	Geen of South Molton		A
MPX 945R	1977	Ford Transit	Robin Hood C-F	Angela of Bursledon		A

Registration	Date	Chassis	Body	New to	Fleet No	Status
RUF 40R	1977	Leyland National 11351/2R	Leyland National B23D	Southdown Motor Services	40	R
UPB 308S	1977	Leyland National 11351A/1R	Leyland National B41F	London Country Bus Services	SNB 308	A
UPB 309S	1977	Leyland National 11351A/1R	Leyland National B41F	London Country Bus Services	SNB 309	A
CRM 927T	1979	Leyland/DAB	Leyland B64T	South Yorkshire PTE	2006	A
Q995 CPE	1979	AEC Regent III O961 RT	Park Royal O30/26R	London Transport	RT 4588	A
DBV 32W	1980	Bristol VRTSL/3/6LXB	ECW H43/31F	Ribble	2032	R
DBV 43W	1980	Leyland Leopard PSU4E/4R	East Lancs B47F	Burnley and Pendle	43	A
LFJ 862W	1980	Bristol VRTSL3/6LXB	ECW	Western National Omnibus Co	1215	RP
RLN 237W	1981	Leyland-DAB 6-35-690/4	Roe AB—T	British Airways	C310	A
A749 NTA	1984	Ford Transit	Ford	Devon County Council		A
C748 FFJ	1985	Ford Transit 190D	Carlyle B16F	Devon General Ltd	748	A
C671 FFJ	1986	Ford Transit	Carlyle B16F	Devon General Ltd	671	RP

Notes:

UO 2331	Body new 1940	EFJ 666	Used as a snow plough 1952-6
JY 124	New body and engine fitted in 1947	EFJ 241	Converted to tree-cutter in 1958
OD 5489	Body fitted 1946	ADR 813	Rebodied 1953. Originally torque convertor. Now with crash gearbox.
OD 7500	Rebodied 1949		
ATT 922	Rebodied in the late 1940s	GTA 395	Lengthened and rebodied in 1954
ADV 128	Rebodied 1950	CTT 513C	Restored by the Oxford Bus Museum Trust
AUO 74	Front end of chassis only	31909	Original registration JFJ 498N
FV 5737	Rebodied 1950	RUF 40R	Exhibition vehicle. Originally B44D.
ETT 946	Rebodied 1950	Q995 CPE	Original registration NLP 581
BOW 169	New with Beadle body; acquired by Wilts & Dorset Motor Services (505) in 1952 and converted to breakdown vehicle in 1956	CRM 927T	Articulated prototype (57 ft long)
		RLN 237W	Front portion converted to playbus
		A749 NTA	Fitted with tail lift for wheelchairs

The West of England Transport Collection's Winkleigh base is home to a number of restored and unrestored vehicles. Awaiting attention there is Willowbrook-bodied AEC Reliance saloon Western Welsh 1287 (WKG 287), which is listed here as part of the Quantock Heritage fleet. *Philip Lamb*

Westgate Museum

Contact address: Enquiries: 14 Ilkley Road, Caversham, Reading RG4 7BD
Brief description: The collection, near Doncaster, is housed in a
former Methodist Chapel built in 1865. The vehicles operate at the Trolleybus Museum at Sandtoft from time to time.
Opening days/times: Viewing strictly by appointment.

Registration	Date	Chassis	Body	New to	Fleet No	Status
RC 8472+	1944	Sunbeam W	Weymann UH30/26R	Derby Corporation	172	R
RC 8575+	1945	Sunbeam W	Park Royal UH30/26R	Derby Corporation	175	RP
SVS 281	1945	Daimler CWA6	Duple UH30/26R	Douglas Corporation	52	R
DRD 130+	1949	BUT 9611T	Park Royal H33/26RD	Reading Corporation	144	R
LDP 945	1955	AEC Regent III 6812A	Park Royal L31/26RD	Reading Corporation	98	R
WLT 529	1960	AEC Routemaster R2RH	Park Royal H36/28R	London Transport	RM 529	R

+ Trolleybus

Notes:
RC 8472   On display at Sandtoft Transport Centre
SVS 281   Originally registered FMN 955.

Workington Heritage Transport Trust

Contact Information: 22 Calva Road, Seaton, Workington, Cumbria, CA14 1DF
Telephone: 01900 67389
E-mail: wthc@btopenworld.com
Affiliation: NARTM, Transport Trust
Brief Description: A collection based around buses and rail vehicles from the West Cumberland area. It is the aim to open to the public once a suitable building and funding have been arranged.
Events planned: 1 January 2005 and 29 May 2005, free bus services in Workington. 25/26 June 2005 Free bus service and rally in connection with the Whitehaven Maritime Festival.

Registration	Date	Chassis	Body	New to	Fleet No	Status
109 DRM	1961	Bristol Lodekka FS6G	ECW H33/27RD	Cumberland Motor Services	550	
AAO 34B	1964	Bristol MW6G	ECW B45F	Cumberland Motor Services	231	
KHH 378W	1980	Leyland National 116L11/1R	Leyland National B52F	Cumberland Motor Services	378	R

Notes:
KHH 378W   Restored to post-NBC CMS Cumberland Livery

Above: **Former London Country Leyland Nationals SNC168 and SNB312 are both part of the Three Counties Bus Museum collection. They are seen here in St Albans.** *Philip Lamb*

Left: **A slightly later vehicle in the Three Counties Bus Museum collection is beautifully presented London Country (Green Line) RB51, a Duple Dominant-bodied AEC Reliance.** *Philip Lamb*

Right: **Under restoration and moved to Wythall for Midland Red's centenary celebrations last year is Colin Hawketts' Utility Guy Arab II Midland Red 2574 (HHA 26). Bodywork is by Weymann.** *Philip Lamb*

Part 3

Privately Preserved Buses

This section is included with the help and co-operation of the British Bus Preservation Group (BBPG). There are known to be many excellent privately preserved buses, coaches and some trolleybuses in this country and the list which follows is prepared from data provided by the Group. All the vehicles are owned by BBPG members and every effort has been made to ensure that the information given is correct at the time of going to press.

Condition of the vehicles varies, some having been fully restored (even to public operational standard in some cases); others are undergoing restoration, often a lengthy job with limited resources; some awaiting their turn for the day when the restoration task can be started. Those vehicles which are restored generally make visits to bus rallies up and down the country and details of such events can be found in the bus enthusiast magazines, regularly published.

If you are the owner of a preserved bus, coach or trolleybus which is not listed, you may wish to become a member of the BBPG. Services to their members include a regular Newsletter 'British Bus News', the chance to contact others with similar interests and the ability to share information on vehicle restoration problems, projects and, of course, sources of spare parts. Membership costs is £13 per annum and the BBPG may be contacted at the address below.

British Bus Preservation Group

Contact address: BBPG, 6 Pine Close, Billinghurst, RH14 9NL.
E-mail: info@bbpg.co.uk
Web site: www.bbpg.co.uk
Affiliation: NARTM

Registration	Date	Chassis	Body	New to	Fleet No	Status
DB 5221	1929	Tilling Stevens B10A		North Western Road Car Co		A
FM 6397	1931	Leyland Titan TD1	Leyland L51R	Crosville Motor Services	45	RP
FM 6435	1931	Leyland Lion LT2	Leyland B32F	Crosville Motor Services	L7	RP
MV 8996	1931	Bedford WLB	Duple B20F	Howards of West Byfleet		R
BU 7108	1932	Leyland Titan TD2	Massey H-/-R	Oldham Corporation	69	RP
FM 7443	1932	Leyland Cub KP2	Brush B20F	Crosville Motor Services	716	RP
AOG 638	1934	Daimler COG5		Birmingham City Transport	51	RP
AUF 670	1934	Leyland Titan TD3	East Lancs H26/26R	Southdown Motor Services	970	R
DL 9015	1934	Dennis Ace	Harrington B20F	Southern Vectis Omnibus Co	405	RP
JA 5506	1935	Dennis Lancet	Eastern Counties B31R	North Western Road Car Co	706	RP
CCD 940	1936	Leyland Titan TD4	East Lancs H28/26R	Southdown Motor Services	140	A
FM 9984	1936	Leyland Tiger TS7	Harrington C32F	Crosville Motor Services	K101	RP
JA 5528	1936	Bristol JO5G	Brush B31R	North Western Road Car Co	728	RP
BFM 144	1937	Leyland Tiger TS7	ECW B32F	Crosville Motor Services	KA27	R
EUF 181	1938	Leyland Titan TD5		Southdown Motor Services	0181	RP
FHT 112	1938	Bristol K5G	ECW O30/26R	Bristol Tramways	C3209	RP
JA 7770	1938	Bristol L5G	Burlingham B35R	North Western Road Car Co	346	RP
FUF 181	1939	Dennis Falcon	Harrington B30C	Southdown Motor Services	81	A
JK 8418	1939	Leyland Lion LT9	Leyland B32F	Eastbourne Corporation	12	R
DDL 50	1940	Bristol K5G	ECW O30/26R	Southern Vectis Omnibus Co	703	R
EFM 581	1940	Leyland Tiger TS8	ECW B32F	Crosville Motor Services	KA158	RP
EVC 244	1940	Daimler COG5/40	Park Royal B38F	Coventry City Transport	244	R
FNY 933	1944	Bristol K6A	Park Royal H30/26R	Pontypridd UDC	40	RP
HHA 26	1945	Guy Arab II	Weymann UH30/26R	BMMO ('Midland Red')	2574	RP
HKE 867	1945	Bristol K6A	Weymann H30/26R	Maidstone & District Motor Services	DH159	R
HKL 826	1946	AEC Regal I O662	Beadle OB35F	Maidstone & District Motor Services	OR2	R
ACH 627	1947	Daimler CVD6	Brush H30/26R	Derby Corporation	27	RP
ANH 154	1947	Daimler CVG6	Northern Coachbuilders H30/26R	Northampton Corporation	154	R
GOE 486	1947	Daimler CVA6	MCW H30/24R	Birmingham City Transport	1486	R
HLW 214	1947	AEC Regent III O961 RT	Park Royal H30/26RD	London Transport	RT 227	R
HTC 661	1947	Bedford OB	Scottish Motor Traction C29F	Dean & Pounder of Morecombe		R
JDV 754	1947	Bedford OB	Duple C29F	Woolacombe & Mortehoe		R
JXN 46	1948	AEC Regent III O961 RT	Weymann H30/26R	London Transport	RT 1018	R
KHA 311	1948	BMMO C1	Duple C30C	BMMO ('Midland Red')	3311	R
KNN 254	1948	Leyland Titan PD1A	Duple L29/26F	Barton Transport of Chilwell	580	RP

108

Registration	Date	Chassis	Body	New to	Fleet No	Status
JXC 194	1949	AEC Regent III O961 RT	Cravens H30/26R	London Transport	RT 1431	RP
KGK 758	1949	AEC Regent III O961 RT	Cravens H30/26R	London Transport	RT 1499	RP
LFM 320	1949	Leyland Tiger PS1/1	Weymann B35F	Crosville Motor Services	KA244	R
LUC 250	1949	Leyland Titan 7RT	(chassis only)	London Transport	RTL 1073	RP
HWY 36	1950	Leyland Titan PD2/1	Leyland L27/26R	Todmorden Joint Omnibus Committee	18	RP
JOJ 231	1950	Leyland Tiger PS2	Weymann B34F	Birmingham City Transport	2231	R
JOJ 827	1950	Daimler CVG6	Crossley H30/25R	Birmingham City Transport	2827	RP
JXX 487	1950	Bedford OB	Duple B30F	Ministry of Supply		A
KEL 405	1950	Bristol LL6B	ECW FB37F	Hants & Dorset Motor Services	677	R
KYY 529	1950	AEC Regent III O961 RT	Park Royal H30/26RD	London Transport	RT 1702	R
KYY 615	1950	AEC Regent III O961 RT	Park Royal H30/26R	London Transport	RT 1777	RP
KYY 647	1950	Leyland Titan 7RT	Park Royal F H60F	London Transport	RTL 1004	R
FFN 446	1951	Leyland/Beadle Titan TD5	Beadle C35F	East Kent Road Car Co		RP
HDL 280	1951	Bristol LL5G	ECW B39R	Southern Vectis Omnibus Co	39	RP
JOJ 207	1951	Daimler CVD6		Birmingham City Transport	2707	RP
LUC 381	1951	AEC Regal IV 9821E	ECW C39F	London Transport	RFW 6	RP
LYF 104	1951	Leyland Titan 7RT	Park Royal H30/26R	London Transport	RTL 1163	R
MFM 39	1951	Bedford OB	Duple C29F	Crosville Motor Services	SL71	A
RSK 615	1951	Leyland Royal Tiger PSU1/15	Duple DP41F	Jackson of Castle Bromwich		A
URE 281	1951	AEC Regal III	Harrington FC33F	Lymers of Tean		A
LTX 311	1952	Leyland Tiger PS2/5	Massey B35F	Caerphilly Corporation	1	RP
MLL 555	1952	AEC Regal IV 9821LT RF	Metro Cammell B37F	London Transport	RF 168	RP
MLL 722	1952	AEC Regal IV 9822E	Park Royal RDP—C	British European Airways	1080	A
NLE 534	1952	AEC Regal IV 9821LT RF	Metro Cammell B39F	London Transport	RF 534	R
JDL 40	1953	Bristol KSW5G	ECW L-/-RD	Southern Vectis Omnibus Co	766	A
LWR 424	1953	Bristol KSW6G	ECW -	West Yorkshire Road Car Co	4044	R
MXX 283	1953	AEC Regal IV 9821 LT RF	Metro Cammell B41F	London Transport	RF 395	RP
MXX 292	1953	AEC Regal IV 9821 LT RF	Metro Cammell	London Transport	RF 404	RP
MXX 421	1953	AEC Regal IV 9821 LT RF	Metro Cammell R39F	London Transport	RF 444	R
NLE 673	1953	AEC Regal IV 9821LT RF	Metro Cammell B39F	London Transport	RF 673	R
NXL 847	1953	AEC Regal III	Duple C39F	Eastern Belle of Bow		R
note ab	1954	GMC PD4501 Scenicruiser	GMC RC43F	Greyhound	T-902	RP
RAL 795	1954	Daimler CVG6	Massey H33/28RD	Gash of Newark	DD10	RP
395 DEL	1955	Albion Victor	Heaver B35F	Guernsey Motor Co	71	RP
EXL 892	1955	Guy Arab	Northern Counties	Middlesborough Corporation		RP
JVH 381	1955	AEC Regent III 9613E	East Lancs H35/28R	Huddersfield Corporation	181	A
MDL 954	1956	Bristol Lodekka LD6G	ECW O33/27R	Southern Vectis Omnibus Co	544	R
WUA 832	1956	AEC Regent V MD2RA	Roe H33/27R	Leeds City Transport	832	RP
466 DHN	1957	Guy Arab IV	Roe H33/28R	Darlington Corporation	66	RP
LSV 748	1957	Albion Victor FT39AN	Heaver B31F	Guernsey Motor Co	73	RP
XCV 326	1957	Bedford SBG	Duple B42F	Harper & Kellow of St. Agnes		A
390 DKK	1958	AEC Reliance 2MU3RV	Harrington DP40F	Maidstone & District Motor Services	CO390	RP
875 DTB	1958	Guy Arab IV	Northern Counties H41/32R	Lancashire United Transport	608	A
VFJ 995	1958	Leyland Titan PD2/40	Weymann H31/26R	Exeter Corporation	60	R
120 JRB	1959	Daimler Freeline D650HS	Burlingham C37F	Tailby & George ('Blue Bus Services') Willington		A
129 DPT	1959	AEC Reliance 2MU3RA	Plaxton C41F	OK Motor Services		RP
VLT 250	1960	AEC Routemaster	Park Royal H36/29R	London Transport	RM 244	R
314 PFM	1960	Bristol Lodekka FS6G	ECW	Crosville Motor Services	DFG33	RP
VLT 196	1960	AEC Routemaster	Park Royal H36/28R	London Transport	RM 196	R
314 DBM	1961	Ford	Duple	Travel House of Dunstable		R
8124 WX	1961	Bristol MW6G	ECW C39F	West Yorkshire Road Car Co	CUG27	R
WKG 284	1961	AEC Reliance 2MU3RA	Willowbrook DP41F	Western Welsh Omnibus Co	1284	R
WLT 765	1961	AEC Routemaster	Park Royal H36/28R	London Transport	RM 765	RP
XKO 72A	1961	Leyland Atlantean PDR1/1 Mk II	Metro Cammell O44/33F	Maidstone & District Motor Services	DH572	RP
811 BWR	1962	Bristol SUL4A	ECW B36F	West Yorkshire Road Car Co	SMA5	R
NAT 766A	1962	Daimler CVG6-30	Roe H39/31F	Grimsby - Cleethorpes Transport	57	R
RCK 920	1962	Leyland Titan PD3/5	Metro Cammell FH41/31F	Ribble Motor Services	1775	RP

Registration	Date	Chassis	Body	New to	Fleet No	Status
3747 RH	1963	AEC Bridgemaster 2B3RA	Park Royal H43/29F	East Yorkshire Motor Services	747	RP
AMX 8A	1963	AEC Reliance 2U3RA	Harrington C51F	Valliant of Ealing		RP
ALM 37B	1964	AEC Routemaster	Park Royal H36/28R	London Transport	RM 2037	RP
BCH 156B	1964	Daimler CVG6	Roe H37/28R	Derby Corporation	156	A
BDL 583B	1964	Bristol Lodekka FLF6G	ECW H38/32F	Southern Vectis Omnibus Co	70	A
BKG 713B	1964	AEC Renown 3B3RA	Northern Counties H38/29F	Western Welsh Omnibus Co	713	RP
PEF 21	1964	Leyland Leopard L1	Strachan B45D	West Hartlepool Corporation	21	A
TFA 987	1964	Daimler CCG5	Massey H33/28R	Burton upon Trent Corporation	87	R
WOW 993T	1964	Leyland Titan PD3/4	Northern Counties FCO39/30F	Southdown Motor Services	423	RP
BED 732C	1965	Leyland Titan PD2/40	East Lancs H34/30F	Warrington Corporation	51	RP
BEF 28C	1965	Leyland Titan PD2/40	Roe H37/28RD	West Hartlepool Corporation	28	RP
BOW 503C	1965	AEC Regent V 2D3RA	East Lancs/Neepsend H37/29R	Southampton Corporation	366	RP
BUF 272C	1965	Leyland Titan PD3/4	Northern Counties FH39/30F	Southdown Motor Services	272	RP
CTT 774C	1965	Bedford VAS1	Duple C29F	Heard of Bideford		RP
CUV 116C	1965	AEC Routemaster R2RH	Park Royal H36/28R	London Transport	RM 2116	R
EKP 234C	1965	Leyland Atlantean PDR1/1	Massey H—/—F	Maidstone Borough Council	34	RP
FDB 328C	1965	Leyland Titan PD2/40	East Lancs H36/28R	Stockport Corporation	28	RP
FDB 334C	1965	Leyland Titan PD2/40	East Lancs H36/28R	Stockport Corporation	34	R
FPT 590C	1965	AEC Routemaster 3R2RH	Park Royal H41/31F	Northern General Transport	2120	R
CHB 407D	1966	Leyland Titan PD3/4	East Lancs H41/29F	Merthyr Tydfil	142	RP
EDV 505D	1966	Bristol MW6G	ECW C39F	Western National Omnibus Co (Royal Blue)	1423	RP
GEE 418D	1966	Daimler Fleetline SRG6LW	Willowbrook B42D	Grimsby-Cleethorpes Transport	35	R
HAD 915D	1966	Bedford VAM5	Plaxton C45F	Princess Mary Coaches		RP
HDV 638E	1967	Bristol MW6G	ECW C39F	Western National Omnibus Co (Royal Blue)	1433	RP
JRH 414E	1967	Leyland Atlantean PDR1/1	Roe H44/31F	Kingston upon Hull Corporation	214	A
JRH 417E	1967	Leyland Atlantean PDR1/1	Roe H44/31F	Kingston upon Hull Corporation	217	A
LAX 101E	1967	Bristol RESL6L	ECW B46F	Red & White Services	RS167	R
NDM 950E	1967	Bedford VAM14	Duple Midland DP45F	Phillips of Holywell		A
JVV 267G	1968	Daimler CVG6	Roe H33/26R	Northampton Corporation	267	RP
PRH 244G	1968	Leyland Atlantean PDR1A/1	Roe H44/31F	Kingston upon Hull Corporation	244	A
PYM 108F	1968	AEC Reliance 6MU3R	Plaxton C30C	Glenton Tours of London		R
STH 100F	1968	Bedford VAM14		Davies Brothers		RP
YNU 351G	1968	Bristol Lodekka FLF6G	ECW H38/32F	Midland General Omnibus Co	313	R
MJA 895G	1969	Leyland Titan PD3/14	East Lancs H38/32F	Stockport Corporation	95	RP
SVF 896G	1969	Bristol RELH6G	ECW C47F	Eastern Counties Omnibus Co	RE896	RP
UTG 312G	1969	AEC Regent V 2MD3RA	Willowbrook	Pontypridd UDC	7	RP
UTG 313G	1969	AEC Regent V 2MD3RA	Willowbrook H34/26F	Pontypridd UDC	8	RP
WYP 203G	1969	AEC Reliance 6MU3R	Plaxton C41F	Surrey Motors		R
XCH 425G	1969	Daimler Fleetline CRG6LX	Roe H44/34F	Derby Corporation	225	A
LEF 60H	1970	Bristol RELL6L	ECW B46D	Hartlepool Corporation	60	RP
IJI 5367	1971	Bristol RELH6L	Plaxton C49F	Greenslades Tours of Exeter	300	RP
STL 725J	1971	Bedford YRQ	Willowbrook DP43F	Simmonds of Great Gonnerby		RP
VOD 123K	1971	Bristol LHS6L	Marshall B33F	Western National Omnibus Co	1253	RP
CRU 301L	1972	Bristol VRT6G	ECW	Hants & Dorset Motor Services	3301	RP
GBB 516K	1972	Leyland Atlantean PDR2/1	Alexander H48/30F	Tyneside PTE	680	RP
HOR 413L	1972	Leyland National 1151/2R/0403	Leyland National B44D	Gosport & Fareham Omnibus Co	13	RP
JMC 123K	1972	AEC Reliance 6MU4R	Plaxton C34F	Glenton Tours of London	123	RP
NHN 260K	1972	Daimler Fleetline SRG6LX-36	Roe B48D	Darlington Corporation	60	RP
NPD 108L	1972	Leyland National 1151/2R/0402	Leyland National B18D	London Country Bus Services	LN8	R
RWC 637K	1972	Bedford		Harris of Grays		RP
TDL 566K	1972	Bristol RELL6G	ECW B53F	Southern Vectis Omnibus Co	866	A
TSP 939K	1972	Leyland Leopard PSU4B/4R	Plaxton C45F	Rennie of Dunfermline		RP
ATA 563L	1973	Bristol VR	ECW	Western National (Devon General)	563	RP
BPT 672L	1973	Leyland Leopard PSU3B4R	Plaxton C53F	Trimdon Motor Services		RP

Registration	Date	Chassis	Body	New to	Fleet No	Status
HKE 680L	1973	Bristol VRTSL6LX	ECW H43/29F	Maidstone & District Motor Services	680	A
NCD 559M	1973	Bristol VRTSL6LX	ECW	Southdown Motor Services	559	RP
NPD 128L	1973	Leyland National 1151/1R/0402	Leyland National B28F	London Country Bus Services	LNC 28	R
OCH 261L	1973	Daimler Fleetline CRG6LX	Roe H44/34F	Derby Corporation	261	RP
OWC 720M	1973	Bristol RELL6L	ECW B53F	Colchester Corporation	20	RP
PKG 587M	1973	Bristol VRTSL6LX	ECW	Cardiff Corporation	587	RP
TGY 102M	1973	Leyland National	Leyland National B36D	London Transport	LS2	A
THM 515M	1973	Daimler Fleetline		London Transport	DMS 1515	A
THM 712M	1973	Daimler Fleetline		London Transport	DM 1712	RP
GEF 191N	1974	Bristol RELL6L	ECW DP48F	Hartlepool Corporation	91	RP
GHV 2N	1974	Daimler Fleetline CRL6	Park Royal H44/27D	London Transport	DM 1002	RP
GLJ 467N	1974	Bristol VRTSL6LX	ECW H43/31F	Hants & Dorset Motor Services	3315	R
GLJ 677N	1974	Leyland National 1151/1R/SC	Leyland National DP48F	Hants & Dorset Motor Services	3641	A
HPK 503N	1974	Leyland National 11351/1R	Leyland National B49F	Alder Valley	201	RP
PKH 600M	1974	Bedford VAS	Plaxton C29F	Hull City Football Club		R
RNV 810M	1974	Bristol VRT		United Counties Omnibus Co		RP
RPU 869M	1974	Bristol RELH6G	ECW DP49F	Eastern Counties Omnibus Co	RE849	RP
UMO 180N	1974	Leyland National 11351/1R	Leyland National B49F	Alder Valley	180	R
WPG 217M	1974	Leyland National 10351/1R/SC	Leyland National DP39F	London Country Bus Services	SNC117	A
GPD 318N	1975	Bristol LHS6L	ECW B35F	London Country Bus Services	BN 50	RP
JAJ 296N	1975	Bristol RELL6L	ECW B46D	Hartlepool Corporation	96	RP
KDW 347P	1975	Leyland National 11351/1R/SC	Leyland National	Western Welsh Omnibus Co	ND3975	RP
KDW 362P	1975	Leyland National 11351/1R/SC	Leyland National	Western Welsh Omnibus Co	ND5475	RP
KPA 369P	1975	Leyland National	Leyland National	Alder Valley	218	RP
KJD 507P	1976	Leyland National 11351A/2R	Leyland National DP36D	London Transport	LS7	A
KOU 795P	1976	Bristol VRTSL3/6LXB	ECW H39/31F	Bristol Omnibus Co	5509	A
LDV 176P	1976	Leyland Leopard PSU3C/4R	Plaxton C47F	Western National Omnibus Co	2436	RP
LWB 377P	1976	Ailsa B55-10	Van Hool McArdle H44/31D	South Yorkshire PTE	377	RP
NDP 38R	1976	Bristol VRT/LL3/6LXB	Northern Counties H47/29D	Reading Corporation	38	RP
NOE 576R	1976	Leyland National 11351A/1R	Leyland National	Red & White Services	654	A
NWO 462R	1976	Leyland National 11351A/1R	Leyland National DP48F	Western Welsh Omnibus Co	ND1776	A
UGR 698R	1976	Bristol VRT/SL3/6LXB	ECW H43/31F	United Automobile Services	698	RP
OJD 357R	1977	Leyland Fleetline FE30ALR	Park Royal H44/24D	London Transport	DMS 2357	RP
RJT 146R	1977	Leyland National 11351A/1R	Leyland National B49F	Hants & Dorset Motor Services	3698	RP
WCW 308R	1977	Leyland Leopard PSU3D/2R	Alexander B53F	Lancaster City Transport	308	A
THX 220S	1978	Leyland National 10351A/1R	Leyland National B36D	London Transport	LS220	RP
THX 580S	1978	Leyland Fleetline FE30ALR Special	MCW H44/28D	London Transport	DM 2580	RP
VDV 107S	1978	Bristol LH6L	ECW B43F	Western National (Devon General)	127	RP
WKO 138S	1978	Bristol VRT/SL3/6LXB	ECW H43/31F	Maidstone & District Motor Services	5138	RP
WUH 173T	1978	Leyland National 11351A/1R	Leyland National B52F	National Welsh Omnibus Services	N2978	A
YRC 420	1978	AEC Reliance 6U3ZR	Plaxton C48FL	Silver Line Coaches		
AYR 300T	1979	Leyland National 10351A/2R	Leyland National B36D	London Transport	LS 300	RP
BUH 239V	1979	Leyland National 2 NL106L11/1R	Leyland National	National Welsh Omnibus Services	NS493	A
DNW 840T	1979	Leyland National 10351B/1R	Leyland National B44F	West Yorkshire Road Car Co	1002	RP
EPD 511V	1979	Leyland National 10351B/1R	Leyland National	London Country Bus Services	SNB 511	A
EPD 543V	1979	Leyland National 10351B/1R	Leyland National B41F	London Country Bus Services	SNB 543	A
FVM 191V	1979	Bedford CF		Shearings		RP
HIL 7081	1979	Bedford CFL	Plaxton C17F	Golden Miller of Feltham		R
TWM 220V	1979	Leyland Atlantean AN68A/1R	East Lancs H45/33F	Merseyside PTE	1836	R
WDA 986T	1979	Leyland Fleetline FE30AGR	MCW H43/33F	West Midlands PTE	6986	R
WYW 72T	1979	Metrobus DR101/9	MCW H43/28D	London Transport	M 72	A
YPL 433T	1979	Leyland National 10351B/1R	Leyland National B41F	London Country Bus Services	SNB 433	R
AFB 593V	1980	Bristol LH6L	ECW B43F	Bristol Omnibus Co	462	A

Registration	Date	Chassis	Body	New to	Fleet No	Status
AVP 369W	1980	Leyland Atlantean	Roe H73F	Northern General Transport Co	3469	RP
HFG 923V	1980	Leyland National II NL116L11/1R	Leyland National B52F	Southdown Motor Services	123	R
SNS 823W	1980	Leyland National NL116L11/1R	Leyland National B52F	Central SMT Co	N37	A
JCK 852W	1981	Leyland National 2 NL106AL11/1R	East Lancs National Greenway B41F	Ribble Motor Services	852	RP
OCW 8X	1981	Leyland Atlantean AN68C/1R	East Lancs H43/31F	Blackburn Corporation	8	R
RNE 692W	1981	Bedford CF	Plaxton C17F	Shearings of Altrincham		R
XFG 25Y	1983	Leyland National NL1161HLXB/1R	ECW Leyland B49F	Brighton Corporation Brighton Borough Transport	25 25	RP RP
AXI 2534	1982	Bristol RELL6G	Alexander B45F	Citybus, Belfast	2534	A
UKE 830X	1982	Leyland Leopard PSU3G/4R	ECW C49F	East Kent Road Car Co	8830	A
A537 TYW	1983	Dodge G08	Wadham Stringer	British Rail		RP
VCO 802	1983	Leyland Tiger TRCTL11/3R	Plaxton C49F	East Kent Road Car Co	8840	R
C41 HDT	1985	Dennis Domino SDA1202	Optare B33F	South Yorkshire PTE	41	RP
C46 HDT	1985	Dennis Domino SDA1202	Optare B33F	South Yorkshire PTE	46	RP
C501 DYM	1986	Iveco 49-10	Robin Hood DP21F	Roundabout	RH1	A
D825 PUK	1986	Leyland Sherpa	Carlyle B20F	Ribble Motor Services		R
E523 TOV	1999	Iveco 49-1	Carlyle B21F	Carlyle		RP

Notes:

AOG 638	Converted to lorry	note ab	Unregistered
CCD 940	Originally Beadle L26/26R - rebodied 1950.	395 DEL	Guernsey registration was 2027
EUF 181	Coverted to Recovery Vehicle	LSV 748	Original Guernsey registration was 4029
HKE 867	Rebodied 1953	NAT 766A	Originally registered TJV 100
KYY 615	Previously a training bus	WOW 993T	Originally registered 423 DCD
RSK 615	Originally registered LOE 300	MJA 895G	For continued preservation in Portsmouth
FFN 446	Chassis parts from 1938 Leyland	IJI 5367	Originally registered UFJ 229J
LWR 424	Originally bus 858 (later DGW4); converted to a towing vehicle and renumbered 4044 in 1972	HIL 7081	Originally registered DJF 631T
		VCO 802	Originally registered FKK 840Y

Below: **Seen in Winchester is Hants & Dorset 677 (KEL 405). This ex-coach was lengthened and bodied in 1961 for use as a bus. Later its rear end was modified for use on the Sandbanks ferry.** *Philip Lamb*

Part 4

Heritage Bus Services

One of the most significant restorations of last year, Ribble 'White Lady' Leyland PD2/3/East Lancs Ribble 1248 (DCK 219) is to be found amongst the large collection of diverse vehicles with Quantock Heritage. *Philip Lamb*

Blue Triangle
Rainham

Contact address: Unit 3C, Denver Industrial Estate, Ferry Lane, Rainham, Essex, RM13 7MD.
Phone: 01708 631001
Operations planned for 2005: Scheduled heritage services not finalised at time of publication, but vehicles frequently appear on rail replacement services.

Registration	Date	Chassis	Body	New to	Fleet No	Status
HLW 178	1947	AEC Regent III O961 RT	Weymann H30/26R	London Transport	RT 191	R
KGK 959	1949	AEC Regent III O961 RT	Weymann H30/26R	London Transport	RT 2150	
KXW 171	1950	AEC Regent III O961 RT	Saunders Roe H30/26R	London Transport	RT 3062	
LLU 670	1950	AEC Regent III O961 RT	Park Royal H30/26R	London Transport	RT 3871	R
LYR 854	1950	AEC Regent III O961 RT	Weymann O30/26R	London Transport	RT 3435	R
LYR 969	1952	AEC Regent III O961 RT	Weymann H30/26R	London Transport	RT 2799	
MXX 289	1952	AEC Regal IV 9821LT RF	Metro Cammell B39F	London Transport	RF 401	
VLT 268	1960	AEC Routemaster R2RH	Park Royal H36/28R	London Transport	RM 268	RP
VLT 298	1960	AEC Routemaster R2RH	Park Royal H36/28R	London Transport	RM 298	R
WLT 900	1961	AEC Routemaster R2RH/1	Park Royal H40/32R	London Transport	RML 900	
CUV 260C	1965	AEC Routemaster R2RH/1	Park Royal H36/29RD	London Transport	RCL 2260	R

Notes:
LYR 854   Converted to open top following de-roofing in 1976

Buckland Omnibus Co
Woodbridge

Contact address: Wayside, The Street, Bredfield, Woodbridge, IP13 6AX.
Phone: 01394 380125
E-mail: ajb@bucklandbuses.co.uk
Web site: www.bucklandbuses.co.uk
Operations planned for 2005: Vehicles available for private hire. Occasional special Felixstowe sea front service — phone for details.

Registration	Date	Chassis	Body	New to	Fleet No	Status
TE 7870	1929	Dennis ES	Brush B29D	Accrington Corporation	57	R
GRP 260D	1966	Bristol MW6G	ECW C39F	United Counties Omnibus Co	260	R
KUL 331D	1966	Bedford VAS2	Willowbrook B29F	Greater London Council	331	A

Notes:
TE 7870   Body rebuilt 1974 by Wyatt

Carmel Coaches
Okehampton

Contact address: Mr A. G. Hazell, Northlew, Okehampton, Devon.
Phone: 01409 221237
Operations planned for 2005: Vehicles will operate on Dartmoor Rover Network. Please enquire for details. Sundays and Bank Holidays, May to September.

Registration	Date	Chassis	Body	New to	Fleet No	Status
LOD 495	1950	Albion Victor FT39N	Duple C31F	Way of Crediton		R
MTT 640	1951	Leyland Titan PD2/1	Leyland L27/26R	Devon General	DL640	R

Cosy Coaches
Killamarsh

Contact address: Cosy Coach Tours, 5 Meynell Way, Killamarsh, Derbyshire, S21 1HG.
Phone: 0114 248 9139
Operations planned for 2005: Please telephone for details.

Registration	Date	Chassis	Body	New to	Fleet No	Status
ATS 408	1948	Bedford OB	Duple C29F	James Mefflan of Kirriemuir		R
MRB 765	1949	Bedford OB	Duple C29F	H D Andrew of Tideswell		RP
CCB 300	1950	Albion Victor FT39N	Duple C31F	Cronshaw of Blackburn		A
ERG 164	1950	Bedford OB	Duple C29F	Paterson of Aberdeen		RP
TDT 344	1955	AEC Regent V	Roe H34/28R	Doncaster Corporation	144	RP
YBD 201	1961	Bristol MW6G	ECW C34F	United Counties Omnibus Co	201	A

Cumbria Classic Coaches
Kirkby Stephen

Contact address: Bowber Head, Ravenstonedale, Kirkby Stephen, Cumbria, CA17 4NL.
Phone: 015396 23254
Website: www.cumbriaclassiccoaches.co.uk
E-mail: coaches@cumbriaclassiccoaches.co.uk
Operations planned for 2005: Route 569: Ravenstonedale–Kirkby Stephen–Hawes, Tues (Hawes market day) Easter to October. Kendal Clipper (circular tour of Kendal), half-hourly, seven days a week during School Summer Holidays. Route 570: Hawes to Ribblehead viaduct Tuesdays Easter to October

Registration	Date	Chassis	Body	New to	Fleet No	Status
JTB 749	1948	AEC Regal III O962	Burlingham C33F	Florence Motors of Morcambe		R
CRN 80	1949	Leyland Tiger PS1	East Lancs B34R	Preston Corporation	75	R
TSK 736	1949	Commer Commando	Scottish Aviation C29F	David Lawson	C8	RP
CWG 286	1950	Leyland Tiger PS1/1	Alexander C35F	W Alexander & Sons (Northern)	PA184	R
MTJ 84	1951	Guy Arab III	Roe C31F	Lancashire United Transport	440	R
JPY 985	1953	Commer Avenger I	Plaxton C29F	Heather Coaches of Robin Hood Bay		R
627 HFM	1959	Bristol Lodekka LD6G	ECW CO33/27RD	Crosville Motor Services	DLB978	

Notes:
TSK 736   Original registration CMS 9. To be returned to original colours.
JPY 985   Converted to LPG/Petrol

Green Bus Service
Great Wyrley

Contact address: Warstone Motors Ltd, The Garage,
Jacobs Hall Lane, Great Wyrley, Staffordshire WS6 6AD
Phone: 01922 414141
Operations planned for 2005: Please telephone for details
Note: No vehicle data update received since 2000

Registration	Date	Chassis	Body	New to	Fleet No	Status
GZ 2248	1944	Bedford OWB	Duple B32F	Northern Ireland Road Transport Board		
GCA 747	1950	Bedford OB	Duple C29F	Owen of Rhostyllen		
GNY 432C	1965	Leyland Titan PD3/4	Massey L35/35RD	Caerphilly Corporation	32	

MacTours & Majestic Tour
Edinburgh

Contact address: Edinburgh Vintage Bus Company,
11A James Court, Lawnmarket, Edinburgh EH1 2PB.
Phone: 0131 477 4771
Operations planned for 2005: Hop-on, hop-off open-top tours of Edinburgh operate seven days a week, most of the year.

Registration	Date	Chassis	Body	New to	Fleet No	Status
OAS 624	1951	Leyland Tiger PS1	Guernseybus B31F	Jersey Motor Transport Co		
YSL 334	1951	Leyland Tiger PS1	Guernseybus OB34F	Jersey Motor Transport Co	44	
LST 873	1958	Leyland Titan PD2/40	Park Royal O27/26RO	Barrow in Furness Corporation	165	
JSJ 746	1959	AEC Routemaster ERM	Park Royal O75R	London Transport	RM 90	
JSJ 747	1959	AEC Routemaster ERM	Park Royal O75R	London Transport	RM 84	
JSJ 748	1959	AEC Routemaster ERM	Park Royal O75R	London Transport	RM 80	
JSJ 749	1959	AEC Routemaster ERM	Park Royal O76R	London Transport	RM 94	
WLT 371	1959	AEC Routemaster R2RH	Park Royal O63R	London Transport	RM 371	
VLT 143	1960	AEC Routemaster ERM	Park Royal O75R	London Transport	RM 143	
VLT 163	1960	AEC Routemaster ERM	Park Royal O75R	London Transport	RM 163	
VLT 235	1960	AEC Routemaster ERM	Park Royal O75R	London Transport	RM 235	
VLT 237	1960	AEC Routemaster ERM	Park Royal O75R	London Transport	RM 237	
VLT 242	1960	AEC Routemaster ERM	Park Royal O71R	London Transport	RM 242	
VLT 281	1960	AEC Routemaster ERM	Park Royal O71R	London Transport	RM 281	
858 DYE	1961	AEC Routemaster R2RH	Park Royal O63R	London Transport	RM 727	
485 CLT	1962	AEC Routemaster R2RH	Park Royal H32/25RD	London Transport	RMC 1485	
803 DYE	1962	AEC Routemaster R2RH	Park Royal O63R	London Transport	RM 1010	
CUV 203C	1965	AEC Routemaster R2RH	Park Royal H36/28R	London Transport	RM 2203	
CUV 210C	1965	AEC Routemaster R2RH	Park Royal O63R	London Transport	RM 2210	
CUV 241C	1965	AEC Routemaster R2RH/3	Park Royal CO65RD	London Transport	RCL 2241	
CUV 248C	1965	AEC Routemaster R2RH/3	Park Royal CO65RD	London Transport	RCL 2248	
NMY 634E	1967	AEC Routemaster R2RH/2	Park Royal H32/24F	British European Airways	8241	
NMY 646E	1967	AEC Routemaster R2RH/2	Park Royal H32/24F	British European Airways	8253	
OSJ 636R	1977	Leyland Leopard PSU3C/3R	Alexander OB49F	Western SMT Co	2636	R

Notes:

OAS 624	Originally registered J 5560 and fitted with Reading body.
YSL 334	Originally registered J 5567 and fitted with Reading B34F body.
LST 873	Originally registered CEO 952. Rebuilt to open staircase configuration.
JSJ 747	Originally registered VLT 84. Extended and converted to open top.

JSJ 748	Originally registered VLT 80. Extended and converted to open top.	
JSJ 746	Originally registered VLT 90. Extended and converted to open top.	
JSJ 749	Originally registered VLT 94. Extended and converted to open top.	
WLT 371	Converted to open top.	
VLT 235	Extended and converted to open top.	
VLT 163	Extended and converted to open top.	
VLT 143	Extended and converted to open top.	
VLT 237	Extended and converted to open top.	
VLT 242	Extended and converted to open top.	
VLT 281	Extended and converted to open top.	
858 DYE	Originally registered WLT 727. Converted to open top.	
803 DYE	Originally registered 10 CLT. Converted to open top.	
CUV 210C	Converted to open top.	
NMY 634E	Passed to London Transport (RMA50) in 1979; acquired by Stagecoach at Perth in 1987	
NMY 646E	Passed to London Transport (RMA9) in 1979	
OSJ 636R	Converted to open top.	
All Routemasters converted to Cummins engine with Allison automatic gearbox.		

Memory Lane Vintage Omnibus Services
Maidenhead

Contact address: 78 Lillibrooke Crescent, Maidenhead, Berkshire, SL6 3XQ.
Phone: 01628 825050
Fax: 01628 825851
E-mail: info@memorylane.co.uk

Registration	Date	Chassis	Body	New to	Fleet No	Status
KGU 290	1949	AEC Regent III O961 RT	Weymann H30/26R	London Transport	RT 1530	RP
KYY 628	1950	AEC Regent III O961 RT	Park Royal H30/26R	London Transport	RT 1790	R
LYF 377	1951	AEC Regal IV 9821LT RF	Metro Cammell B37F	London Transport	RF 26	R
MLL 943	1952	AEC Regal IV 9821LT RF	Metro Cammell B39F	London Transport	RF 525	A
NLE 643	1953	AEC Regal IV 9821LT RF	Metro Cammell B39F	London Transport	RF 643	RP
617 DDV	1960	Bristol MW6G	ECW C39F	Southern National Omnibus Co (Royal Blue)	2250	R
VLT 216	1960	AEC Routemaster R2RH	Park Royal H36/28R	London Transport	RM 216	R
253 KTA	1962	Bristol MW6G	ECW C39F	Western National Omnibus Co (Royal Blue)	2270	

Quantock Heritage
Wiveliscombe

Contact address: Bishop's Lydeard, Somerset.
Phone: 01823 251140
Affiliations: NARTM
Operations planned for 2005: Please telephone for details

Registration	Date	Chassis	Body	New to	Fleet No	Status
JG 9938	1937	Leyland Tiger TS8	Park Royal C32R	East Kent Road Car Co		R
AJA 132	1938	Bristol L5G	Burlingham B35R	North Western Road Car Co	372	R
EMW 893	1947	Daimler CVD6	Park Royal B35C	Swindon Corporation	57	A
HUO 510	1947	AEC Regal I O662	Weymann B35F	Devon General	SR510	R
JUO 992	1947	Leyland Titan PD1	ECW L27/26R	Southern National Omnibus Co	2932	A
ACH 441	1948	AEC Regal III O682	Windover C32F	Trent Motor Traction Co	611	R
JFM 575	1948	AEC Regal III 6821A	Strachan's B35R	Crosville Motor Services	TA5	RP
JNN 384	1948	Leyland Titan PD1	Duple L29/26F	Barton Transport	467	A
JTE 546	1948	AEC Regent III 6811A	Park Royal H33/26R	Morecambe & Heysham Corporation	20	R
JLJ 402	1949	Leyland Tiger PS2/3	Burlingham FDP35F	Bournemouth Corporation	45	R
KTF 594	1949	AEC Regent III 9621E	Park Royal O33/26R	Morecambe & Heysham Corporation	65	R
LJH 665	1949	Dennis Lancet J3	Duple C35F	Lee of Barnet		RP

Registration	Date	Chassis	Body	New to	Fleet No	Status
CHL 772	1950	Daimler CVD6	Willowbrook DP35F	Bullock of Featherstone		R
GWN 432	1950	Dennis Lancet J3	Thurgood FC37F	Super of Tottenham		R
JFJ 875	1950	Daimler CVD6	Weymann B35F	Exeter City Transport	75	R
KFM 767	1950	Bristol L5G	ECW B35R	Crosville Motor Services	KG117	R
KFM 893	1950	Bristol L5G	ECW DP31R	Crosville Motor Services	KG131	R
LFM 302	1950	Leyland Tiger PS1	Weymann B35F	Crosville Motor Services	KA226	R
LFM 717	1950	Bristol L5G	ECW B35R	Crosville Motor Services	KG136	A
LFM 734	1950	Bristol LL5G	ECW B39R	Crosville Motor Services	KG153	A
LUO 692	1950	Leyland Tiger PS2	Burlingham C33F	Pridham of Lamerton		A
DCK 219	1951	Leyland Titan PD2/3	East Lancs FCL27/22RD	Ribble Motor Services	1248	R
PHN 699	1952	Guy Arab III	Roe B41C	Darlington Corporation	26	RP
CHG 545	1954	Leyland Tiger PS2/14	East Lancs B39F	Burnley Colne & Nelson	45	R
BAS 562	1956	Bristol Lodekka LD6G	ECW O33/27R	Southern Vectis Omnibus Co	507	R
BAS 563	1956	Bristol Lodekka LD6G	ECW O33/27R	Southern Vectis Omnibus Co	501	R
BAS 564	1956	Bristol Lodekka LD6G	ECW O33/27R	Southern Vectis Omnibus Co	500	R
701 AEH	1957	Leyland Titan PD3/4	MCW O36/32F	Potteries Motor Traction Co	H701	RP
VDV 752	1957	Bristol Lodekka LDL6G	ECW O37/33RD	Western National Omnibus Co	1935	R
VDV 753	1957	Bristol Lodekka LDL6G	ECW O37/33RD	Western National Omnibus Co	1936	R
GSU 678	1958	Leyland Titan PD2/40	Metro Cammell	Portsmouth Corporation	114	A
NDB 356	1958	Leyland Tiger Cub PSUC1/1	Crossley B44F	Stockport Corporation	403	R
890 ADV	1959	AEC Reliance 2MU3RV	Willowbrook C41F	Devon General Grey Cars	TCR890	R
805 EVT	1960	AEC Reliance 2MU3RV	Weymann DP41F	Potteries Motor Traction Co	SL805	RP
LDB 796	1960	Leyland Tiger Cub PSUC1	Willowbrook DP43F	North Western Road Car Co		R
WKG 287	1961	AEC Reliance 2MU3RA	Willowbrook B41F	Western Welsh Omnibus Co	1287	A
3655 NE	1962	Leyland Tiger Cub PSUC1/12	Park Royal DP38D	Manchester City Transport	55	A
572 CNW	1962	Daimler CVG6LX-30	Roe H39/31F	Leeds City Transport	572	RP
DPV 65D	1966	AEC Regent V 2D2RA	Neepsend H37/28R	Ipswich Corporation	65	R
HJA 965E	1967	Leyland Titan PD2/40	East Lancs Neepsend H36/28R	Stockport Corporation	65	R
TDK 686J	1971	AEC Reliance 6U3ZR	Plaxton C53F	Yelloway Motor Services of Rochdale		A
HVU 247N	1975	AEC Reliance 6U3ZR	Plaxton C53F	Yelloway Motor Services of Rochdale		RP
NNC 854P	1976	AEC Reliance 6U3ZR	Plaxton C53F	Yelloway Motor Services of Rochdale		A
WDK 562T	1979	AEC Reliance 6U3ZR	Plaxton C49F	Yelloway Motor Services of Rochdale		R

Notes:

GWN 432	Rebodied 1960		701 AEH	Converted to open top by Sundekker
DCK 219	White Lady double deck coach		GSU 678	Converted to breakdown vehicle. Originally registered ORV 991.
BAS 562	Originally registered MDL 953			
BAS 564	Originally registered MDL 955		572 CNW	Converted to exhibition vehicle
BAS 563	Originally registered MDL 952		HVU 247N	Did carry registration 146 FLD

Southcoast Motor Services
Croydon

Contact address: PO Box 1029, Croydon, CR9 6AA
Phone: 0870 3215767
Operations planned for 2005: Services as advertised in the enthusiast press.
Note: No recent data from this collection.

Registration	Date	Chassis	Body	New to	Fleet No	Status
406 DCD	1964	Leyland Titan PD3/4	Northern Counties FCO39/30F	Southdown Motor Services	406	R
HCD 350E	1967	Leyland Titan PD3/4	Northern Counties FH39/30F	Southdown Motor Services	350	R

Indices

Listed here under the British Bus Preservation Group, London Transport Cravens-bodied RT1431 has recently passed into the care of Ensignbus at Purfleet. Restored to Class 6 standard, this bus may now be seen out and about on special duties in the London area.
Philip Lamb

Index of Vehicles by Registration Number

Reg	Page	Reg	Page	Reg	Page	Reg	Page	Reg	Page
101 CLT	63	314 DBM	109	47638	81	6342 HA	22	85 D 2412	25
105 UTU	58	314 PFM	109	484 EFJ	103	6370 HA	16	850 ABK	51
109 DRM	105	318 AOW	98	485 CLT	116	643 MIP	25	858 DYE	116
116 JTD	41	3190 UN	99	488 KOT	66	6545 HA	20	862 RAE	22
120 JRB	109	31909	103	501 KD	88	657 BWB	62	866 HAL	50
122 JTD	41	326 CAA	79	503 RUO	76	66	62	869 NHT	70
1252 EV	53	332 RJO	73	504 EBL	46	675 AAM	72	871 KHA	20
129 DPT	109	333 CRW	29	5056 HA	95	675 COD	72	872 ATA	76
1294 RE	16	334 CRW	16	507 OHU	22	675 OCV	79	875 DTB	109
1322 WA	58	335 AOW	98	5073 HA	20	675 OCV	79	881 BTF	91
138 CLT	24	3655 NE	118	5212 HA	20	6769	80	8860 VR	41
14 LFC	51	370 FCR	98	528 CTF	91	6801 FN	78	890 ADV	118
14 PKR	81	373 FCR	103	532 DWW	103	694 ZO	60	891 XFM	72
1425 P	61	373 WPU	24	534 RTB	86	70 AUF	98	9 RDV	76
177 IK	25	3747 RH	110	56 GUO	95	701 AEH	118	90 HBC	87
191 AWL	73	375 GWN	72	561 TD	86	71 AHI	25	904 OFM	22
1925 WA	82	381 BKM	24	562 RTF	48	7209 PW	58	913 DTT	76
198 CUS	80	386 DD	99	566 JFM	72	737 DYE	39	918 NRT	24
201 YTE	48	390 DKK	109	569 KKK	30	7424 SP	53	924 AHY	70
214 CLT	82	3916 UB	82	57 GUO	22	7514 UA	35	931 GTA	76
217 AJF	87	3945 UE	25	572 CNW	118	756 KFC	51	932 GTA	76
217 MHK	24	395 DEL	109	574 CNW	77	760 CTD	86	935 GTA	76
221 JVK	90	404 RIU	59	574 TD	48	773 FHA	16	943 KHA	20
236 LNO	24	406 DCD	118	5789 AH	79	78 D 140	25	952 JUB	38
248 NEA	20	410 DCD	76	5789 AH	79	78 D 824	25	956 AJO	51
253 KTA	117	414 CLT	41	583 CLT	86	780 GHA	95	960 HTT	76
264 ERY	16	416 DCD	98	595 LCG	79	7874 WJ	58	9629 WU	62
264 KTA	72	419 DCD	98	596 LCG	79	80 NVO	50	964 H87	61
268 KTA	72	422 CAX	58	604 JPU	72	802 MHW	20	969 EHW	70
28 TKR	24	422 DCD	76	6167 RU	69	803 DYE	116	972 CUF	98
297 LJ	69	4227 FM	48	617 DDV	117	805 EVT	118	972 EHW	70
301 LJ	23	433 MDT	62	6203 KW	35	811 BWR	109	974 AFJ	103
3016 HA	20	434 BTE	48	6204 KW	35	8124 WX	109	975 CWL	73
3035 HA	16	436 KOV	102	6219 TF	48	815 KDV	103	9797 DP	99
304 GHN	67	461 CLT	28	6220 KW	35	8154 EL	69	980 DAE	72
304 KFC	51	462 EOT	66	6249 UP	90	8156 EL	69	991 MDV	103
305 KFC	51	4632 VM	41	627 HFM	115	827 BWY	77	99-64-HB	21
312 MFC	73	466 DHN	109	6330 WJ	58	828 SHW	80		
A101 HLV	88	ACB 904	91	AFJ 764T	102	AJA 139B	48	AOG 638	108
A112 HLV	88	ACC 88	48	AFM 103G	48	AJA 152	41	AOG 679	16
A30 ORJ	97	ACH 441	117	AFN 488B	78	AJA 408L	96	AOR 158B	98
A472 HNC	97	ACH 627	108	AFN 780B	78	AJX 369	82	APA 46B	50
A537 TYW	112	ACK 796	91	AFS 91B	53	ALJ 340B	69	APR 167A	49
A706 LNC	42	AC-L 379	71	AFT 930	90	ALJ 973	71	APW 829B	33
A749 NTA	104	ACU 304B	90	AFY 971	48	ALM 37B	110	ARC 515	16
A765 NNA	97	AD 7156	83	AHA 451J	21	ALS 102Y	81	ARD 676	71
A869 SUL	51	ADL 459B	34	AHA 582	20	AML 582H	39	ARG 17B	53
A927 MDV	102	ADR 813	103	AHC 442	73	AMX 8A	110	ARN 811C	94
AAA 503C	66	ADV 128	103	AHE 163	38	ANA 1Y	97	ARP 601X	72
AAA 506C	66	ADX 1	33	AHF 850	63	ANA 601Y	97	ARY 225K	87
AAA 508C	66	ADX 196	33	AHG 334V	86	ANA 645Y	97	ASC 665B	53
AAA 756	52	ADX 63B	33	AHL 694	89	ANB 851	16	ATA 536L	110
AAO 34B	105	AED 31B	68	AHN 451B	67	ANH 154	108	ATD 281J	86
AAO 771A	86	AEL 170B	69	AHU 803	70	ANJ 306T	99	ATD 683	48
ABD 253B	72	AFB 592V	70	AIT 934	60	ANQ 778	48	ATF 477	52
ABR 433	89	AFB 593V	111	AJA 118	22	ANV 775J	101	ATS 408	115
ACB 902	48	AFJ 727T	102	AJA 132	117	ANW 682	34	ATT 922	103

AUD 310J	73	BMS 222	52	CC 7745	20	CSG 29C	53	DDR 414	103
AUF 670	108	BMS 405	52	CC 8671	66	CSG 43C	55	DDW 431V	81
AUO 74	103	BNC 960T	97	CC 9305	30	CSG 773S	56	DED 797	48
AUX 296	52	BND 874C	41	CC 9424	66	CSG 792S	56	DEK 3D	101
AVP 369W	112	BNE 729N	96	CCB 300	115	CTF 627B	86	DFE 383	38
AVX 975G	24	BNE 751N	96	CCD 940	108	CTP 200	73	DFE 963D	22
AWA 124B	53	BNE 764N	96	CCG 296K	66	CTT 23C	76	DFM 347H	48
AWG 393	52	BOK 1V	21	CCG 704C	79	CTT 513C	103	DFV 146	86
AWG 623	52	BON 474C	20	CCK 359	91	CTT 518C	82	DGS 536	52
AWG 639	52	BOW 162	69	CCK 663	86	CTT 774C	110	DGS 625	52
AXI 2259	83	BOW 169	103	CD 4867	17	CU 3593	71	DHC 784E	99
AXI 2534	112	BOW 503C	110	CD 5125	17	CUV 116C	110	DHN 475	77
AXJ 857	40	BOW 507C	98	CD 7045	52	CUV 121C	80	DHR 192	46
AXM 649	39	BP 9822	17	CDB 224	41	CUV 203C	116	DHW 293K	71
AXM 693	28	BPL 469T	101	CDC 166K	100	CUV 208C	77	DIV 83	60
AYJ 379	52	BPT 672L	111	CDC 168K	100	CUV 210C	116	DJF 349	49
AYR 300T	111	BPV 9	33	CDH 501	16	CUV 219C	20	DJG 619C	78
AYV 651	39	BR 7132	17	CDJ 878	48	CUV 229C	39	DJP 468E	94
AZD 203	25	BRS 37	52	CDL 479C	34	CUV 233C	24	DJP 754	41
B106 XJO	51	BTB 23T	68	CDR 679	52	CUV 241C	116	DKT 11	34
B177 FFS	81	BTF 25	91	CDT 636	61	CUV 248C	116	DKY 703	61
B349 LSO	56	BTN 113	89	CDX 516	28	CUV 260C	114	DKY 704	71
B401 NJF	16	BTR 361B	98	CEO 720W	67	CVF 874	33	DKY 706	61
B901 TVR	97	BTW 488	24	CEO 723W	67	CVH 741	61	DKY 712	69
B926 KWM	63	BU 7108	108	CEO 956	67	CVL 850D	38	DKY 713	48
BAS 562	118	BUF 122C	99	CEO 957	67	CVP 207	20	DKY 735	22
BAS 563	118	BUF 260C	99	CET 613	95	CWG 206	41	DL 5084	33
BAS 564	118	BUF 272C	110	CFK 340	89	CWG 283	52	DL 9015	108
BBA 560	41	BUF 277C	99	CFM 354	34	CWG 286	115	DL 9706	101
BBK 236B	73	BUF 426C	99	CFM 86S	49	CWG 696V	49	DLJ 111L	69
BBW 21V	51	BUH 239V	111	CFN 104	100	CWG 756V	58	DLU 92	28
BCD 820L	46	BVP 784V	17	CFV 851	24	CWH 717	41	DM 2583	89
BCH 156B	110	BWG 39	52	CGJ 188	28	CWN 629C	70	DM 6228	91
BCK 367C	48	BWG 833L	56	CHB 407D	110	CWU 136T	35	DMS 325C	55
BCK 939	61	BWO 585B	58	CHF 565	63	CWU 146T	63	DMS 359C	55
BCP 671	82	BWS 105L	56	CHG 541	52	CWX 671	34	DMS 820	52
BCR 379K	98	BXA 452B	53	CHG 545	118	CXX 171	28	DMS 823	52
BD 209	89	BXA 464B	53	CHL 772	118	CYI 621	59	DNF 204	58
BDJ 808	48	BXD 576	39	CHY 419C	72	CYJ 252	52	DNF 708C	96
BDJ 87	62	BXI 2583	83	CJG 959	30	CZ 7013	63	DNW 840T	111
BDL 583B	110	C 2367	89	CK 3825	40	D122 PTT	51	DOD 474	103
BED 731C	48	C208 FVU	42	CK 4474	91	D275 OOJ	35	DPT 848	89
BED 732C	110	C24 NVV	101	CK 4518	89	D320 LNB	97	DPV 65D	118
BEF 28C	110	C41 HDT	112	CKG 193	71	D509 MJA	97	DPV 68D	33
BEN 177	41	C416 AHT	23	CLE 122	39	D63 NOF	42	DR 4902	46
BFE 419	38	C45 HDT	62	CMS 201	96	D676 NNE	42	DRD 130	105
BFM 144	108	C46 HDT	112	CN 2870	20	D825 PUK	112	DRN 289	91
BFS 1L	56	C501 DYM	112	CN 4740	89	DAU 370C	50	DSD 936V	56
BFS 463L	56	C519 FFJ	77	CN 6100	89	DB 5070	40	DSG 169	52
BFS 471L	56	C526 DYT	40	CNH 699	22	DB 5221	108	DTP 823	73
BG 8557	63	C53 HDT	58	CNH 860	72	DBA 214C	41	DU 4838	50
BG 9225	63	C671 FFJ	104	CNH 862	72	DBC 190C	87	DUK 278	102
BHA 399C	20	C724 JJO	51	CPM 61	46	DBL 154	100	DUK 833	22
BHA 656C	20	C729 JJO	73	CPU 979G	24	DBN 978	58	DWB 54H	58
BHH 83J	99	C748 FFJ	104	CRC 911	58	DBU 100W	94	DWG 526	52
BHL 682	77	C751 YBA	97	CRG 811	91	DBV 32W	104	DWH 706W	97
BHO 670J	100	C777 SFS	56	CRM 927T	104	DBV 43W	104	DX 3988+	32
BHU 92C	70	C801 FRL	102	CRN 80	115	DBW 613	50	DX 5610	32
BJA 425	41	C823 CBU	97	CRS 834	91	DBY 001	80	DX 5629	32
BJK 672D	99	CAH 923	33	CRU 103C	69	DCK 219	118	DX 6591	32
BJX 848C	80	CAP 234	34	CRU 180C	69	DCN 83	90	DX 7812	32
BK 2986	73	CBC 921	16	CRU 187C	69	DCS 616	52	DX 8871	46
BKG 713B	110	CBR 539	90	CRU 197C	69	DDB 174C	41	DY 5029	81
BLH 123B	25	CC 1087	89	CRU 301L	110	DDL 50	108	E523 TOV	112

E570 MAC	67	ESF 647W	56	FGS 59D	52	GDJ 435	48	GSC 667X	56
E901 DRG	90	ESF 801C	55	FHF 451	63	GDL 764	34	GSI 353	60
E903 DRG	90	ESG 652	52	FHF 456	48	GDT 421	61	GSO 80V	56
EA 4181	16	ESV 811	43	FHN 833	38	GE 2446	52	GSU 678	118
EAS 284	63	ETJ 108	52	FHT 112	108	GEA 174	22	GTA 395	103
EBO 919	71	ETO 452C	50	FJF 40D	87	GEE 418D	110	GTB 903	86
ECD 524	17	ETS 964	53	FJJ 774	39	GEF 191N	111	GTJ 694	82
ECK 934	91	ETT 946	103	FJW 616	20	GFN 273	78	GTP 175F	73
ECU 201E	90	EUD 256K	51	FKF 933G	88	GFU 692	62	GTV 666	61
ECX 425	82	EUF 181	108	FKU 758	62	GFY 406	48	GTX 761W	50
ED 6141	48	EUF 184	17	FLD 447Y	81	GGA 670	52	GUE 247	20
EDB 549	41	EUF 198	34	FM 6397	108	GGR 103N	90	GUF 191	98
EDB 562	41	EUP 405B	90	FM 6435	108	GHA 327D	22	GUJ 608	16
EDB 575	41	EVA 324	52	FM 7443	108	GHA 333	20	GUP 907N	90
EDG 250L	103	EVC 244	108	FM 9984	108	GHA 337	20	GUW 443W	101
EDS 288A	53	EVL 549E	38	FNY 933	108	GHA 415D	20	GUW 444W	101
EDS 320A	53	EWM 358	48	FOI 1629	83	GHD 215	82	GUX 188	59
EDT 703	61	EWS 130D	55	FON 630	16	GHD 765	58	GVD 47	52
EDV 505D	110	EWS 168D	55	FOP 429	24	GHN 189	67	GW 713	46
EDV 555D	72	EXL 892	109	FPT 590C	110	GHN 574	61	GWJ 724	57
EF 7380	89	EXV 253	39	FPT 6G	94	GHT 127	70	GWM 816	96
EFJ 241	103	EZH 155	25	FR 1347	46	GHT 154	70	GWN 432	118
EFJ 666	103	EZH 17	60	FRB 211H	21	GHV 2N	111	GWY 690N	35
EFJ 92	41	EZH 170	25	FRC 956	20	GJ 2098	28	GYC 160K	23
EFM 581	108	EZH 231	60	FRJ 254D	41	GJB 254	51	GYS 896D	80
EFM 631C	101	EZH 64	60	FRJ 511	58	GJB 279	63	GZ 2248	116
EFN 178L	78	EZL 1	60	FRP 692	72	GJF 301N	87	GZ 7638	59
EFN 592	78	F115 PHM	40	FRP 828	72	GJG 739D	78	H74 ANG	79
EFV 300	82	F300 SSX	81	FRU 224	69	GJG 751D	30	HA 3501	20
EGA 79	43	F575 RCW	86	FRU 305	59	GJX 331	35	HA 4963	16
EGN 369J	28	F685 YOG	17	FSC 182	52	GK 3192	39	HA 8047	22
EGO 426	28	FAE 60	22	FTB 11	48	GK 5323	39	HAD 915D	110
EGP 1J	39	FAR 724K	100	FTO 614	61	GK 5486	39	HAH 537L	72
EHA 415D	16	FAS 982	53	FTR 511	98	GKP 511	61	HAX 399N	23
EHA 424D	95	FBG 910	63	FTT 704	70	GKV 94	94	HBD 919T	72
EHA 767D	20	FBN 232C	68	FUF 181	108	GLJ 467N	111	HBF 679D	21
EHA 775	16	FBR 53D	90	FV 5737	103	GLJ 677N	111	HCD 347E	76
EHL 344	77	FBU 827	48	FVM 191V	111	GLJ 957	103	HCD 350E	118
EHL 472D	99	FCD 294D	99	FW 5698	38	GM 5875	63	HCK 204G	48
EHO 869	98	FCI 323	25	FW 8990	61	GM 6384	53	HD 7905	57
EHT 108C	77	FCK 884	91	FWG 846	53	GM 9287	53	HDG 448	20
EHV 65	73	FDB 328C	110	FWH 461Y	97	GN 8242	28	HDL 280	109
EKP 234C	110	FDB 334C	110	FWL 371E	51	GNB 518D	96	HDV 638E	110
EKU 743	61	FDL 676	34	FWX 914	35	GNC 276N	42	HDV 639E	55
EKU 746	61	FDL 927D	34	FXT 122	100	GNF 15V	97	HE 12	89
EKV 966	29	FDM 724	20	FYG 663J	99	GNF 16V	97	HEK 705	41
EKY 558	61	FDO 573	38	FYS 839	71	GNG 125C	33	HET 513	46
ELP 228	28	FDV 829V	77	FYS 988	43	GNM 232N	24	HF 9126	52
EMS 362V	81	FEA156	22	FYS 998	43	GNM 235N	103	HFG 923V	112
EMW 893	117	FEL 105L	69	FZ 7897	63	GNY 432C	116	HFM 561D	72
EN 9965	96	FEL 209V	69	GAA 580	66	GO 5170	28	HFO 659	52
END 832D	96	FEL 751D	50	GAA 616	66	GO 5198	39	HFR 501E	80
ENW 980D	35	FES 831W	56	GAJ 12	61	GOE 486	108	HFR 512E	86
EO 9051	67	FET 617	95	GAM 216	22	GOH 357N	17	HFR 516E	86
EO 9177	67	FET 618	61	GAN 744J	90	GOU 732	94	HG 9651	58
EOD 524D	50	FFM 135C	48	GAX 2C	72	GOU 845	66	HGA 983D	80
EOI 4857	63	FFN 399	78	GAY 171	16	GPD 313N	101	HGG 359	80
EPD 511V	111	FFN 446	109	GBB 516K	110	GPD 318N	111	HGM 335E	55
EPD 543V	111	FFU 860	38	GBB 524K	90	GRP 260D	114	HGM 346E	55
EPM 134V	101	FFV 447D	55	GBU 1V	97	GRS 334E	80	HHA 26	108
ERD 152	61	FFY 401	48	GCA 747	116	GRS 343E	55	HHA 637	20
ERG 164	115	FFY 402	20	GCD 48	76	GRY 48D	87	HHN 202	89
ERN 700	91	FFY 403	48	GCK 279S	101	GRY 60D	21	HHP 755	82
ERV 252D	69	FFY 404	48	GCM 152E	63	GSC 658X	56	HHW 920L	70

HIL 7081	111	JA 5528	108	JOV 714P	17	JXX 487	109	KNG 374	33
HJA 121N	96	JA 7585	41	JOV 738P	102	JY 124	103	KNG 718	79
HJA 965E	118	JA 7770	108	JOV 741P	102	JYC 855	94	KNG 718	79
HKE 680L	111	JAA 708	79	JOW 499E	98	K232 DAC	29	KNN 254	108
HKE 867	108	JAJ 296N	111	JOW 928	98	KAG 856	80	KNV 337	72
HKL 826	108	JAP 698	100	JP 4712	41	KAH 407	33	KOD 585	76
HKR 11	61	JBD 975	72	JPA 190K	28	KAL 579	20	KOM 150	29
HKW 82	35	JBN 153	41	JPL 153K	101	KAZ 6703	99	KON 311P	21
HLJ 44	69	JC 5313	81	JPT 544	89	KBD 712D	101	KOU 791P	23
HLW 159	48	JCK 530	86	JPT 901T	90	KBD 715D	101	KOU 795P	111
HLW 178	114	JCK 542	91	JPT 906T	90	KBO 961	71	KOW 909F	98
HLW 214	108	JCK 852W	112	JPY 985	115	KCG 627L	66	KOW 910F	98
HLX 410	28	JCP 60F	46	JRA 635	89	KCK 869	94	KOX 663F	16
HLY 524V	56	JDJ 260K	49	JRH 414E	110	KCK 914	94	KOX 780F	21
HMA 99W	49	JDL 40	109	JRH 417E	110	KD 3185	81	KPA 369P	111
HNB 24N	96	JDN 668	62	JRJ 281E	41	KDB 408F	41	KPM 91E	56
HNP 154S	99	JDV 754	108	JRN 29	23	KDB 696	79	KPT 909	46
HNP 989J	98	JEL 257	22	JRN 41	91	KDB 696	79	KR 1728	48
HNW 131D	35	JF 2378	16	JRR 404	20	KDJ 999	48	KRH 411P	80
HOR 413L	110	JFJ 500N	103	JRT 82K	33	KDL 885F	34	KRN 422	48
HOR 590E	79	JFJ 506N	72	JRX 823	88	KDT 206D	62	KRR 255	43
HOR 592E	79	JFJ 606	103	JSC 900E	55	KDT 393	62	KRU 55F	69
HOU 904	66	JFJ 875	118	JSF 928T	56	KDW 347P	111	KSV 102	83
HOV 685	20	JFM 238D	31	JSJ 746	116	KDW 362P	111	KSX 102X	56
HPF 318N	101	JFM 575	117	JSJ 747	116	KED 546F	86	KTC 615	48
HPK 503N	111	JFM 650J	48	JSJ 748	116	KEL 110	69	KTD 768	48
HPW 133	38	JFT 413X	90	JSJ 749	116	KEL 131	16	KTF 594	117
HRG 209	53	JFV 527	91	JSX 595T	56	KEL 133	69	KTJ 502	89
HRN 249G	94	JG 8720	66	JT 8077	34	KEL 405	109	KTT 42P	103
HRN 31	91	JG 9938	117	JTB 749	115	KET 220	58	KTT 689	16
HRN 39	91	JHA 227L	100	JTD 300B	48	KFM 767	118	KTV 493	61
HRN 99N	86	JHA 868E	21	JTE 546	117	KFM 775	20	KTV 506	62
HSC 173X	56	JHL 701	90	JTF 920B	62	KFM 893	118	KUF 199F	99
HTB 656	41	JHL 708	77	JTH 100F	99	KFN 239	78	KUL 331D	114
HTC 661	108	JHL 983	77	JTU 588T	56	KGG 184N	90	KUS 607E	68
HTF 586	41	JHT 802	70	JUB 29	82	KGK 529	95	KVF 658E	79
HTF 644B	48	JJG 1P	78	JUD 597W	51	KGK 575	95	KVF 658E	79
HTT 487	76	JK 8418	108	JUE 349	20	KGK 758	109	KVH 219	62
HUD 476S	51	JLJ 402	117	JUM 505V	35	KGK 803	28	KVH 473E	35
HUO 510	117	JLJ 403	69	JUO 992	117	KGK 959	114	KVO 429P	50
HUP 236	89	JMC 121K	16	JV 9901	61	KGM 664F	56	KW 2260	34
HVH 472D	83	JMC 123K	110	JVF 528	50	KGU 284	23	KW 474	38
HVM 901F	41	JMN 727	61	JVH 373	82	KGU 290	117	KW 6052	61
HVO 937	43	JMS 452E	80	JVH 378	82	KGY 4D	39	KW 7604	38
HVU 244N	42	JN 5783	46	JVH 381	109	KHA 301	16	KWE 255	57
HVU 247N	118	JNA 467	41	JVO 230	49	KHA 311	108	KWT 642D	35
HWO 334	20	JNB 416	29	JVS 541	53	KHA 352	16	KWY 228V	35
HWV 294	72	JND 646	41	JVU 755	41	KHC 367	88	KXW 171	114
HWY 36	109	JND 728	58	JVV 267G	110	KHH 378W	105	KXW 435	95
HX 2756	39	JND 791	41	JVW 430	24	KHL 855	77	KY 9106	34
HYM 768	39	JNN 384	117	JVW 976W	76	KHU 28	22	KYY 529	109
HYM 812	71	JO 5032	50	JWB 416	57	KHU 326P	23	KYY 615	109
HZA 230	59	JO 5403	50	JWS 594	52	KHU 624	103	KYY 622	101
HZA 279	59	JOJ 207	109	JWU 307	101	KHW 306E	21	KYY 628	117
HZD 593	59	JOJ 222	16	JWU 886	35	KHW 630	22	KYY 647	109
IB 552	17	JOJ 231	109	JWW 375	62	KID 154	25	L247 FDV	51
IJI 5367	110	JOJ 245	20	JWW 376	62	KJ 2578	48	L929 CTT	102
ILI 98	25	JOJ 526	16	JWW 377	62	KJA 299G	48	LA 9928	39
IY 1940	59	JOJ 533	20	JX 7046	82	KJA 871F	41	LAA 231	66
IY 7383	25	JOJ 548	16	JX 9106	82	KJD 401P	39	LAE 13	70
IY 7384	59	JOJ 827	109	JXC 194	109	KJD 507P	111	LAK 309G	35
IY 8044	25	JOJ 847	16	JXC 288	28	KLB 908	95	LAK 313G	35
J 2503	47	JOJ 976	20	JXC 432	20	KLB 915	95	LAX 101E	110
JA 5506	108	JOV 613P	21	JXN 46	108	KLJ 346	69	LC 3701	39

LDB 796	118	LRN 321J	94	MNS 10Y	81	NEA 101F	21	NWO 462R	111
LDJ 985	48	LRN 60J	23	MNW 86	35	NEH 453	24	NWU 265D	35
LDP 945	105	LRV 996	73	MO 9324	17	NFN 84R	78	NWW 89E	77
LDS 201A	53	LST 873	116	MOD 978	69	NFS 176Y	56	NXL 847	109
LDV 176P	111	LSV 748	109	MOF 90	16	NG 1109	33	NXL 847	109
LED 71P	49	LSX 16P	56	MOO 177	79	NGE 172P	80	NXL 874	94
LEF 60H	110	LTA 772	46	MOO 177	79	NHA 744	20	NXP 506	52
LEN 101	77	LTA 813	94	MOR 581	66	NHA 795	20	NXP 997	39
LEO 734Y	67	LTC 774	41	MPU 21	72	NHN 250K	90	NZE 598	59
LEO 735Y	67	LTF 254	82	MPU 52	24	NHN 260K	110	NZE 620	60
LEV 917	83	LTN 501	47	MPX 945R	103	NHU 2	70	NZE 629	60
LF 9967	89	LTU 869	59	MRB 765	115	NJA 568W	97	O 9926	20
LFJ 862W	104	LTV 702	103	MSD 407	48	NJO 703	50	OAE 954M	70
LFM 302	118	LTX 311	109	MSD 408	80	NJW 719E	21	OAE 957M	103
LFM 320	109	LUC 210	28	MSF 122P	80	NKD 536	88	OAS 624	116
LFM 717	118	LUC 250	109	MSF 465P	80	NKD 540	88	OBN 502R	96
LFM 734	118	LUC 381	109	MSF 750P	56	NKJ 849P	79	OC 527	20
LFM 753	22	LUO 692	118	MTB 848	41	NKU 245X	35	OCH 261L	111
LFM 767	35	LUS 524E	56	MTC 540	91	NLE 534	109	OCK 997K	86
LFR 529F	86	LVK 123	89	MTE 639	52	NLE 537	39	OCU 769R	90
LFR 540G	86	LVR 508W	50	MTJ 84	115	NLE 643	117	OCU 807R	90
LFR 866X	49	LWB 377P	111	MTL 750	16	NLE 672	28	OCW 8X	112
LFS 288F	56	LWB 388P	58	MTT 640	115	NLE 673	109	OD 5489	103
LFS 294F	56	LWR 424	109	MUA 865P	77	NLE 939	102	OD 5868	103
LFS 296F	99	LYF 104	109	MUN 942R	103	NLJ 268	69	OD 7497	76
LFS 303F	56	LYF 377	117	MV 8996	108	NLJ 272	69	OD 7500	103
LFS 480	53	LYM 729	90	MWW 114D	77	NLP 645	46	ODE 182	82
LFW 326	38	LYR 533	35	MXX 23	20	NMA 328D	58	ODK 705	82
LG 2637	58	LYR 542	62	MXX 283	109	NMR 345	69	ODL 400	34
LHA 870F	16	LYR 826	28	MXX 289	114	NMS 358	80	OED 217	23
LHC 919P	68	LYR 854	114	MXX 292	109	NMS 366	53	OFC 205	51
LHL 164F	77	LYR 910	28	MXX 332	101	NMY 634E	116	OFC 393	50
LHN 784	61	LYR 915	101	MXX 334	28	NMY 636E	56	OFC 902H	73
LHN 785	82	LYR 969	114	MXX 364	39	NMY 646E	116	OFM 957K	63
LHN 860	67	LYR 997	24	MXX 410	102	NNB 125	41	OFN 721F	78
LHS 748V	80	M627 HDV	102	MXX 421	109	NNB 547H	96	OFR 970M	86
LHW 918	22	M939 XKA	42	MXX 430	102	NNB 589H	96	OFR 989M	17
LHY 937	24	MAH 744	33	MXX 434	101	NNC 854P	118	OFS 777	53
LHY 976	70	MAL 310	49	MXX 481	79	NNU 123M	43	OFS 798	53
LIL 9929	56	MAN 1378	88	MXX 481	79	NNU 124M	43	OHK 432	38
LJ 500	68	MAP 340W	99	MXX 489	101	NNU 234	69	OHU 770F	22
LJF 31F	68	MBN 177	94	MYA 590	28	NOC 600R	102	OHY 938	70
LJH 665	117	MCK 229J	77	MZ 7396	59	NOE 544R	21	OJ 9347	16
LJW 336	16	MCN 30K	90	NAC 416F	51	NOE 576R	111	OJD 357R	111
LJX 198	82	MDJ 555E	48	NAE 3	72	NOV 880G	102	OJD 903R	80
LJX 215	82	MDL 880R	34	NAG 120G	56	NPD 108L	110	OJF 191	87
LLU 670	114	MDL 954	109	NAH 135P	79	NPD 128L	111	OJI 4371	86
LLU 957	95	MDT 222	62	NAH 135P	79	NPJ 472R	66	OJO 727	73
LLU 987	95	MFM 39	109	NAH 941	79	NRA 78F	43	OLD 589	39
LMA 284	41	MFN 898	78	NAT 766A	109	NRG 154M	31	OLD 714	38
LMG 952C	55	MFR 306P	94	NBD 311F	101	NRG 26H	80	OLJ 291	46
LMJ 653G	46	MHU 49	22	NBN 436	68	NRH 802A	68	ONF 865H	96
LMS 168W	81	MHY 765	57	NBU 494	41	NRN 586	94	ONO 49	24
LMS 374W	56	MJ 4549	66	NCD 559M	111	NSF 757	80	ONO 59	38
LN 4743	32	MJA 891G	41	NCK 338J	94	NSJ 502	53	ONU 425	72
LN 7270	89	MJA 895G	110	NCS 16P	56	NTF 466	48	OOX 825R	17
LNA 166G	96	MJA 897G	41	NDB 356	118	NTT 661	76	OP 237	16
LNN 89E	50	MLL 555	109	NDH 959	71	NTT 679	76	OPV 821	99
LOD 495	115	MLL 722	109	NDK 980	41	NTU 125	94	ORB 277	20
LOG 301	16	MLL 740	28	NDL 656R	56	NTW 942C	24	ORC 545P	50
LOG 302	16	MLL 817	101	NDL 769G	67	NTY 416F	56	ORJ 83W	42
LOU 48	66	MLL 943	117	NDM 950E	110	NUD 105L	73	ORS 60R	56
LOW 217	98	MMW 354G	72	NDP 38R	111	NUW 567Y	40	ORU 230G	69
LRA 801P	43	MN 2615	39	NDV 537G	77	NVK 341	89	ORV 989	73

OSJ 620R	83	PKH 600M	111	RFE 416	38	SHA 645G	21	TDV217J	102
OSJ 629R	56	PND 460	41	RFM 408	72	SHL 917	82	TE 5110	59
OSJ 636R	116	PNF 941J	96	RFM 641	63	SHN 301	90	TE 5780	81
OSK 831	90	PNU 114K	43	RFM 644	48	SHN 80L	43	TE 7870	114
OST 502	25	POR 428	66	RFN 953G	78	SJ 1340	52	TE 8318	38
OT 8283	66	POU 494	79	RFU 689	72	SKB 695G	88	TET 135	58
OT 8592	66	PRA 109R	80	RGS 598R	79	SLT 56	39	TF 6860	34
OT 8898	66	PRH 244G	110	RGS 598R	79	SLT 57	39	TF 818	38
OT 8902	66	PRN 145	94	RHS 400W	56	SLT 58	28	TFA 987	110
OTA 632G	21	PRN 79K	94	RJT 146R	111	SMS 120P	56	TFF 251	72
OTA 640G	95	PRN 906	94	RLN 237W	104	SND 455X	97	TFN 980T	78
OTB 26W	68	PRX 187B	98	RMS 400W	81	SND 460X	97	TFU 90	53
OTT 43	94	PRX 200B	98	RN 7588	91	SNS 823W	112	TGM 214J	56
OTT 55	46	PRX 206B	98	RN 7824	41	SO 3740	52	TGY 102M	111
OTV 137	62	PSJ 480	48	RN 8622	34	SOA 674S	101	THL 261H	77
OTV 161	49	PSJ 825R	58	RNA 220J	96	SOE 913H	21	THM 515M	111
OU 9286	79	PTC 114C	41	RNA 236J	100	SOI 3591	83	THM 692M	63
OUM 727P	16	PTD 640S	97	RNE 692W	112	SOU 456	66	THM 712M	111
OV 4090	20	PTE 944C	41	RNV 810M	111	SOU 465	66	THX 220S	111
OV 4486	20	PTF 718L	94	ROD 765	82	SP 5139	31	THX 580S	111
OVF 229	79	PTF 727L	94	RPU 869M	111	SPT 65	90	TJ 6760	91
OVF 229	79	PTW 110	24	RRM 386X	81	SR 1266	29	TJO 56K	73
OVL 473	101	PUA 294W	35	RRN 405	86	SRB 424	29	TKU 467K	35
OWC 182D	72	PUF 165H	99	RRN 428	94	SRJ 328H	48	TMS 403X	81
OWC 720M	111	PUM 149W	35	RRS 46R	56	SS 7486	52	TMS 585H	56
OWE 116	57	PUO 331M	23	RRU 901	69	SS 7501	52	TNA 496	41
OWE 271K	21	PV 817	33	RRU 903	16	SSA 5X	81	TNA 520	41
OWS 620	53	PV 8270	33	RRU 904	69	SSF 237H	56	TNB 759K	96
OWW 905P	77	PV 9371	33	RSD 973R	80	SSN 248S	80	TOB 997H	102
OWX 167	77	PVH 931	71	RSG 825V	81	SSX 602V	56	TPD 109X	101
OWY 750K	77	PW 8605	89	RSJ 747	101	STH 100F	110	TPJ 61S	39
OZ 6686	59	PWL 413	51	RSK 615	109	STJ 847L	86	TRJ 109	48
PAJ 829X	90	PWL 999W	73	RSL 905	90	STL 725J	110	TRJ 112	41
PAU 204R	80	PWS 492S	86	RT 4539	66	STO 523H	50	TRN 481V	94
PBC 113G	87	PYM 108F	110	RTC 645L	49	SUK 3	20	TRN 731	35
PBC 734	29	Q124 VOE	21	RTJ 422L	86	SV 6107	91	TRR 814R	102
PBC 98G	87	Q507 OHR	22	RU 2266	68	SVF 896G	110	TRY 122H	87
PBJ 2F	79	Q995 CPE	104	RU 8678	52	SVS 281	105	TSJ 272	82
PBJ 2F	79	RAG 400	80	RUF 186	76	SVS 904	35	TSJ 47S	80
PCG 888G	98	RAG 411	53	RUF 37R	99	SVV 587W	101	TSK 736	115
PCG 889G	98	RAG 578	53	RUF 40R	104	SWS 671	53	TSP 939K	110
PCK 618	94	RAL 795	109	RV 3411	73	SWS 715	53	TTD 386H	42
PCN 762	90	RAR 690J	100	RV 4649	73	SWV 155J	90	TTR 167H	98
PCW 203J	90	RB 4757	81	RV 6360	48	SYK 569F	99	TTT 781	82
PDH 808	20	RBC 345G	99	RV 6368	73	TBC 164	16	TUG 20	90
PDJ 269L	49	RBD 111M	101	RWB 87	58	TBD 279G	72	TUO 497	72
PDL 519	34	RBD 319G	101	RWC 637K	110	TBK 190K	73	TUO 74J	77
PDU 125M	29	RBW 87M	73	SB 8155	16	TCD 374J	99	TUP 329R	90
PDU 135M	21	RC 2721	38	SBD 525R	101	TCD 383J	99	TUP 859	90
PEF 21	110	RC 4615	20	SBF 233	20	TCD 490J	99	TV 4484	61
PFE 542V	38	RC 8472	105	SCD 731N	99	TCH 274L	21	TV 9333	61
PFN 788M	78	RC 8575	105	SCH 117X	50	TCK 465	94	TVS 367	80
PFN 865	49	RCH 518F	50	SCH 237	22	TCK 494	94	TWH 807K	68
PFR 346	48	RCH 629L	43	SCS 333M	56	TCK 726	94	TWH 809K	68
PFR 554H	86	RCK 920	110	SCS 366M	56	TCK 821	80	TWL 928	51
PFR 747	100	RCM 493	63	SDL 268	34	TCO 537	90	TWM 220V	111
PHA 319M	17	RCP 237	88	SDL 638J	34	TDH 912	22	TWS 910T	23
PHA 370M	21	RCS 382	53	SDX 33R	68	TDJ 612	48	TWT 123	77
PHJ 954	24	RCU 588S	90	SDX 57	24	TDK 322	58	TWW 766F	35
PHN 699	118	RCU 838S	90	SEO 209M	67	TDK 686J	118	TWY 8	77
PHN 831	90	RD 7127	71	SFC 610	51	TDL 564K	34	TXJ 507K	42
PJX 232	35	RDB 872	22	SFV 421	94	TDL 566K	110	TY 9608	77
PJX 35	77	RDH 505	20	SGD 407	24	TDL 998	88	TYD 888	53
PKG 587M	111	REN 116	41	SHA 431	20	TDT 344	115	TYJ 4S	99

Reg	No	Reg	No	Reg	No	Reg	No	Reg	No
UBD 757H	101	UVL 873M	38	VRC 612Y	50	WT 7101	34	XVU 352M	42
UBN 902	68	UWH 185	68	VRD 193	62	WT 7108	47	XVU 363M	96
UCS 659	53	UWX 981F	99	VRF 372	100	WT 9156	81	XVX 19	24
UCX 275	22	UXD 129G	101	VRU 124J	69	WTE 155D	55	XW 9892	23
UDT 189S	58	UZG 100	60	VSC 86	53	WTS 266T	56	XWS 165K	56
UDT 455F	62	UZH 258	25	VTU 76	35	WTS 270T	80	XWW 474G	77
UEO 478T	67	VAE 499T	23	VTY 543J	90	WTS 708A	90	XWX 795	62
UF 1517	17	VBA 151S	49	VUD 30X	73	WUA 832	109	XX 9591	28
UF 4813	17	VBD 310H	100	VUP 328	90	WUH 173T	111	YBD 201	115
UF 6473	17	VCO 802	112	VV 5696	72	WV 1209	32	YD 9533	66
UF 6805	17	VCW 597Y	90	VVP 911	20	WW 4688	71	YDB 453L	96
UF 7428	17	VD 3433	52	VY 957	40	WWH 43L	96	YDK 590	41
UFC 430K	51	VDL 264K	34	VYO 767	101	WWJ 754M	62	YDL 135T	34
UFF 178	53	VDV 107S	111	VZI 44	60	WWM 904W	88	YDL 315	88
UFJ 292	90	VDV 752	118	VZL 179	60	WWY 115G	99	YFM 283L	72
UFJ 296	76	VDV 753	118	WAD 640S	79	WYP 203G	110	YFR 351	86
UFM 52F	63	VDV 760	58	WAJ 112	53	WYW 6T	28	YG 7831	89
UFM 53F	72	VDV 798	76	WBN 955L	96	WYW 72T	111	YHT 958	22
UFP 233S	87	VDV 817	103	WBR 246	35	WYW 82T	68	YHY 80	70
UGR 698R	111	VER 262L	51	WBR 248	90	WZJ 724	60	YJG 807	78
UHA 255	20	VF 2788	32	WCG 104	79	XAK 355L	35	YL 740	50
UHA 941H	21	VF 8157	32	WCW 308R	111	XBO 121T	56	YLG 717F	35
UHA 956H	21	VFJ 995	109	WDA 700T	17	XBU 17S	42	YLJ 147	69
UHA 969H	17	VH 2088	81	WDA 835T	102	XBU 1S	97	YNA 321M	96
UHA 981H	21	VH 6188	68	WDA 956T	102	XC 8059	39	YNU 351G	110
UHG 141V	81	VH 6217	69	WDA 986T	111	XCH 425G	110	YNX 478	51
UHY 359	22	VHB 678S	80	WDF 569	20	XCV 326	109	YPL 433T	111
UHY 360	70	VJG 187J	78	WDK 562T	118	XCW 955R	94	YPT 796	90
UHY 362	102	VJO 201X	73	WEX 685M	77	XDH 516G	21	YR 3844	39
UHY 384	70	VK 5401	47	WFM 801K	35	XDH 519G	22	YRC 194	50
UK 9978	22	VKB 711	88	WFN 513	30	XDH 56G	21	YRC 420	111
UKA 562H	88	VL 1263	38	WFN 912	30	XDH 72	71	YSG 101	53
UKE 830X	112	VLT 140	46	WG 1620	89	XEM 898W	63	YSL 334	116
ULS 716X	56	VLT 143	116	WG 2373	80	XFG 25Y	112	YT 3738	23
ULS 717X	56	VLT 163	116	WG 3260	52	XFM 42G	56	YTE 587V	97
UMA 370	41	VLT 196	109	WG 4445	80	XG 9304	52	YWB 494M	51
UMO 180N	111	VLT 216	117	WG 8107	52	XGM 450L	80	YWL 134K	73
UNA 848S	97	VLT 235	116	WG 8790	52	XHA 482	20	YYB 118	100
UNB 629	41	VLT 237	116	WG 9180	57	XHA 496	20	YYJ 914	53
UO 2331	103	VLT 242	116	WH 1553	38	XHO 370	66	YYS 174	80
UOA 322L	43	VLT 250	109	WHA 237H	90	XJA 534L	96	ZC 714	59
UOU 417H	79	VLT 268	114	WHL 970	77	XKO 72A	109	ZD 7163	59
UOU 419H	79	VLT 281	116	WHN 411G	90	XLG 477	35	ZH 3926	59
UP 551	47	VLT 298	114	WJY 758	35	XLV 140W	49	ZH 3937	59
UPB 308S	104	VLT 44	24	WKG 284	109	XM 7399	39	ZH 4538	59
UPB 309S	104	VLW 444G	101	WKG 287	118	XMS 252R	56	ZI 9708	59
UPB 312S	101	VM 4439	40	WKJ 787	94	XMS 422Y	81	ZJ 5904	25
UPE 203M	101	VMO 234H	101	WKO 138S	111	XNG 770S	33	ZJ 5933	59
URE 281	109	VMP 8G	56	WLT 371	116	XNX 136H	17	ZL 2718	59
USV 324	99	VMP 10G	80	WLT 506	16	XON 41J	17	ZL 6816	59
UTC 672	41	VNB 101L	42	WLT 529	105	XPK 51T	101	ZO 6819	59
UTF 732M	94	VNB 132L	96	WLT 765	109	XRU 277K	69	ZO 6857	59
UTG 312G	110	VNB 173L	96	WLT 900	114	XSL 945A	53	ZO 6881	59
UTG 313G	110	VNB 177L	96	WNG 864H	21	XSN 25A	53	ZO 6949	59
UTN 501Y	90	VNB 203L	96	WNL 259A	90	XTA 839	76	ZO 6960	25
UTU 596J	20	VO 6806	46	WNO 478	24	XTC 530H	80	ZS 8621	25
UTV 229	82	VO 8846	49	WOW 993T	110	XTP 287L	73	ZU 5000	25
UU 6646	28	VOD 123K	110	WPG 217M	111	XU 7498	89	ZU 9241	59
UUA 212	90	VOD 550K	77	WRA 12	58	XUA 73X	77	ZY 1715	25
UUA 214	35	VOD 88K	103	WRL 16	103	XUF 141	98	ZY 79	59
UUF 110J	76	VOI 8415	83	WRP 767J	101	XUO 721	76		
UUF 116J	99	VPT 598R	90	WS 4522	52	XUS 575S	80		
UUF 328J	99	VR 5742	40	WSD 756K	80	XVU 341M	96		

Index of Museums, Collections and Heritage Bus Services

* Operators using historic vehicles

Abbey Pumping Station, Leicester. 16
Aldershot & District Bus Interest Group 66
Alford, Grampian Transport Museum. 31
Amberley Museum 17
Aston Manor Road Transport Museum, Aston. 17
Aycliffe & District Bus Preservation Society. 67
Beamish, North of England Open Air Museum 46
Birkenhead, Wirral Transport Museum. 63
Birmingham & Midland Museum of Transport, Wythall 19
Black Country Living Museum, Dudley 21
Blue Triangle, Rainham*. 114
Bohemia-Sachsen Transport Heritage Park. 67
Bolton Bus Group 68
Bournemouth Heritage Transport Collection 68
Bristol Road Transport Collection, Kemble 22
Bristol Onmibus Vehicle Collection 69
Bristol Vintage Bus Group 70
British Commercial Vehicle Museum, Leyland. 23
British Trolleybus Society 70
Buckland Omnibus Co, Woodbridge* 114
Butterley, Midland Road Transport Group 42
Canvey Island, Castle Point Transport Museum 24
Cardiff & South Wales Trolleybus Project 71
Carlton Colville, East Anglia Transport Museum, ... 30
Carmel Coaches, Okehampton*. 114
Castle Point Transport Museum, Canvey Island 24
Cavan & Leitrim Railway, Dromod 25
Cheetham, Manchester Museum of Transport 40
Chelveston Preservation Society. 71
Cherwell Bus Preservation Group 72
City of Portsmouth Preserved Transport Depot, Portsmouth. . . 73
Classic Southdown Omnibuses 76
Cobham Bus Museum 28
Cosy Coaches, Killamarsh* 115
Covent Garden, London's Transport Museum 39
Coventry, Museum of British Road Transport 39
Croydon, Southcoast Motor Services* 118
Cultra, Ulster Folk & Transport Museum 62
Cumbria Classic Coaches, Kirkby Stephen* 115
Devon General Society 76
Denholme, Keighley Bus Museum 74
Dewsbury Bus Museum 77
Dover Transport Museum, Whitfield. 29
Dromod, Cavan & Leitrim Railway 25
Dudley, Black Country Living Museum. 21
East Anglia Transport Museum, Carlton Colville 30
Eastern Transport Collection Society 78
Edinburgh, MacTours* 116
Edinburgh, Majestic Tour*. 116
Friends of King Alfred Buses 79
Glasgow Vintage Vehicle Trust 80
Glasgow, Museum of Transport 43
Golcar Transport Collection 81
Grampian Transport Museum, Alford. 31
Great Wyrley, Green Bus Services* 116
Green Bus Services, Great Wyrley*. 116
Halifax Bus Museum 82
Howth, Transport Museum Society of Ireland 59
Huddersfield Passenger Transport Group 82
Imperial War Museum, London 32

Ipswich Transport Museum 32
Irish Transport Trust 83
Isle of Wight Bus Museum, Newport (IoW) 33
John Shearman Collection. 83
Keighley Bus Museum, Denholme. 34
Kelvin Amos Collection. 86
Kemble, Bristol Road Transport Collection 22
Killamarsh, Cosy Coaches* 115
Kirkby Stephen, Cumbria Classic Coaches* 115
Lancastrian Transport Trust 86
Lathalmond, Scottish Vintage Bus Museum 51
Legionnaire Group 87
Leicester, Abbey Pumping Station 16
Leicester Corporation Bus Owners Group. 87
Leyland, British Commercial Vehicle Museum. 23
Lincolnshire Road Transport Museum, North Hykeham 38
London, Imperial War Museum 32
London's Transport Museum, Covent Garden 39
Long Hanborough, Oxford Bus Museum 50
MacTours, Edinburgh* 116
Maidenhead, Memory Lane Vintage Omnibus Services*. 117
Majestic Tour, Edinburgh*. 116
Manchester Museum of Transport, Cheetham. 40
Medstead Depot Omnibus Group 88
Memory Lane Vintage Omnibus Services, Maidenhead*. 117
Merseyside Transport Trust 88
Midland Road Transport Group, Butterley 42
Mike Sutcliffe Collection 88
Mossley, Tameside Transport Collection 58
Museum of British Road Transport, Coventry 29
Museum of Transport, Glasgow. 43
National Museum of Science and Industry, Wroughton. 46
Newport (IoW), Isle of Wight Bus Museum 33
North East Bus Preservation Trust Ltd. 89
North Hykeham, Lincolnshire Road Transport Museum, ... 38
North of England Open Air Museum, Beamish 46
North West Museum of Road Transport, St Helens 47
Nottingham Transport Heritage Centre, Ruddington 49
Okehampton, Carmel Coaches*. 114
Oxford Bus Museum, Long Hanborough 50
Peter Stanier Collection 91
Portsmouth, City of Portsmouth Preserved Transport Depot. . . 73
Quantock Heritage, Wiveliscombe* 117
Rainham, Blue Triangle 114
Ribble Vehicle Preservation Trust 92
Roger Burdett Collection 94
Rotherham Trolleybus Group. 95
RTW Group 95
Ruddington, Nottingham Transport Heritage Centre 49
St Helens, North West Museum of Road Transport. 47
St Margarets School Transport Society 96
Sandtoft, Trolleybus Museum at 61
Scottish Vintage Bus Museum, Lathalmond 51
SELNEC Preservation Society. 96
Sheffield Bus Museum, Tinsley 57
Southcoast Motor Services, Croydon* 118
Southampton & District Transport Heritage Trust 98
Southdown Historic Vehicle Group. 98
Tameside Transport Collection, Mossley 58
Telford Bus Group 99

TH Collection	100	West of England Transport Collection	102
Three Counties Bus Museum	100	Westgate Museum	105
Tinsley, Sheffield Bus Museum	57	Whitfield, Dover Transport Museum	29
Transport Museum Society of Ireland, Howth	59	Wirral Transport Museum, Birkenhead	63
Trolleybus Museum at Sandtoft	61	Wiveliscombe, Quontock Heritage*	117
Ulster Folk & Transport Museum, Cultra	62	Woodbridge, Buckland Omnibus Co*	114
Wealdstone & District Vintage Vehicle Collection	101	Workington Transport Heritage Trust	105
West Country Historic Omnibus & Transport Trust	102	Wroughton, National Museum of Science & Industry	46
West Midlands Bus Preservation Society	102	Wythall, Birmingham & Midland Museum of Transport	19

Former North Western 372 (AJA 132) is a 1938 Bristol L5G rebodied by Burlingham in 1950. Seen near Winchester on 1 January 2005, this attractive little saloon is currently with Quantock Heritage.
Philip Lamb